ANCIENT
EGYPT
39,000 BCE

ANCIENT EGYPT 39,000 BCE

The History, Technology, and Philosophy of Civilization X

EDWARD F. MALKOWSKI

Bear & Company
Rochester, Vermont • Toronto, Canada

Bear & Company
One Park Street
Rochester, Vermont 05767
www.BearandCompanyBooks.com

Bear & Company is a division of Inner Traditions International

Library of Congress Cataloging-in-Publication Data

Malkowski, Edward F.
  Ancient Egypt 39,000 BCE : the history, technology, and philosophy of
Civilization X / Edward F. Malkowski.
      p. cm.
  Includes bibliographical references and index.
  Summary: "A view into the sophisticated and highly advanced civilization that
preceded the world of the pharaohs"—Provided by publisher.
  ISBN 978-1-59143-109-1 (pbk.)
  1. Egypt—Civilization—To 332 B.C. 2. Civilization, Ancient. I. Title.
DT61.M2929 2010
932'.011—dc22
                                                                    2009052900

Printed and bound in the United States by Lake Book Manufacturing

10 9 8 7 6 5 4 3 2 1

Text design by Jon Desautels and layout by Priscilla Baker
This book was typeset in Garamond Premier Pro with Stone Sans used as a display
typeface

The following images are reproduced courtesy of Jupiter Images: figures 5.3, 5.4,
5.7, 5.9, and 10.8 and plates 29, 30, 32, 39, and 40.

To send correspondence to the author of this book, mail a first-class letter to the
author c/o Inner Traditions • Bear & Company, One Park Street, Rochester, VT
05767, and we will forward the communication.

CONTENTS

FOREWORD

My own journey into the subject of ancient Egypt began in early 1999. At that time I had no interest in the pyramids, and like most people, I assumed they were little more than overrated piles of rock that had been used for someone's burial. Also at that time I never dreamed I would one day be writing a foreword to one of the most fascinating books regarding ancient Egypt.

Winters are dark and rainy in northwest Washington. With little else to do, I had made a habit of exploring local bookstores. On one such outing in 1999 I came across Edward Kunkel's book *The Pharaoh's Pump,* which put forth an interesting proposition: the Great Pyramid had a hydraulic ram pump built into the subterranean section. Although Kunkel's work had been around since the early 1960s, I had never heard of it, and after reading it, it made no sense to me—except for one section. Kunkel claimed that an advanced whirlpool had once existed within the subterranean chamber. For me, that not only seemed plausible, but quite ingenious.

Intrigued, I sorted through dozens of books and scoured the Internet for pictures and descriptions of the subterranean section of the Great Pyramid. As a result of this research, my interest continued to grow, and I soon embarked on a quest to build a model of the subterranean section. Almost exactly a year after learning of Kunkel's theory, I completed a running model of this subterranean section, 1:48 scale (¼ inch to the foot). My approach was scientific. In addition to building the model, I described specific experimental setups and recording designs. I reported all the results; these can be viewed on my website.*

That was seven years ago. Since then, my work—unaltered since 2002 when the final subterranean flows were determined—has been critiqued by some of the top people in the engineering field and has held strong. The models that I built can be built by anyone, which I strongly encourage anyone with a keen interest to do. (For you *Mythbusters* fans, I have submitted my work on the Great Pyramid's subterranean chamber to them.)

A year ago Edward Malkowski informed me that he intended to describe my work in his book *Ancient Egypt 39,000 BCE* and that my work was going to be the basis for a new theory on the purpose of the pyramids and the Great Pyramid. Much of the evidence he describes in this book is scientific and backed by substantial data, and I am proud to be part of it.

For me, *Ancient Egypt 39,000 BCE* is the culmination of years of discovery by a number of people that comes together to paint a fascinating picture of the past. These individuals present not only their views, but their personal research, undertaken over the decades. John Anthony West and Robert Schoch's research and compelling theory is presented here: that rainfall eroded the Great Sphinx, thus redating its carving by thousands of years. Sir William Flinders Petrie and Christopher Dunn's insightful analysis of precision granite artifacts is covered extensively, with beautiful photos. However, the most important artifact, in my opinion, is "the stone at Abu Rawash," dubbed by Malkowski "the new Rosetta Stone." I completely agree with him that its discovery will eventually change how we view history.

Indeed, my own research into the past parallels Malkowski's, particularly one of the least understood events—the end of the Ice Age and the death of millions of animals and numerous species. Around 9750 BCE, with the end of the Ice Age, came the formation of the Carolina Bays, more than 500,000 shallow elliptical depressions found along North America's Atlantic coastal plain from New Jersey to Florida. At the bottom of these "bays" is an unusual blue clay containing iridium, carbon spherules, and nanodiamonds,

---

*http://sentinelkennels.com/Research_Article_V41.html

which have been determined to be extraterrestrial markers. Ted Bunch, Richard Firestone, and Ken Tankersley propose that the formation of these bays is linked to the Younger Dryas impact event, which may have led to the extinction of large mammals, such as mammoths, and the Clovis people, the first inhabitants of North America.

I especially appreciate Malkowski's coverage of this episode in Earth's history in chapter 11, "An Invisible Cataclysm." Any civilization that existed prior to the end of the Ice Age would have suffered as greatly as the animals did. The decimation of a technical society would certainly explain the evidence put forth here.

After being captivated by ancient Egypt in 1999, I purchased a great number of orthodox and alternative books about Egypt and trawled the Internet to uncover a wealth of information on the topic. If I were to recommend a single book on this subject, *Ancient Egypt 39,000 BCE* would be the one I'd share with my friends. Edward Malkowski has assembled the best pictures and data, and I believe it is very important to know what others have already discovered and the wealth of historical information that has been put forth. It is my hope that you read this book with an open mind and enjoy the theories and opinions contained herein. And while we need to be open to new discoveries, these discoveries must be rigorously tested and analyzed.

It is also my wish that you pursue your own research to the best of your ability and always use your intuition and imagination. This was absolutely key for me.

JOHN CADMAN

John Cadman is a marine engineer who spent three years scientifically investigating the subterranean chamber of the Great Pyramid. As a consequence of his investigation, he invented the self-powered pulse pump, which pumps water without the aid of electricity. He also spent a number of years as the chief engineer of a king crab boat sailing the Bering Sea.

TIMELINE OF EGYPT'S PERIODS AND DYNASTIES

Predynastic Period   (5500–3100 BCE)

Early Dynastic Period

    1st Dynasty   (2920–2770 BCE)

    2nd Dynasty   (2770–2650 BCE)

Old Kingdom

    3rd Dynasty   (2650–2575 BCE)

    4th Dynasty   (2575–2467 BCE)

    5th Dynasty   (2465–2323 BCE)

    6th Dynasty   (2323–2152 BCE)

First Intermediate Period

    7th Dynasty   (2160–2152 BCE)

    8th Dynasty   (2159–2130 BCE)

    9th Dynasty   (2130–2080 BCE)

    10th Dynasty   (2080–2040 BCE)

Middle Kingdom

    11th Dynasty   (1986–1937 BCE)

    12th Dynasty   (1937–1759 BCE)

    13th Dynasty   (1759–1633 BCE)

    14th Dynasty   (1786–1603 BCE)

Second Intermediate Period

    15th Dynasty   (1674–1567 BCE)

    16th Dynasty   (1684–1567 BCE)

    17th Dynasty   (1650–1539 BCE)

New Kingdom

    18th Dynasty   (1539–1295 BCE)

    19th Dynasty   (1295–1186 BCE)

    20th Dynasty   (1186–1069 BCE)

Third Intermediate Period

    21st Dynasty   (1070–945 BCE)

    22nd Dynasty   (945–712 BCE)

    23rd Dynasty   (828–725 BCE)

    24th Dynasty   (725–715 BCE)

    25th Dynasty   (712–657 BCE)

Late Dynastic Period

    26th Dynasty   (664–525 BCE)

    27th Dynasty   (525–404 BCE)

    28th Dynasty   (404–399 BCE)

    29th Dynasty   (399–380 BCE)

    30th Dynasty   (380–343 BCE)

    31st Dynasty   (343–332 BCE)

Note to the Reader: Some of these dynastic dates overlap, which is endemic to the field of Egyptology given the speculative nature of the discussion.

PREFACE

In the spring of 2004 I began work on my second book, *Before the Pharaohs: Egypt's Mysterious Prehistory,* a digest of John Anthony West and Robert Schoch's investigation into the possible prehistoric origin of ancient Egypt's Great Sphinx. Aside from telling the story of West and Schoch's research, I also searched for any evidence in the historical record indicating that a culture sophisticated and ambitious enough to carve a 200-foot-long lion out of bedrock might have existed. What I found was a mystery.

On one hand, I found no obvious physical evidence suggestive of the existence of an advanced prehistoric civilization—one that had some knowledge of physics and the means to implement that knowledge to create useful products. On the other hand, however, oral history as well as the historical record do claim that such a civilization existed; it was often referred to as the Golden Age. Most oral histories claim this civilization was antediluvian, and that it was destroyed by a great deluge. Unfortunately, there is no evidence that a worldwide flood ever occurred. Nor does a worldwide flood make any sense, since a flood of that proportion would have seriously altered Earth's atmosphere and would have required five times the amount of water already existing in the oceans.

Perhaps the deluge originally referred to something other than water, but after many generations, its meaning was altered. If so, then it is also plausible that an advanced civilization existed at that time, just as the ancient historians describe. In this book, I call this culture Civilization X.

A perfunctory treatment of ancient Egypt's history, such as in a world history class, typically makes a straightforward case that the Old Kingdom pharaohs were responsible for some of the greatest monuments and temples in Egypt, most notably Giza's pyramids. But a closer look into the organization, materials, and labor required to erect these monuments, particularly the tunneling performed on the Giza Plateau, raises too many questions. These technical and organizational requirements create a set of assumptions for the historian that cannot be reconciled with today's technology. The broadest assumption is that people of the second millennium BCE had the level of skill required to quarry and move large quantities of stone from as far away as 500 miles and then use this stone in the construction of the temples and pyramids.

No civilization has reproduced these accomplishments. Even today, using modern technology, constructing the Great Pyramid would prove to be a difficult and very expensive task. And yet we are supposed to believe that a people who had emerged from the Stone Age just a few hundred years earlier were able to accomplish this?

Common sense says they could not. But despite common sense, there is a long-standing belief that they built on a vast scale with the simplest of tools. It is belief because there is no evidence to support the assumption that people of the second millennium had the level of technology required. Furthermore, there are too many anomalies and anachronisms that need to be explained, the most obvious one being the Great Pyramid itself, with its extraordinary size and unusual internal design.

All the magnificent structures of the Old Kingdom are attributed to copper chisels and stone hammers. That's the paradigm that has been in place since the late nineteenth century. However, paradigms change, if society is working as it should, when enough people reject the orthodoxy in favor of a new standard. Even so, paradigm changes are never easy. With exclusive influence in public school systems and a noncritical approach to history, the paradigm is perpetuated. Change almost always occurs very slowly and is not final until the old guard of the orthodoxy retires or passes away, leaving a new, younger generation to interpret the evidence and form their own theories and opinions.

The media is always at the cusp of change in public opinion, and through books and the cinema new ideas that were once lunatic or fringe or even taboo find an audience that senses a correction in thinking may be needed. During the 1970s, for instance, there were no television shows that embraced the paranormal. In 1972, ABC tried to get one off the ground with a series called *The Sixth Sense*, starring Gary Collins, but it lasted only a single season. Later in the '70s, *The Night Stalker* achieved some faint success. Today, however, with shows like *Charmed, Medium, The Ghost Whisperer, Angel, Buffy the Vampire Slayer,* and *Supernatural,* to name just a few, this once-atypical genre is now commonplace. And, of course, in the 1990s there was the phenomenally successful television series *The X-Files*—my own personal favorite.

Why have these shows become so popular?

People accept the idea that there is more to life than the physical world and have opted for nontraditional ways of expressing and entertaining that view. They also seek knowledge about a whole host of alternative subjects, such as consciousness, for example, which is at the core of understanding the human experience. Amazon.com lists more than 108,000 nonfiction titles for "consciousness": 47,000 under Religion and Spirituality, 41,000 under Health, Mind, and Body, and 44,000 under Science. The same is true for history, particularly ancient Egyptian history, which lists more than 200,000 books.

I was surprised and intrigued that the film *10,000 BC* (released in March 2008) portrayed an Egyptian-type civilization as an advanced prehistoric society—pyramids and all. (The producers of the film did an extraordinary job creating the visual effects of pyramid building, but the true majesty and scale of the pyramids can only be appreciated in person.) Although the film was a work of fiction, and not a very good one according to most film critics, such a portrayal of ancient Egypt as a "lost civilization" hints at a growing curiosity about prehistory and continued uncertainty about the identity of the builders of ancient Egypt's temples and pyramids.

Of course, there are those who will vehemently object to this type of imaginative and exploratory approach to history on the grounds that it's not scientific. But the truth is that history is not scientific and never will be. The inductive approach cannot be considered the definitive means by which to ascertain the truth. In the case of the pyramids, one must see the evidence firsthand to truly begin to understand the truth. There is no substitute for visiting Egypt and walking among the ancient ruins.

No documentary or book has ever truly captured the essence of Egypt's ancient temples or temple ruins. There is granite everywhere—ashlars, columns, broken temple edifices, fields of rubble, and piles of rubble. The ancient Egyptians built public buildings out of limestone and dressed them in solid granite.

Being the hardest known rock, granite is difficult to work with, even with current technology. This makes it very expensive in today's world. So how could such an ancient culture build a civilization out of granite using simple hand tools? No civilization has done so before or since.

How could the dynastic Egyptians* have done it?

They shouldn't have, couldn't have. But there has never been irrefutable evidence to suggest otherwise, according to the orthodoxy. *Now, in this volume, there is. Ancient Egypt 39,000 BCE* is the sequel to *Before the Pharaohs: Egypt's Mysterious Prehistory*. For readers of the latter, chapter 2 in this volume, "A Prehistoric Sphinx," is an updated and abridged version of chapters 1 and 2 in *Before the Pharaohs: Egypt's Mysterious Prehistory*. Eight new photographs have been added—five of which depict the eroded Sphinx and its enclosure—as well as a 2004 study of limestone erosion that supports a prehistoric age for the Sphinx. Although the evidence concerning the great antiquity of the Sphinx is covered in depth in *Before the Pharaohs*, I wanted this volume to include all the conclusive evidence for the existence of Civilization X that I have discovered. This volume, *Ancient Egypt 39,000 BCE*, is part travelogue, part history, and part science.† As such, it is intended to present ancient Egypt's ruins as I have experienced them and to explain them to the best of my abilities.

---

*The period known as dynastic Eygpt stretched from approximately 2920 BCE to 332 BCE.

†Author's Note: Much of the evidence in this book is visual. All photos and diagrams in it are also available for viewing at *www.civilizationx.com*. Further information concerning John Cadman's research is available at *http://sentinelkennels.com/Research_Article_V41.html*.

ACKNOWLEDGMENTS

It has been a pleasure working with two progressive and open-minded scientists: John Cadman and Thomas Malkowski. Their scientific insights have been an invaluable source.

John Cadman, I believe, will someday go down in the history books for his experiments and modeling of the Great Pyramid's subterranean chamber and passageways. To the best of my knowledge, he is the only person to experimentally demonstrate something, anything, about Giza's Great Pyramid. In my opinion, his work is the discovery of the century.

Thomas Malkowski, my son, has proven over the years to be a challenging antagonist. As a studying physicist, he has more than once steered me in the correct direction while I've been in the process of building a viable theory to explain ancient Egypt's network of pyramids. He shares the credit with me for the pyramid theory put forth in this book.

The quest to understand ancient Egyptian civilization encompasses many years of work by many researchers, including John Burke and Philip Callahan and their research about ancient agriculture; John Anthony West and Robert Schoch for their research into the age of the Sphinx; Christopher Dunn for his work in discovering proof positive that the civilization that built the pyramids employed some type of machine tools; Dr. Paul LaViolette and his research into galactic core bursts; and Richard Firestone, Allen West, and Simon Warwick-Smith for their work in discovering evidence of prehistoric gamma-ray bursts and their consequences for life on Earth.

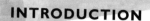

APOCALYPSE NOW

Our civilization lives in precarious equilibrium between its distance from the sun and the emptiness of space. Whether you believe that global warming is the result of civilization's emission of greenhouse gases or that it is a natural cycle, the evidence points to global warming as a real phenomenon. But the fact is, global warming has been occurring for the past 13,000 years. Before Earth began its warming trend, the northern climes that are so agriculturally productive today were buried under miles of ice and snow.

Scientists claim that our world could return to such a harsh climate in as little as ten years if the ocean conveyor that pumps warm water into the North Atlantic ceases to do so. There is also the possibility of an Armageddon asteroid, an asteroid sufficiently large to create a "total evaporation impact" that would scour the planet's surface down to the bedrock.

Curiously, however, before the 1960s there was no proof that rocks from space entered Earth's atmosphere and hit the ground. No one believed in the reality of asteroid impacts, and it was only the determination of astronomer Gene Shoemaker through his work at Arizona's Meteor Crater that science took notice. Apparently, space rocks did fall to earth, and now we know that asteroids have been striking Earth from the very beginning of Earth's history.

Today, asteroids whose orbits are close to Earth have become a serious topic for some astronomers. There are more than a few, astronomers have discovered. Alarmingly, it takes only a single rock greater than a few miles across to pummel us into a dark age. The most likely site of a meteor impact would be one of the oceans, given that two-thirds of the planet is covered by water. Although this may seem like a relatively safe place for an impact, the energy created by vaporizing rock would generate a tsunami of unprecedented proportions, one that might be perceived as a great flood. Trillions of tons of displaced water would create a wave so large it is difficult to imagine. It could never happen in our lifetime, could it?

Although such devastation has never occurred within the memory of our civilization, we have been periodically reminded of nature's power. Almost 100 years before the 2004 Sumatra tsunami, in 1908 near Russia's Tunguska River, a comet exploded in the atmosphere, releasing energy somewhere between the equivalent of five and thirty-five tons of TNT. It destroyed 800 square miles of forest. If the Tunguska comet had exploded over a densely populated area, millions of people would have been killed.

What if the Tunguska comet had been significantly larger? Would it have destroyed our civilization? How much destruction does it take to erase civilization? If a global catastrophe occurred today, like the meteor strike astronomers warn us will eventually happen, what *would* be the impact on civilization?

The impact on civilization, of course, would depend on the size of the projectile. If the extraterrestrial body were the size of a planetoid, like the moon, for example, nothing of Earth's surface would be left. Except for microbes buried in Earth's crust, all life would be annihilated. A much smaller meteor would still do significant damage, such as that which ended the Age of the Dinosaurs. Paleontologists are convinced by the evidence that a six-mile-wide meteor struck in Mexico's Yucatan Peninsula sixty-five million years ago, leaving a crater 112 miles wide and three thousand feet deep. What effect this size impact would have on human populations is unknown, although the fossil record indicates even such a small impact would be devastating.

No such devastating impacts have been recorded in human history, but some scientists, such as Dr. Stanley Ambrose of the University of Illinois, believe that a supervolcanic eruption seventy-three thousand years ago wreaked havoc on our planet, leaving a crater thirty miles wide and sixty miles long. According to Ambrose, the fallout from the Toba eruption reduced the human population to possibly as few as several thousand individuals, which, according to geneticists, helps explain the similarity in all human DNA. All of us living today are the descendents of a handful of survivors from the Toba eruption.

If a global catastrophe occurred today, such as Earth being struck by the Armageddon asteroid or an eruption of Yellowstone's caldera, and reduced the world's population to a billion people or less, could our technical society survive? Could the county or state you live in continue with more than 80 percent of its inhabitants gone?

No one knows for sure, although studies have been made on the subject, albeit involving a lesser magnitude of destruction. In 1972, the Office of Technology Assessment—the U.S. government's advisory group of scientists, technologists, and engineers—performed a study on the effects of a limited nuclear war. They concluded that the *best case* scenario was that civilization would return to a medieval-style society.

In 1998, a small preview of such a tragedy occurred in Quebec. An ice storm knocked out power and demonstrated the frailty of modern civilization and the dependence it has on its technology. The vital infrastructure of society—energy distribution for heating, food production, a clean water supply, telecommunications, information technology, the transportation of people and goods, hospitals, and banking—was crippled. Within a few days, people were burning their furniture to stay warm.

What would have happened if the situation had not been corrected?

Any modern equipment that survived would be scavenged and used for as long as possible, but without the manufacturing of replacement parts, the equipment would eventually become useless. For equipment requiring fuel of some type, how long would existing supplies last? Regardless of how long fuel supplies lasted, over time the caustic forces of nature would have their way, and any surviving equipment would return to the mineral elements from which it was originally forged.

According to a recent documentary entitled *Life After People,* experts in civil engineering and geology testify to the speed in which civilization's infrastructure would erode into nothing. If the human species were to succumb to extinction, within a few hundred years all buildings, regardless of their composition, would begin to crumble, and after a thousand years there would be very little evidence that cities of steel and concrete had ever existed. Only objects made from the hardest rock or the thickest concrete would survive. Hoover Dam might last for ten thousand years, but after that only Mount Rushmore and its solid granite faces would remain.

As for future generations, only the tools necessary to survive and eke out a living would be those that provided an advantage in the hunt or in the fields. Forget about machines and electronics, even paper and pencil. Individuals born post-apocalypse would have to begin again and forge a new society. In a few thousand years, maybe less, the civilization that once was would be nothing more than a dim memory, and within ten thousand years all traces of civilization would have vanished.

If there were various pockets of survivors scattered across the globe, different civilizations would begin to emerge, most likely with a culture and language specific to each region. Precisely how long it would take for these civilizations to emerge no one knows. Nonetheless, they would emerge all at about the same time, for human beings are inherently social and naturally organize themselves into a form that benefits the group. Once a threshold of manpower was reached, specialization would occur. Thus, civilization would be reborn. Science, trade, education, and all the other aspects of civilization would develop. Eventually, thousands of years later, civilization would reach a level comparable to what it had been eons ago, yet it might never know that a previous civilization had ever existed.

How would those later archaeologists who were excavating this civilization know that such a break in civilization had occurred? What form would the evidence take?

A large meteor impact or the eruption of a supervolcano would result in nearly everything being buried under leagues of ash, as it was sixty-five million years ago in Central America's Yucatan Peninsula, or seventy-three thousand years ago in the Toba supereruption.

In the Toba eruption, 1,740 cubic miles of magma was ejected; it covered two hundred thousand square miles of land and sea. If the Yellowstone caldera erupted, the continental United States would be devastated by a blast equivalent to that detonated by millions of Hiroshima-sized nuclear bombs, the long-term consequences of which are truly unimaginable.

The toughest of buildings farthest away from ground zero would likely survive and might still be standing if they were not subsequently disassembled for use as materials in new construction by the first few generations of survivors. So too any large monuments carved in stone.

To the new civilization many thousands of years later, Rushmore's emboldened faces would be meaningless, as would be the engraved plates within the mountain's hall of records. The new civilization would infer that the heads of Rushmore had been carved in relatively recent times by the native population of the Black Hills, even though how they accomplished such a feat would remain a mystery.

If not buried in ash, heavy structures made from thick reinforced concrete would lightly pepper the landscape. But with their chambers gutted by scavengers and their exteriors plain, there would be no way of assigning them a history. They too would be designated as structures built by primitive yet extraordinarily resourceful inhabitants.

When the new civilization reached a certain point of sophistication, its archaeologists and historians would assess and reassemble what could be determined about these structures from what legends and stories survived. They would also dig into the soil and discover other structures of a similar nature. Without any other evidence to go on, these enigmatic structures might be categorized as part of some primitive people's religious traditions, just as the more recent ancestors of the new civilization built massive religious structures to honor their god. As with all cultures, the ancient inhabitants who built these majestic temples must have been motivated completely by religious beliefs.

As years pass, the new civilization would become increasingly knowledgeable and its science would progress in unimaginable ways. Such would be its progress that life would become easy, and thus ample time would exist for many to reflect on life and on history. A number of people would become interested in the ancient ruins that dotted the countryside, and after decades of work, they would be able to recognize some of the unusual technology that previous civilizations employed. Yet, even though they were scientists and engineers, they would remain baffled by their conclusions.

Although the scenario of global cataclysm presented here is hypothetical, it hints at the technical and historical evidence you are about to read. One need only review the effect of Hurricane Katrina on the city of New

Orleans in 2005 or the Sumatra tsunami of 2004 to get a glimpse of how devastating natural catastrophes can be. The effect on civilization of a large meteor impact or a supervolcanic eruption would be so vast and so damaging that a hurricane or tsunami would be dwarfed in comparison; a whole new scale of destruction would have to be invented. Yet in our resilience, we humans would likely survive while other species became extinct.

In light of recent archaeological discoveries, such a scenario of cataclysmic decimation appears to be the best explanation for what science simply refers to as "the end of the Ice Age." It also appears to have been recorded in the most ancient of human histories, what our civilization has labeled as myth.

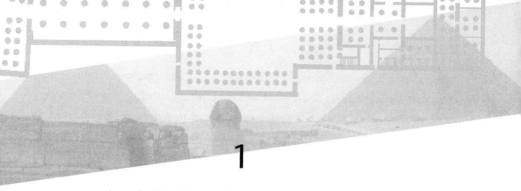

1

A CIVILIZATION IN GRANITE

Egypt might be the single most visited place in the world. It may also be the most documented place in the world. More books have been written and more documentaries have been filmed about Giza and ancient Egypt than any other ancient civilization or place. And this is for good reason: there are no other man-made monuments more grandiose than the pyramids and the Great Sphinx, and there is no temple more mysterious and majestic than Luxor's Temple of Amun-Mut-Khonsu. So large are the Giza pyramids that it wasn't until the Eiffel Tower's completion in 1889 that a building taller than the Great Pyramid was erected. Even so, the Great Pyramid still ranks as one of the most massive structures in existence. Little wonder that it is the Seventh Wonder of the World and is still standing.

In the numerous books and documentaries about ancient Egypt, what is seldom addressed in a meaningful way is the volume of granite still remaining on the plateau—even after thousands of years of scavenging. *The Oxford History of Ancient Egypt* barely mentions it except to state that "the pyramid of Menkaure shows extensive use of granite."[1] Although this is true, granite rubble can be found nearly everywhere on the Giza Plateau, particularly on the south side of the middle pyramid and to the east and south of the Valley Temple.

Without knowing its significance, tourists capture on film Giza's fields of granite rubble. Granite rubble is not majestic, nor is it anything special to show your family and friends in presentation of your vacation. In fact, granite rubble is close to being uninviting. To the average tourist the rubble scattered about the plateau might even be perceived as an eyesore compared with the majesty of the pyramids and the Sphinx. However, among the rubble there are large, beautifully crafted pieces of ornate granite displaying the handiwork of Giza's builders.

Two characteristics, each of which required a great deal of skill, distinguish the buildings of this "granite" civilization. First, the ancient Egyptians built on a colossal scale. Why they did this is a matter of conjecture, but for whatever reason, it is a good bet that they considered it necessary. The second characteristic is that the structures are finished with granite. Although most of the granite casings, facings, and columns of ancient Egypt's structures have been either destroyed or scavenged, stored in the Cairo Museum, or reduced to rubble, the granite workmanship that still exists speaks of a grand unified ancient civilization. For those who want to know not only why but also how, the abundance of granite used in the building of these structures is problematic, given the rudimentary level of skill that existed in dynastic Egypt.

Granite is the hardest rock there is. Cutting it into shapes and sizes to build a structure or carve a forty-foot statue is a feat that is today best left to modern technology and machines that use diamonds for tooling. Yet whoever built the ancient civilization that we see remnants of in Egypt were clearly experts in granite quarrying, transporting, and finishing. There is no statistic as to how much granite was used in ancient Egypt, but at nearly every ancient site there *is* granite, and a lot of it. At some sites there are multiton granite artifacts, evidence of the technical means and knowledge necessary to efficiently quarry, cut, shape, and assemble mass quantities of granite.

THE GIZA PYRAMIDS

Despite a small army of local salesmen hawking trinkets, souvenirs, and camel rides, as one wanders across the Giza Plateau it's difficult not to be awestruck by the pyramids—simply because of their sheer size. Large blocks of limestone and granite that were once part of these giant stone hills pepper the landscape as a testament to the sense of permanence the builders desired. Standing between the third and second pyramids, a local saying comes to mind: "Man fears time but time fears the pyramids." There is no sensation or vista in the world like it. From a distance, people walking along the base of the second pyramid look like an army of ants marching in rhythm to the feast of the day. The pyramids dwarf everything man-made I have ever seen, except perhaps the presidents of Mount Rushmore.

The scale of construction exceeds everything known to mankind except for the most recent projects built with twentieth-century construction technology. Each monumental pyramid on the plateau was built on the scale of Arizona's Hoover Dam. It is as if some ancient civilization's Department of the Interior decided to build not one dam but three, all within a quarter mile of each other, and then coat two of them with granite.

Today, however, these structures have been stripped of their granite glory and stand as mountains of coarse limestone blocks. Seeing them as they appeared soon after completion must have been a sight almost more spectacular than can be imagined: two large mountain peaks of pink granite and a third peak of white limestone—the brilliant sun dancing off the surfaces of all three.

The Great Pyramid, the crowning glory of the plateau and the focus of speculation for many an author, has been picked clean of its limestone casing. Only a few casing stones remain, most of which are in sorry shape. Why the builders of the Great Pyramid chose limestone as its siding is unknown. Limestone is softer than granite and easier to work with, so it is no surprise that the limestone casing of the Great Pyramid has been completely removed.

The pyramid builders also used granite in various parts of the Great Pyramid. In its interior, the uppermost chamber (more commonly known as the King's Chamber) was constructed out of smooth, solid granite slabs, some of which weigh seventy tons. Although not polished, the slabs that make up the uppermost chamber walls feel as if they were run through a planer machine. Only minute depressions remain where crystals once existed but were torn out by whatever process surfaced the slab.

The second (middle) and third pyramids were cased in granite, and amazingly some of these casings still remain today. Even more remarkable is that the second pyramid has retained its pinnacle of granite casing.

Neither the third pyramid nor the Great Pyramid have held onto casing stones near their peaks.

Why the second and third pyramids were cased in granite is a mystery. It may have been due to the beauty of granite's sparkling quartz, yet a sizable portion of the third pyramid's casing stones were never finished, but were left rough and uneven. Its uneven and bumpy exterior makes for a curious sight. An area of smooth, finished casing stones rests next to another area where each and every stone is rounded, displaying a "bumpy" appearance. Evidently it was more important for the granite casing stones to fit the inner limestone course work than to have a smooth, finished appearance. Some theorists believe that the granite casing stones were first put in place, then cut to a smooth, flat finish. Such a technique would ensure flat and even sides for the pyramid, but enough granite exists at the base of the pyramid to suggest that it had been fully cased. However, only a small section of granite casing stones near the ground level appears to have been leveled.

It might also be the case that granite was chosen for its functionality and not for its aesthetics. Granite is erosion resistant and would have been an apt choice for siding if the desired structure was intended to last for an indefinite period. On that point, it certainly appears that the pyramid builders succeeded.

Uniquely, and although no one knows why, the third pyramid has retained a greater percentage of its casing stones than the other two, and it boasts a granite pavement of megalithic proportion. Each pavement stone is nearly four feet high. Standing amid these humongous blocks, I felt as if I was in the *Land of the Giants*. Around the base of the third pyramid are piles of granite rubble, or I should say piles of boulders, really, since the blocks are incredibly large.

The descending passage of the third pyramid is also lined with granite. Discovered in 1908 by Egyptologist George Reisner, the passageway was buried, "covered with a tangled mass of great granite blocks." According to Reisner, under his direction Egyptian workers removed several hundred pieces of granite weighing anywhere from one to eleven tons from around the pyramid's entrance.[2]

How the granite casing stones of the pyramids were removed is unknown. Perhaps a major earthquake occurred at some time in the

Fig. 1.1. Vast amounts of granite rubble surround Giza's third pyramid. Notice that some of the pyramid's granite casing stones remain in place.

Fig. 1.2. Not all casing stones of the third pyramid were cut smooth. Granite may have been chosen for its durability as opposed to its beauty.

Fig. 1.3. Megalithic granite paving blocks at the base of Giza's third pyramid

remote past. The field of rubble on the east and south sides of the middle pyramid and the piles of blocks and rubble around the third pyramid suggest that an earthquake might have been the cause. Perhaps later, scavengers pilfered only the lighter stones that offered the easiest access. It might also be the case that demolition teams climbed to the top of these stone peaks and pried away the casing blocks one by one.

Whatever happened during more recent times, scavenger crews attempting to harvest the granite crop met the stubbornness of hardened volcanic stone. Whoever was attempting to break and tow away ready-made granite blocks found it a futile venture. A good portion of the granite blocks littering Giza's landscape display chisel furrows—deep cuts where someone attempted to split the block in half. Today, such acts are no doubt a crime, but for those who chose to scavenge the pyramids, it certainly was easy access to granite that had already been quarried. Prior to the eighteenth century, the pyramids were likely to have been derelict structures anyway.

Fig. 1.4. Numerous granite blocks with chisel grooves litter the base of the third pyramid. In vain, scavengers tried to split these blocks.

Fig. 1.5. Close-up of the chisel groove

Unlike the third pyramid, the second pyramid has no piles of rubble at its base. However, on the east side of the middle pyramid, within a field of granite and limestone rubble there is a clue as to the pyramid's purpose: a granite trough emerges from the sand. (See plate 1 of the color insert.) That a trough was a part of the pyramid complex suggests that its builders built for functionality. Presumably the complex might have had something to do with water, possibly irrigation.

A few hundred feet east of Giza's middle pyramid, among strewn-about granite blocks, lies another testament to the genius of the pyramid builders. Exactly what this large granite object was may never be known (speculatively, it may be the pillar of an entranceway), but its smooth surface and perfectly curved shape is an incredible feat of technology. I cannot imagine how it was carved to perfection, perfectly round and smooth to the touch. (See plate 2 of the color insert.)

The most striking aspect of this granite pillar, besides its perfect shape and smoothness, is that three surfaces—two flat surfaces and one curved—come together at its base. Next to this granite marvel lies a square pillar inscribed with hieroglyphs and another piece of curved,

Fig. 1.6. Granite and limestone rubble field on the south side of the second pyramid

Fig. 1.7. Curved granite object within a few hundred feet east of the middle pyramid

Fig. 1.8. Close-up view from the north

smooth granite. Built on a smaller scale than the pyramids and carved with elegance, the buildings from which these pieces came must have been for human occupancy or use.

There is nothing left of the structure or structures of which these unique granite artifacts were once a part. Like the casing stones of the pyramids, the buildings near the pyramids offered easy access to already finished granite. Close to the ground, they were likely the first structures to be disassembled and carried away to be used as building materials elsewhere.

THE SPHINX AND VALLEY TEMPLES

In front of the Sphinx, Giza's builders erected two temples. The northern temple is known as the Sphinx Temple and the other, the Valley Temple. Like the area surrounding the middle and third pyramids, the area surrounding the Sphinx complex, particularly in the Valley Temple's east yard, is littered with granite rubble.

Although the Sphinx Temple was at one time faced with granite, all that remains is its inner limestone core. However, much of the Valley Temple's granite is still in place. The Valley Temple's front side (east) is lined with megalithic granite blocks, each nearly six feet tall. (See plates 3 and 4 of the color insert.) The granite pillars and lintels that make up the temple's interior are also largely still intact. A puzzling feature of the corners of the Valley Temple is their strange construction. (See plate 5 of the color insert.)

A more exquisite example of technical know-how rests on the south side of the Valley Temple and is perhaps the most precise granite carving in Lower Egypt. Although what this broken block of granite was used for is unknown, it was obviously sculpted for decorative purposes.

The face of the granite block was carved in the shape of the letter S (figure 1.9), and at the end of the rolling S curve, the granite squares off to form a squared face. Its surface is still smooth to the touch.

My guide assured me that this unique granite block *was carved by hand* but did not comment on exactly how it was carved by hand or what tools were used. Considering that this ornate block is nearly four feet tall and six feet long, weighing many tons, and was part of a much larger piece, the idea that it was carved into a perfect S shape by hand defies common sense, in my opinion, given the simple hand tools available to the ancient Egyptians.

Further west along the Valley Temple there lies a second block of granite with its face also curved in an S shape. Although this second block is not a mate to the first block, its appearance is similar; it may have been used for the same purpose as the first block. One possible use for this style of block is as decorative trimming on the top of the temple wall, such as is found in the temples of Esna and Edfu in Upper Egypt.

Fig. 1.9 (right). Ornate granite block on the south side of the Valley Temple

Fig. 1.10 (below left). Ornate granite viewed on end from the west

Fig. 1.11 (below right). Ornate granite viewed on end from the east

Walking west past the Valley Temple, east of the middle pyramid, and south of the causeway, there is a maze of rock-cut tombs and crypts built into the small rolling hills of the plateau. Rock, sand, ancient brick structures, and modern restorations all blur together. It is a desolate site. The rock in which these tombs are carved is the same yellow limestone formation from which the Sphinx is carved. (See plate 6 of the color insert.) For some reason, the guides call this area "the Sphinx Museum."

I followed my guide though this long-abandoned cemetery, which resembles the no-man's-land that one might see in an old World War I film. Almost everything of interest has been moved to the Cairo Museum. The only statues that remain are those carved into walls or so broken that there is little need to pay someone to move them.

What is very noticeable is that the tombs in the area were hand cut with chisels, and the statues as well. Chisel marks are well defined in tunnels and chambers throughout the area. In a few crypts, doorposts and headers were finished and inscribed with hieroglyphs. But nowhere in this area does anything resemble the magnificence and the precision of the pyramids or the granite pillars of the Valley Temple. Then, out of the

Fig. 1.12. Second granite block ornately carved in an S shape

corner of my eye, far to the south, I noticed four dark-red pillars lightly coated with Saharan dust.

Giza's Unknown Temple

Standing at the far southern edge of this no-man's-land of rock-cut tombs is a place not featured on any Giza map, at least the maps I have seen. Yet even from a distance it is easy to see, once you crest the cemetery's final dune. Four red pillars stand erect in front of what appears to be a rock shelter, one pillar taller than the rest. It's an unusual scene for the area. The dark-red pillars stand out against a background of Sahara yellow. Beyond these giant pillars of granite the land flattens out into a cordoned area reserved for archaeologists currently working on the plateau. There, behind barbed wire, ten huge granite blocks lie neatly in a row. Armed guards are on station at various strategic points, overhead on the rocks above as well as in the distance at the area's perimeter. Most likely this is an important site, since it is also off limits.

I visited the so-called Sphinx Museum twice, each visit separated by a week. The second time a man dressed in a long blue tunic stopped my friend and me and would not let us pass into the area of the giant pillars, the point where I took the photo in figure 1.14. I desperately wanted another look. Nonetheless, the man in the blue tunic looked serious as he walked toward us with outstretched hands. My friend tried to snap a photo, but the man waved his hands in an attempt to spoil his picture. Whatever he was saying in Arabic, my Sphinx Museum guide that day understood and quickly turned us back.

I asked why and received the answer I was expecting. The area below, where the red granite pillars were, was a restricted area. Ironically, the man who turned us back had been *my guide* the previous week! And a week ago he took me wherever I wanted to go, including to the red granite pillars of the unknown temple. He spoke English quite well and without a doubt was the most cordial guide I encountered.

The week before I received a close-up view of the giant pillars. Like the Valley Temple, they were made from solid granite. But these pillars are very different. Fluted along their vertical axis and inscribed with hieroglyphs, they must have held a simple yet powerful beauty for the temple's builders (figures 1.16 and 1.17). Although the structure these stones are

Fig. 1.13 (above and opposite). Megalithic granite blocks behind the unknown temple (and barbed wire)

from no longer exists, they must have been a part of the building's exterior. I wonder: Do the hieroglyphs tell of a king or queen? Or do they pay tribute to a god? Perhaps they tell of neither and are simply a testament to the knowledge and skill of the civilization that created them.

Fig. 1.14. Granite pillars of an unknown temple

One of the pillars, the only pillar not fluted, likely weighs in excess of fifty tons. When new and unbroken, it may have weighed over one hundred tons. On the pillars that are fluted, the channels in the granite are nearly an inch deep (figure 1.16) and perfect in each pillar. The southernmost pillar, still anchored in its original paving stones, is also fluted on its backside's corners, a most impressive display of skill (figures

Fig. 1.15. Close-up of granite pillars in figure 1.14

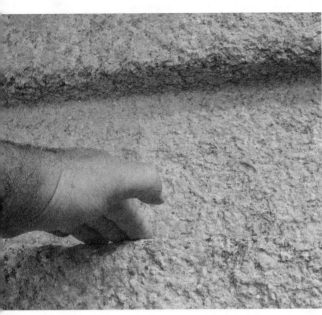

Fig. 1.16. Fluting on the granite pillars is nearly an inch deep.

Fig. 1.17. Hieroglyphs carved into granite pillars of the unknown temple

1.18 and 1.19). Although the surfaces of the pillars are not smooth, they are flat. The wind appears to have taken its toll over thousands of years and blasted out the weaker parts of the rock, resulting in a slightly rough texture to the surface.

There is more to this unknown temple than I had access to, although the rest of it lies behind locked iron gates. One pillar is visible just beyond the yellow-painted iron bars (figure 1.21).

Fig. 1.18. Fluted, red granite pillar of an unknown Giza temple

Fig. 1.19. Reverse side of pillar in figure 1.18

Fig. 1.20. My guide adds perspective to the size of the unknown temple's pillars.

Fig. 1.21. Another part of the temple sits behind iron gates.

A New Discovery at Giza

Aside from the magnificent red granite pillars of the unknown temple, the rock-cut cemetery contained another surprise, which, according to my guide, was the latest discovery on the plateau. He asked if I would like to see it. "Sure," I replied, although unsure if it was the latest discovery or not. After seeing it, I decided the baksheesh I paid to the guard for a peek was worth it.

We approached an area that was fenced off with barbed wire. Beyond the barbed wire another man waited for us; he took us down a northerly path with a turn here and a turn there. We ended up at a passageway in the west side of the short limestone cliff. Down we went. I didn't have a flashlight, but the guardian of this chamber had a small candle. He lit it with my lighter, and all at once a beautifully carved stone box came into view. (See plate 7 of the color insert.)

I am not sure if the box was carved from granite, diorite, limestone, or another type of rock. Whatever it was, the inside corners of the box were square. Its exterior was also square except for the lower right-hand side, which appeared to be damaged. The lid was intact, complete with lifting nodes at each end, and curved across the width of its body. Although the surface of the box was flat, in most areas it was not smooth. The texture of the box's surface was rough in spots. Whether this roughness was unique to the original stone or was a byproduct of the box's construction is unclear. Traditionally, all stone boxes are referred to as sarcophagi regardless of the box's style. However, sarcophagi typically are attributed to later periods of Egyptian civilization. This granite box, if created when the structures were believed to have been built, is attributable to the Fourth or Fifth Dynasty, which means it was more than four thousand years old.

SAKKARA

About ten miles south of Giza is Sakkara, which, according to Egyptologists, is the Old Kingdom's capital of the First and Second Dynasties (2920–2650 BCE) and the birthplace of the pyramid. According to Egyptologists, during the Third Dynasty (ca. 2600 BCE) the Pharaoh Djoser decided that the standard mastaba wasn't enough for a tomb. So, under the guidance of the architect Imhotep, a standard mastaba was transformed into a stepped pyramid.

Sakkara is also the only place where a large cache of unique types of stone housewares has been found, although Sir William Petrie also found fragments of similar bowls at Giza during the late nineteenth century. The stoneware was discovered in an elaborate underground tunnel system, and much of it is inscribed with symbols from the earliest kings of the predynastic era. Some have argued, because of the primitive style of the inscriptions, that it is unlikely that those who fashioned the bowls also made those signatures. It is possible that predynastic Egyptians acquired the stoneware some time after it was made, and then marked it with their sign of ownership. A number of these stone artifacts are on display at the Cairo Museum. Unfortunately, photographs are no longer allowed inside the museum.

Fig. 1.22. Sakkara's Step Pyramid

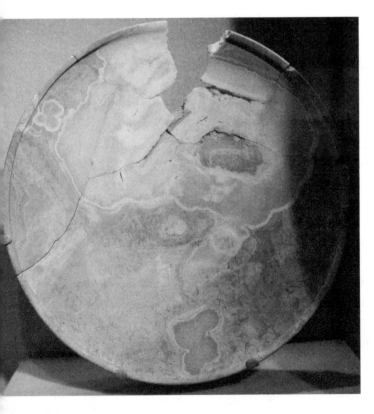

Fig. 1.23. A finely carved alabaster plate from the University of Illinois' Spurlock Museum. It was found at El Qara and dated to between 2800 and 2675 BCE.

In the center of the open bowls and plates, where the angle of the cut changes rapidly, one can see a clean, narrow, and perfectly circular line made by the tip of a cutting tool. Unmistakably, these tool marks were from lathe manufacturing (rotating an item on two spindles so the reduction of material is even on all sides). Soft stone is relatively simple to machine and can be worked with simple tools and abrasives; however, the level of precision in the manufacture of these items rivals twentieth-century industry. Delicate vases made of brittle stone such as schist were finished, turned, and polished to a flawless, paper-thin edge. One nine-inch bowl, hollowed out with a three-inch opening at its top, was flaw-lessly turned so that it balances perfectly on a rounded and tipped bottom. This tip is the size of an egg's rounded point, requiring a symmetrical wall thickness without any substantial error.

Elegant items made from granite indicate not only an accomplished level of skill, but perhaps an advanced method of cutting. Pieces made from granite, porphyry, or basalt cores were hollowed out with a narrow and flared opening, some of which have long necks.

Fig. 1.24. Granite debris at Sakkara

*Fig. 1.25 (above).
Granite column at
Sakkara*

*Fig. 1.26 (right).
Uniquely carved
granite at Sakkara*

*Fig. 1.27 (below).
Inscribed column at
Sakkara*

▲

The most historically intriguing discoveries at Sakkara are the pyramids that house what have become known as the Pyramid Texts, a set of hieroglyphics dating to the Fifth, Sixth, and Eighth Dynasties inscribed on the walls of five pyramids. In 1952, the renowned Egyptologist and professor of Semitic languages Samuel Mercer (1879–1969) composed the first complete translation of Sakkara's Pyramid Texts and concluded that they appear to have emerged as a fully fledged collection of mortuary texts without any precedent in the archaeological record. Since the texts are composed of distinct utterances, with no strict narrative sequence linking them together, scholars believe they were not composed specifically for the purpose of pyramid inscription, but may have had earlier uses.

Like Giza, Sakkara is littered with granite debris. Although whatever structures that existed have been destroyed, the evidence that remains suggests that these structures were also made of or cased in granite.

ABU SIR AND ABU GORAB

At the twin sites of Abu Sir and Abu Gorab, not far from Sakkara and a few miles south of Giza, two granite columns of Egypt's Fifth Dynasty rise into blue skies amid a field of granite ruins in front of three pyramids. Standing on the remnants of a black basalt stone patio, once a center of activity, you're compelled to wonder what happened to create the granite and limestone rubble that surrounds you. Was the destruction a result of a war or catastrophe? Even in its ruinous state, Abu Sir is beautiful.

A granite pillar ornate with hieroglyphs lies next to two standing granite "palm" columns, as does the fallen capital of a third column. Another column made from solid granite lies on the ground amid a vast amount of granite chunks weighing anywhere from one hundred pounds to several tons. The bright pink, beautifully carved granite column sparkles in the sunshine. I have never seen a column made from solid granite so intricately carved with perfect precision. It looks as if it could be new, placed there by some Hollywood production crew as a prop. (See plate 8 of the color insert.)

While standing before this broken beauty of a column, I couldn't help but think of the table legs I had made more than thirty years ago in a high school shop class. The legs of the table I created nearly matched the mix of cylindrical and square features of this granite column. I used a lathe, but how the columns at Abu Sir came to be is a mystery. They appear to be carved from a solid block of granite.

At the twin complexes of Abu Sir and Abu Gorab, the suggestion of water as a motive for building pyramids is much stronger than at Giza. At Abu Sir a trough had been built that runs through the complex and down the hill. At both sites, Abu Sir and Abu Gorab, water basins were clearly part of the structure. (See plate 9 of the color insert.)

Within Abu Sir's temple, which is believed to have been the mortuary temple of King Ptahshepses, two granite boxes were placed in a pit at the west end of the temple courtyard. Although it was apparently off limits, getting there from the temple was easy. At Abu Sir along the eastern wall of the temple and to the rear there is a low three-foot-high wall to be scaled. Over the wall there is a center court with inscribed limestone columns. At its west end, stairs lead to a pit, and in the pit lie two precision-carved pink granite boxes, one smaller than the other. Elegantly and expertly carved, these granite boxes, which are believed to have been part of the ancient Egyptians' burial practices, are nothing short of being an anachronism.

MYSTERIOUS GRANITE BOXES

These granite boxes are one of ancient Egypt's greatest mysteries. Several boxes have been found still sealed, yet when opened they were empty. Whatever the boxes may have been used for, today such workmanship requires not only mechanization (i.e., the use of machines versus hand tools), but a bit sharp enough and hard enough to remove granite. The construction of such artifacts as the granite columns and boxes receives little attention by historical "experts." It's not easy to understand why. The beauty and level of precision—particularly in the flowing palm leaves at the top of the column and the square-shouldered box lid with a rounded belly—is unsurpassed even today.

Fig. 1.28 (right). Remnant of an ornate pink granite column at Abu Sir

Fig. 1.29 (opposite and below). Columns of Abu Sir amid limestone and granite ruins

Fig. 1.30 (left). Limestone trough built on the slope of the hill that leads to the Abu Sir complex

Fig. 1.31 (below). Stone water basin at Abu Gorab

Fig. 1.32 (bottom). Nine water basins lined up at Abu Gorab

Fig. 1.33. Granite boxes of Abu Sir

If the designer's intent was that the granite box be a coffin, then why are there two at Abu Sir? Was the larger one for the king and the smaller one for the queen? If so, why do they lack inscriptions?

In the course of three thousand years of ancient Egyptian civilization, two types of granite boxes were constructed. One type is clearly a coffin and is inscribed with hieroglyphs. A number of these are on display at the British Museum in London and at the Cairo Museum in Egypt.

The second type lacks inscription and is perfectly square, and its lid is curved across the width of its body. Some of the lids have lifting nodes, bulbous protrusions at each end of the lid. It's easy to distinguish between these two types of boxes not only because of the difference in appearance, but also because of the quality of the workmanship. The quality of the first type of granite box is high, while the quality of the second type of granite box is lower, having obviously been created by hand with simple tools such as stone hammers.

There is a third type of granite box that is found only at Sakkara. This type 3 granite box is located underground in a long tunnel carved into the bedrock a little northwest of the Step Pyramid. Officially, the underground tunnel was dug during the Eighteenth Dynasty as a sacred tomb for the Apis bull. According to Egyptologists, this special bull lived a life of royalty as the physical manifestation of Ptah, the god of creation who spoke the world into existence. In myth, the Apis bull was born of a lightning bolt. When the royal bull died he was embalmed at Memphis and then buried in Sakkara's Serapeum in an extraordinarily large granite sarcophagus, a type 3 granite box nearly six feet tall.

The Serapeum was first discovered by Paul Lucas in 1851. A year later, Auguste Mariette uncovered an ancient processional route that the Greek geographer Strabo had described in the first century. Later, he unearthed the entranceway to a grand underground tunnel and discovered it contained twenty-four massive granite boxes, each weighing close to eighty tons. The huge granite boxes were empty, and it was believed that they had been emptied of their contents long ago. Later, however, Mariette did uncover intact burials. One was attributed to the reign of Horemheb and two others to the reign of Ramses II. The burials attributed to Ramses, which were two large gold coffins, contained the remains of Apis bulls, which had been dismembered and individually wrapped. Also discovered were four large canopic jars, each displaying the head of a man and containing the internal organs of the bulls. A third coffin contained a mask made of hammered gold and mummified remains believed to be those of Khamwese, the son of Ramses II.

Like the type 1 granite boxes at Abu Sir, the British Museum, and the Cairo Museum, the Serapeum's granite boxes were finished with a high degree of accuracy. According to expert machinist Christopher Dunn, their corners, both inside and outside, are incredibly square. The inside corner of one box measured $5/32$ inch, a very tight corner even in today's world of computerized precision manufacturing. Dunn also measured the flatness of a twenty-seven-ton granite lid to be accurate to 0.0002 inches.[3]

The precision that these granite boxes display is very difficult if not impossible to explain, especially when excluding the use of high-quality and high-precision tools. It is a matter of physical geometry, meaning that for the box's lid to be square with its two inside walls, the inside walls have to be exactly parallel along its vertical axis. Furthermore, the top edges of the box (all four sides) need to be exactly the same height to

Fig. 1.34 (top). Type 1 (high quality) pink granite box at the British Museum
Fig. 1.35 (bottom). Type 1 (high quality) pink granite box at the Cairo Museum

establish a plane that is square to the sides. Whoever created these boxes made sure that the inside walls were flat vertically as well as horizontally, and also made sure that the surfaces were square and parallel. This is a very difficult task to accomplish without precision measuring and cutting tools, even more so when the sides of the box are nearly six feet apart.

In London's British Museum two granite boxes share the general construction specifications but diverge in the quality of their workmanship. A pink granite box, nearly identical to the one at Abu Sir, is a precision-quality product, symmetrical in its creation (figure 1.34). Its overall shape is square, with beautiful fluting evenly spaced on each of the box's four sides. Its lid has square shoulders that are rounded along the vertical axis. In contrast, the black granite box (figure 1.36) is roughly square at one end but rounded at the other. The hieroglyphs carved on its exterior resemble scratches more than they do inscriptions. The same is true of granite boxes at the Cairo Museum. How can the divergence of quality be explained?

One explanation is that the boxes of lesser quality were crafted by amateurs who were trying to replicate the work of a professional. Another explanation is that boxes of lesser quality are older and that a progression of workmanship occurred over thousands of years. A third explanation is that the difference in the quality of workmanship is because the boxes are from two different civilizations. Whatever the case, the *official* explanation is that the boxes are from different periods of the same civilization. However, the difficulty with this last explanation is that *the older boxes are the ones that display a higher quality of workmanship.* The granite boxes from Abu Sir and Sakkara are from the Old Kingdom era, which would mean that ancient Egypt's technical skills declined over time.

How is it explained that ancient Egypt began civilization with the ability to carve high-quality objects and then lost that ability through the course of the next thousand years? A more baffling question: Why would anyone quarry a one-hundred-ton block of granite for the purpose of hollowing it out to make a covered box, and then bury it deep within the earth? And how could they accomplish it with such precision that today's mechanized granite industry would be hard-pressed to duplicate their efforts? (See plate 10 of the color insert.)

As stated earlier, it is argued by Egyptologists that everything in ancient

Fig. 1.36 (top). Type 2 (low quality) granite box at the British Museum
Fig. 1.37 (bottom). Type 2 (low quality) granite box at the Cairo Museum

Egypt was manufactured with the simplest of tools, specifically copper chisels. wooden mallets, and stone hammers. But there is great difficulty in accepting this explanation. Whoever pilfered the Giza Plateau in search of building materials for their own needs used chisels, and possibly chisels that were made of iron, to break the available stones into more manageable blocks. The futility they faced in using hand tools is obvious. More importantly, the quality of chisel work, as seen in figure 1.38 (which is a typical sight near Giza's third pyramid), is nothing like the precision found in such artifacts as the granite boxes of Abu Sir or the Serapeum.

Whoever crafted the four-thousand-year-old granite boxes did so with incredible skill. Perfectly straight and square corners are easy enough to do with wood, but with granite the weight of the material and strength of the tool tip required to make the cuts are prohibiting factors. Added to that is the difficulty of making an even curvature of the lid (see figure 1.33 on page 33).

Fig. 1.38. Attempt to split a granite block using hand tools

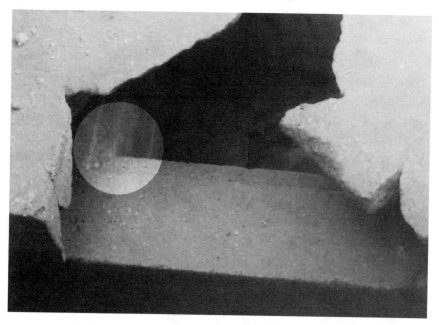

Fig. 1.39. A beveled lip perfectly cut into the top of a box

Fig. 1.40. The four shoulders of Abu Sir's granite box lid where the shoulders meet the curved body of the lid

Still, the most interesting aspect of Abu Sir's pink granite boxes is that a mistake is visible on the lid of the larger box; this was noticed by Christopher Dunn[4] (figure 1.40). As the arrow indicates, a rounded gouge is visible where the square shoulder of the box meets the curved part of the lid. Clearly, a workman would not have stood over this granite, pounding away to make this indentation. The only reasonable explanation is that the operator of some kind of powered machine* pressed in too deeply and made this mark by accident. But that requires the presence of a civilization still unrecognized in history, a civilization that I call Civilization X.

Although the precision with which these granite boxes were carved is incredible, a more incredible feat of workmanship is the carving of the Great Sphinx. Despite its advanced state of erosion, the Sphinx is the most elegant monument not just in Egypt, but the world. No one knows why it was carved, or even when it was carved, although Egyptology's preferred date is during the Old Kingdom's Fourth Dynasty, around 2500 BCE.

However, there are difficulties accepting this date, and the problem has as much to do with history as it does with the geological evidence.

---

*By "powered machine" I am referring to a device powered by nonhuman energy, however, the exact type of power that may have been used is unknown. Some speculate that it might have been sound, in the same way that compressed air is used to power tools today.

2

A PREHISTORIC SPHINX

The Great Sphinx is an enduring, enigmatic icon of ancient civilization. It is also one of history's biggest mysteries. There's nothing else like Giza's incredible Sphinx. Although a consensus of Egyptologists places its carving at around 2600 BCE by the Fourth Dynasty Pharaoh Khafre, there are no Old Kingdom records or any other ancient Egyptian records that state Khafre ordered it carved. In fact, according to Pliny the Elder (23–79 CE), the Egyptians of the first century passed over it in silence.[1]

Sphinx is derived from the Greek word *sphingo* or *sphingein*, which means to strangle or to bind tight. Although no one knows for sure what the earliest Egyptians called the Sphinx, its name is believed to be linked to the Egyptian phrase *shesep-ank*, which translates as "living image." During the latter half of the second millennium BCE it was referred to as Hor-em-akht (Horus in the Horizon), as Bw-How (Place of Horus), and also as Ra-horakhty (Ra of Two Horizons).

Sitting in a rectangular hollow, the Sphinx was excavated and carved from the bedrock limestone permeating the Giza Plateau. Only the head and uppermost portions of this monstrous lion lie above the surface of the plateau. When the Sphinx was being carved, the limestone rock removed from this area was used to build a temple directly in front of the Sphinx, to the east. According to Egyptologists, this was accomplished during the Old Kingdom's Fourth Dynasty, between 2575 and 2467 BCE.

However, this history and date were applied to the Sphinx at a time when Western society was moving through a period of great change, particularly in how the philosophical tenets of life were viewed. The latter half of the nineteenth century was a highly charged period of shifting paradigms, particularly in Great Britain. Under the scholarship of Charles Lyell and later Charles Darwin, the biblically based view of history was being replaced with the concepts of evolution and uniformitarianism. Although wary at first, by the turn of the century, academia had wholly embraced this new view. Science became the means by which knowledge was ascertained, and it soon became the mantra of all the academic disciplines, even for those programs of study that had little to do with science. Nonetheless, they too became science, albeit "social science." This is not to say that those disciplines are not scholarly and don't use systematic approaches to understanding history. But it must be recognized that what happened so long ago is more a matter of detective work than it is science. However, in the matter of Egypt's Great Sphinx, the science of geology has been able to interject new insights into an old tradition.

THE SPHINX AND WATER EROSION

In 1990, author and independent researcher John Anthony West teamed up with the Boston University geologist Dr. Robert M. Schoch and embarked on a project to investigate the possibility that the Great Sphinx was carved, at least in part, before 2500 BCE. West believed the weathering of the Sphinx and its enclosure was the result of rainwater, which

Fig. 2.1. The Sphinx in its enclosure

would have to have occurred prior to the third millennium BCE, when North Africa was still receiving rainfall.

Schoch, a scientist and skeptic, initially believed that he would be able to convince West of the error of his unconventional views concerning the Sphinx and its associated structures.[2]

> I found that West had a very extreme idea that the Sphinx was thousands of years older than the Egyptologists thought. Although I considered this view a long shot, I also wondered if he wasn't on to something. Given that I am a curious person, I thought it was worth a further look.[3]

Schoch and West visited Egypt in early 1991 to study the Sphinx and its enclosure. After a detailed survey of the Sphinx's eroded features, Schoch became convinced that there was more to the story than established history was able to explain.

At Giza, Schoch concluded that the Sphinx and the Valley Temple had been constructed in two stages and had undergone repair, even during ancient times. He also ascertained that the Sphinx temple, and possibly the Valley Temple, were constructed from limestone blocks quarried from the Sphinx enclosure, most likely while the Sphinx was being carved. If true, this meant that the temple structures must be as old as the Sphinx itself. Later, according to Schoch, these temples had been faced with granite ashlars (carved smooth stones) to cover weathering that had developed since their construction.

Fig. 2.2. The Sphinx's head and part of its back rise above ground level.

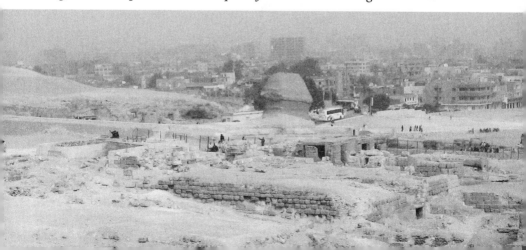

Where the Valley Temple's walls have been stripped of their granite facings, an irregular surface is visible. This uneven surface, "higgledy-piggledy" as Schoch refers to it, is apparently a result of its rehabilitators cutting back and smoothing out the weathered walls before applying the granite facings.[4] It looks "higgledy-piggledy" because only enough limestone was removed to set the granite ashlars in place.

In various places, the backside of the granite siding was cut to fit the bumpy patterns of the wall. In this way, the granite blocks were matched to the shape of the irregular weathering patterns on the limestone substructure. For Schoch, it was apparent that the weathering of the structures was already substantial *even in ancient times*.

Schoch also noted that there were four distinct types of weathering exhibited in the area in and around the Sphinx: rainwater, wind, flaking, and disintegration (or dissolution). Weathering from rainwater, Schoch concluded, is visible on the body of the Sphinx and on its enclosure walls. This is clear, a "textbook example" as Schoch refers to it, from the rolling and undulating profile of the enclosure walls, particularly the southern and western walls. According to Schoch, these eroded features are well developed and prominent within the enclosure. Furthermore, they are also visible where flowing water followed joints and faults in the rock.[5]

Weathering from wind, which is distinctly different from erosion by rain, is also evident on the Giza Plateau. Schoch believes that this weathering probably began during Old Kingdom times (2650–2152 BCE). Various Old Kingdom tombs and land features south and west of the Sphinx, carved from the same layers of limestone as its body, are exemplary of wind erosion. At Giza, on hard layers of rock, faces carved on tombs and statues are still clearly visible. But on softer layers of rock, wind and sand have gouged out deep horizontal tunnels, creating a "wind tunnel" characteristic on the rock's surface.

One way to envision wind erosion is to think of the limestone bedrock as a layer cake. Each alternating layer of cake and icing represents hard and soft layers of stone. When the cake is cut in half, its profile is exposed and its layers are clearly visible. If you run your finger along a cake layer, the cake doesn't give. However, running your finger along an icing layer, representing the soft stone, results in a horizontally scooped-out look. Such is the nature of wind erosion on hard and soft rock layers.

The third type of erosion that has affected the rock surfaces is known as exfoliation or flaking. According to Schoch, the flaking apparent on the Sphinx and temple structures occurred relatively recently (within the last two hundred years) as a result of modern causes such as acid rain and air pollution. A fourth type of weathering, called dissolution, exists in only a few places, such as tombs, as a result of the evaporation cycle occurring in enclosed spaces. The condensation and evaporation of water in the atmosphere covers the rock with a very fine coating of mineral crystals, giving the rock's surface in these areas the appearance of melted wax.

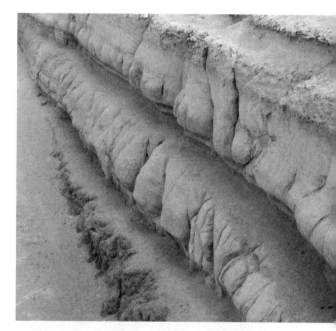

Figs. 2.3 and 2.4. Water erosion on the southeast wall of the Sphinx enclosure

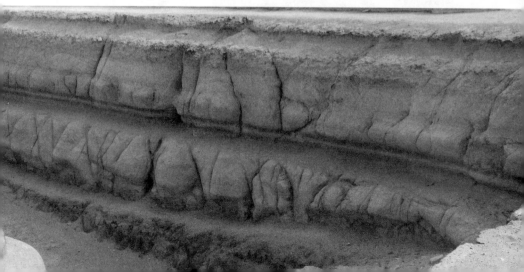

Fig. 2.5 (top). At Sakkara, wind erosion on a minor pyramid's casing stones
Fig. 2.6 (bottom). Wind erosion on limestone hills at Giza

Fig. 2.7. Erosion on the back (west) side of the Sphinx enclosure

According to Schoch, in some cases the four different types of weathering may be difficult to distinguish, with one type overlain by another, but in general, the different forms of weathering are clear and distinct. What Schoch refers to as precipitation-induced weathering is the oldest prevalent type of weathering on the Giza Plateau and is significant only on the oldest Giza structures, such as is seen with the Sphinx body and its enclosure.

Another aspect of the Sphinx that supports Schoch's analysis is the restoration efforts that occurred during Old Kingdom times. Beginning with the ancient Egyptians themselves and continuing to the present, the Sphinx has undergone a number of repair campaigns—during the Old Kingdom in 2500 BCE; in New Kingdom times in 1400 BCE; during the Twenty-Sixth Dynasty, 664–525 BCE; and also during the Greco-Roman era, between 300 BCE and 400 CE.[6] During these repairs, the ruler often excavated the Sphinx enclosure from the sands that would fill its surrounding hollow when left unattended for a few decades. After excavation, repair blocks were often mortared to the weathered body in an attempt to restore the sculpture to its original figure.

According to Schoch, the earliest repair to the Sphinx's surface was performed using what appears to be an Old Kingdom–style masonry technique. If this is true, then the Sphinx would have had to exist well before dynastic Egypt. Obviously, a few hundred years would not be enough time for significant weathering to occur that would require restoration.

DATING THE SPHINX WITH SEISMIC REFRACTION

The surface of limestone rock looks solid, but from a geologic perspective the rock is actually soft and porous. This is because once rock is cut and exposed to the atmosphere it begins to weather, and the depth of weathering below the surface correlates precisely with how long that rock has been exposed to the elements. In this process of weathering, rock becomes softer. Some of the particles that make up the rock dissolve, and it becomes a weaker rock. How deeply the weathering penetrates into the rock below its surface depends on the type of rock it is as well as how long it has been exposed to the elements.

Seismic refraction, which is the charting of geological features through the use of sound waves, enables geologists to map the boundary between weak, weathered rock and the underlying hard limestone. Thus, by locating to what depth the rock has become deteriorated, an estimate can be made as to how long ago the excavation occurred.

With the assistance of seismologist Dr. Thomas Dobecki, Schoch performed a seismic refraction survey to create an image of the Sphinx enclosure's subsurface weathering. The results indicated that the weathering below the surface is not uniform, which strongly suggests, according to Schoch, that the Sphinx area was not quarried all at once. So, by estimating when the least weathered area was excavated and thereby first exposed, he could estimate the minimum age of the Sphinx.

According to Schoch's data, the front and sides of the Sphinx enclosure displayed weathering that measured from 6 to 8 feet in depth. However, along the back (west) side, the limestone had been weathered to a depth of only 4 feet—a finding that was completely unexpected—supporting the theory that the Sphinx was not carved all at once. Alternatively, if the Sphinx had been carved out all at once, it would be reasonable to assume that the surrounding limestone would generally show the same depth of weathering, 6 to 8 feet deep.[7]

One interpretation of these results is that only the sides and front of the Sphinx were initially carved. If so, the Sphinx would have appeared as an outcropping with its rear still part of the natural rock. Schoch believes a likely scenario is that its rear was initially carved but only to the level of the upper terrace, which today remains immediately west of the Sphinx within the enclosure.

An alternative theory is that the rear of the Sphinx was originally carved from the bedrock, but with only a narrow passage existing between it and the enclosure wall. Later that passage was widened. Whatever the case may be, it is clear from the seismic tests performed in April 1991 that the limestone floor behind the Sphinx's rear was exposed after the front part of the Sphinx was carved.

According to Schoch, if the New Kingdom restorations during the Eighteenth Dynasty (1539–1295 BCE) were responsible for detaching the Sphinx's rear from the enclosure wall, then it would not be possible to account for four feet of subsurface weathering, since up to that time the Sphinx enclosure was filled with sand. Therefore, Schoch's opinion is that Khafre uncovered the limestone floor behind the Sphinx in 2500 BCE, and as a result the limestone floor began to weather.

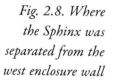

Fig. 2.8. Where the Sphinx was separated from the west enclosure wall

SCHOCH'S CONCLUSION

Based in part on his analysis of the data that the weathering of the limestone floor surrounding the Sphinx is 50 to 100 percent deeper at the front and sides than at the rear, and assuming that the rear floor was first exposed to the air in 2500 BCE, the original carving of the Sphinx (its front and sides) took place between 5000 and 7000 BCE. In other words, the front of the Sphinx is twice as old as its back—somewhere between 2,500 and 5,000 years older.[8]

This is a conservative estimate, however, according to Schoch. Since weathering rates are not constant, *the initial carving may be even older.* If the Sphinx was heavily weathered by precipitation at an early period in its existence, Schoch argues that it may have been carved prior to the last great period of major precipitation in the Nile Valley, which means it may be closer to 10,000 years old.

Egypt experienced a period of unpredictable flooding during this era of high rainfall, referred to as the Nabtian Pluvial. But it is also possible that sporadic heavy rains along the Nile may have lasted until as late as 2350 BCE. Even during historical times, wetter conditions and sporadic and unusually high Nile inundations have been recorded.

However, Nile flooding as a cause for the Sphinx's erosion—rather than ordinary rain erosion—does not stand up to scrutiny, according to Schoch. In the walls of the Sphinx enclosure, the lowest rocks, which are generally softer than the layers higher on the wall, jut out more than the rocks at the very top. If sudden flooding of the area by Nile waters was a significant cause of erosion, then the soft rocks at the bottom of the walls would have eroded farther back. As floodwaters rose, they would have undercut the uppermost rocks. But this is not what is exhibited in the Sphinx enclosure; the topmost layers of rock, which are harder, are receded farther than any other layer.

According to Schoch, it is clearly rain that is responsible for the eroded features on the Sphinx and Sphinx enclosure: "This is a classic, textbook example of what happens to a limestone wall when you have rains beating down on it for thousands of years."[9]

Schoch published his analysis of the Sphinx seventeen years ago, and since that time his work has not been challenged in any scientific way. One man, however, has put forth an alternative theory.

In 1999, an attempt to reconcile the geological features of the Giza Plateau and provide a more palatable date for Egyptologists came from British geologist Colin Reader.[10] Reader reviewed the geology, geomorphology, and surface hydrology of the Giza Plateau and put forth a revised sequence of development for those structures. He also considered the development of ancient Egyptian stone masonry, and in the end reconciled the geological and archaeological evidence, placing the carving of the Sphinx within the context of the First or Second Dynasty (2920–2650 BCE). Reader does agree with Schoch that water was a prominent force of weathering. The quarrying of the Sphinx enclosure, the carving of the Sphinx, and the construction of the Sphinx temple occurred before Khafre's Fourth Dynasty projects, just after 3000 BCE. The relative weakness of the Upper Mokattam limestone, from which the Sphinx was carved, along with the prevailing climatic conditions, makes it conceivable, in Reader's opinion, that intense weathering could have developed within a shorter period.

Although arid conditions were predominant during the early dynasties, conditions were generally not as dry as today's. With less-arid conditions, chemical weathering likely resulted in the leaching of soluble salts from the exposed rock. As this soluble component was removed from the rocks, the potential for further chemical weathering was reduced.

The exposed rock that was not subjected to rainfall runoff became weathered as a result of leaching, the process by which soluble materials in the soil or rock (salts, nutrients, other chemicals or contaminants) are washed into a lower layer or are dissolved and carried away by water. However, in the western area of the Sphinx enclosure, heavy seasonal rainfall runoff removed much of the weathered limestone, exposing comparatively unweathered rock. Given the soluble component of newly exposed rocks, this type of erosion likely promoted a renewed phase of chemical weathering and leaching, which accelerated the deterioration process. Reader believes that these particularly aggressive and repetitive weathering conditions in the western area of the enclosure could have developed over a relatively short time, in geological terms.

In essence, Reader suggests that sporadic but intense thunderstorms were responsible for the erosion on the body of the Sphinx. As heavy rains were unable to soak into the sand, a sheet of water formed on the surface and cascaded down the slope of the plateau and over the southern and western enclosure walls.

SPHINX EROSION: A COMPARATIVE ANALYSIS

All land surfaces can be considered hill slopes, even if they have no incline (a flat surface has a "slope" of zero degrees). In most cases, the erosion of a slope can be considered a system that links together weathering (the breakdown of rock), hill-slope processes (such as mass wasting of solid rock and the movement of loose rock and soil downslope by either gravity or running water), and erosion, which typically occurs from rivers in valley bottoms.

Rainfall is the source of water erosion. Whether the water infiltrates the ground depends on rainfall intensity and the rate of infiltration allowed by surface conditions. Where rainfall intensity exceeds the infiltration capacity of the soil, shallow water flows over the land. This "saturation" overflow occurs mainly at the base of slopes and in concavities. The ground becomes saturated during prolonged rain by a combination of infiltration, the downslope flow within the soil, and groundwater flow. Once the soil is saturated, its infiltration capacity is zero, so any additional rain cannot soak in. When this occurs, it is stored on the surface or becomes overland flow.

Water that infiltrates the ground becomes either soil moisture or groundwater. Just above the water table there is a capillary fringe, where water is drawn up from the water table by capillary action, referred to as "discontinuous saturation." Typically, the water table is not level and follows the shape of the surface—higher under hills, lower in valleys. Because of this, both soil moisture and groundwater can flow from higher to lower elevations, although these flows are usually very slow. A typical flow rate for clean sand is around 10 meters (11 yards) a day; the main contribution of slope erosion is the removal of material by water.

Water flowing overland, whether in a channel or moving across an open plain, transports sediment down a slope. This results in sheet wash, rills, and gullies. Sheet wash is, as the name suggests, a sheet of water flowing across a surface. It is the uniform removal of soil without the development of visible water channels, and it is the least apparent of erosion types. Rills occur when sheet wash concentrates into many small but conspicuous channels. Gullies occur when sheet wash and/or rills concentrate into larger flows. Sheet wash is aided by rain-splash erosion—in which raindrops detach particles from the surface—and is most effective in dry regions that lack protective vegetation. In all cases, the movement of soil and rock particles by flowing water is erosion.

Where infiltration is low and rainfall intensity highly significant, overland flowing water occurs. Infiltration is affected greatly by the presence of vegetation, which promotes water absorption by maintaining an open soil structure. For this reason, so-called Hortonian flows (flows that do not drain into channels or gullies) occur mainly in arid regions with poor vegetation cover. These areas are subject to rare but intense thunderstorms, such as in the southwestern United States, as well as in areas of northern Africa. In these places, intense rain may last only a few minutes, but in that short amount of time significant erosion can occur.

More than twenty-five years of geological and archaeological investigations in the extremely arid regions of southwestern Egypt and northwestern Sudan demonstrate that less-arid conditions existed in these areas beginning around 8000 BCE. At that time, the eastern Sahara changed from an extremely arid, lifeless desert to a semiarid savanna that attracted plants and animals. This life-supporting climate continued for several thousand years and then gradually deteriorated. Around the third millennium BCE the current episode of extreme aridity ensued. This prehistoric wet period can further be broken down into a sequence of three phases. The first existed from 8000 to 6200 BCE, the second from 6100 to 5900 BCE, and the third from 5700 to 2600 BCE.

Reader believes that the rains were heavy enough during this last wet phase to account for the visible erosion. Furthermore, he also believes that rainfall runoff and sheet wash (not direct rainfall) were the source of the water erosion on the Sphinx's western enclosure wall. Thus, any exposed rock would suffer from runoff following the rains and would be heavily eroded. Once the rock from the west of the Sphinx was quarried during the Fourth Dynasty, the potential for runoff erosion of the enclosure walls ended. So the Sphinx was carved before 2500 BCE at least.

The walls of the Sphinx enclosure exhibit erosion to a depth of 3 feet and at its greatest point to a depth of over 6½ feet.[11] So the pertinent question is, how long did it take for this erosion to occur?

According to geology textbooks, the lowering of ground through water erosion is generally a slow process. The rate at which rock erodes depends on the type of rock. In general, igneous and metamorphic rock erodes 0.5 to 7.0 mm every 1,000 years; sandstone, 16 to 34 mm every 1,000 years; and limestone, 22 to 100 mm every 1,000 years.

TABLE 2.1. EROSION RATES FOR ROCK (IN INCHES)

Type	Per 1,000 years	Per 10,000 years
igneous/metamorphic	0.002–0.28	0.02–2.8
sandstone	0.24–1.34	2.4–13.4
limestone	0.87–3.94	8.7–39.4

Although there is no available data for erosion rates on the Giza Plateau, geologists have studied the erosion of rock formations around the world. One of the most well-known eroded features in North America is the Grand Canyon. Geologists have calculated that the canyon is 6 million years old. Since it is 6,000 feet deep at its deepest point, this means that every 1 million years the canyon rock erodes 1,000 feet. In other words, every year for the past 6 million years the Colorado River has eroded the underlying bedrock by 0.001 foot, which is 0.012 inch per year. If we applied this rate of erosion to the Sphinx's enclosure walls, it would take 3,000 years to erode 3 feet, and 6,000 years to erode 6. However, one would expect the steady force of the Colorado River to erode rock at a much faster rate than either rainfall or sheet wash from rainstorms.

All running water gathers and transports particles of soil and fragments of rock. Every stream carries material that has been received from its tributaries or from its own banks, suspended or rolling along its bottom. These particles strike against the bedrock of the stream's channel and literally grind away the surface; they eventually settle out along the channel or get transported out to sea. In this way, the Mississippi River has been reducing the underlying bedrock at the rate of 1 foot every 9,000 years, which is 0.0013 inch per year. If the Sphinx's enclosure walls eroded as the same rate as the Mississippi River's foundations, it would take 28,000 years for 3 feet of erosion and 56,000 for 6 feet. (Of course, a large-volume river has a significantly greater erosional force than does periodic rain or sheet wash, so this is not a comparison of like phenomena.)

In studying the Wutach catchment (a catchment is a geographical area where water collects) in the southeastern region of Germany's Black Forest, European geologists Philippe Morel, Friedhelm von Blackenburg, Mirjam Schaller, Matthias Hinderer, and Peter Kubik calculated the rate of erosion for sandstone at 9 to 14 mm every 1,000 years; granite, 27 to 37 mm every 1,000 years; and limestone, 70 to 90 mm (which is 2¾–3½ inches) every 1,000 years.[12] Using 3 inches as an average rate of limestone erosion every 1,000 years (0.003 inch per year), it would take 12,000 years for the Sphinx enclosure to erode 3 feet and 24,000 for 6 feet.

According to the geologists John Stone and Paulo Vasconcelos, erosion rates in Australia vary with climate and the character of the rock formation, as well as the local landscape. In the highlands of Papua, New Guinea, chlorine-36 measurements on calcite from limestone outcrops around the island indicate that erosion rates from rainfall vary from 1 meter every million years in the arid interior to 150 meters every million years in more humid regions. That's a range of 1 millimeter (0.03937 inch) to 150 millimeters (6 inches) every 1,000 years. According to these rates, it would take anywhere between 6,000 and 1 million years to erode the Sphinx enclosure walls 3 feet, and between 12,000 and 2 million years to erode 6 feet.[13]

More importantly, Stone and Vasconcelos concluded that limestone erosion rates are well correlated with average annual rainfall at values close to those predicted by the equilibrium solubility of calcite. In other words, the more it rains, the greater the rate of erosion in limestone rock.

TABLE 2.2 EROSION RATES PER 1,000 YEARS (IN INCHES) FOR VARIOUS GEOGRAPHIC AREAS[14]

	Minimum	Maximum	Average
Galilee	—	—	0.001
Mississippi	—	—	1.3
Wutach	2.75	3.5	2.0
Australia	0.04	6.0	3.02
Grand Canyon	—	—	12.0
Giza (Schoch)	16	29	22.5
Giza (traditional)	—	—	72.0
Niagara (American Falls)	—	—	250.0

Geologists Ari Matmon, Ezra Zilberman, and Yehouda Enzel, in their study of tectonic activity in the Galilee region of Israel, were able to provide the first estimated rates of landscape-forming processes. According to their study, limestone erosion occurred at a rate of approximately 29 meters every million years, which is 0.029 millimeter (0.00114 inch) per year. At this rate, it would take the Sphinx enclosure wall 32,000 years to erode 3 feet and 64,000 years to erode 6 feet.[15]

One instance where rock rapidly erodes is at Niagara Falls. According to geologists, the falls have receded 11.4 kilometers (7 miles) in 12,400 years, a very fast average rate of nearly 1 meter per year. However, the rate of erosion has decreased recently because of the erosion-resistant limestone caprock the falls now flow over. This limestone layer begins approximately ½ kilometer north of Rainbow Bridge. Still, as the falls continue to erode southward, the erosion rate will, again, increase when the flow reaches another soft layer of rock near Navy Island.

Niagara Falls is actually composed of three falls: the American Falls, between Prospect Point and Luna Island; the Bridal Veil Falls, between Luna Island and Goat Island; and the Horseshoe (Canadian) Falls, between Goat Island and Table Rock. Rock characteristics vary among these different areas. In general, the natural bedrock at the falls is composed of soft shale and limestone. Over the years, the continual flow of water has caused large sections of bedrock to break away. The soft shale erodes faster than limestone, undermining its stability. Today, the American Falls has no regular mode of collapse. So the present amount of water flowing over the American Falls is insufficient to erode the dolostone talus (slope formed by rock debris) at the base of the falls. (Dolostone is similar to limestone but is composed mostly of the mineral dolomite.) The current rate of erosion at the American Falls is estimated at ¼ inch per year—250 inches (20 feet) every 1,000 years. Furthermore, the water flow, which is regulated at a minimum level of 10 percent of the estimated 100,000 cubic feet per second during the summer (half that during winter), is insufficient to cause major erosion.

As various as they may be, environmental influences will always play a role in physical and chemical weathering rates. Records show physical weathering is most pronounced in cool, humid climates, because of water's characteristic of freezing and thawing. On the other hand, rates for chemical weathering are driven by temperature and water supply.

As a result, chemical weathering is most pronounced in hot, humid regions. Since water is a large factor in chemical weathering, as well as erosion when particles are moved away, weathering rates and erosion are slowest in arid environments, which is precisely what Stone and Vasconcelos found in their Australian study. It is also why rivers produce some of the greatest erosion rates.

There is a well-documented correlation of annual rainfall and temperature with weathering and erosion, and this correlation serves as a

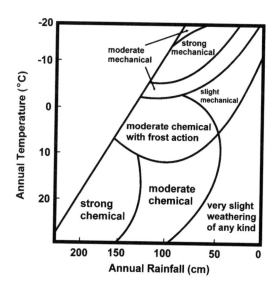

Fig. 2.9. Weathering regions according to temperature and rainfall (from Geological Sciences Department, California State Polytechnic University)

principle for understanding what types of erosion can be expected in various climates. In regions where rainfall and temperature are both relatively high—for example, a tropical rain forest—chemical weathering (the breakdown of rocks resulting from chemical reactions between the minerals in the rocks and substances in the environment such as water and oxygen) is strongest and a predominant feature of exposed rock. At the other extreme, where both temperature and rainfall are relatively low, mechanical weathering is predominant and may be slight to moderate depending on the rainfall.

Mechanical weathering is the process by which frost action, salt-crystal growth, absorption of water, and other physical processes break down a rock to fragments, involving no chemical change. Temperate latitudes in North America and Europe are good examples of regions that experience prominent mechanical weathering, although in some areas annual rainfall may exceed 50 inches.

In extremely arid areas, one would expect to find only very slight weathering of any kind. What *would* be expected is erosion from airborne particles by way of windstorms. North Africa and the Middle East are good examples of this type of erosion, as well as the desert region that stretches from northern Mexico into the southwestern United States.

Geologists seldom generalize about rates of weathering and erosion, because weathering and erosion vary in each climate, and perhaps in microclimates within each climate. There is also the type of rock and terrain to consider. However, for a given area, one would expect a certain range of weathering and erosion that would be consistent with the model presented in figure 2.9. Substantial deviations from those ranges suggest that the climate was different in the past.

The geological principles of weathering and erosion can explain the wide range of erosion rates in the Australian study. In Australia's interior, it is hot and dry with very little weathering. But in New Guinea, where monsoons occur between December and March and again between May and October, weathering occurs at a much greater rate.

The discovery of erosion rates outside a climate's expected erosion range poses a problem that requires an explanation. The greater the deviation, the more difficult it is to explain. At some point the deviation becomes so large that one is forced to reconsider the assumed timeline to bring it into accordance with known geological principles.

Although erosion rates vary from region to region based on climate, rock type, and terrain, geological evidence indicates that limestone rock erodes at a very slow rate unless subject to the force of a mighty river, such as the Niagara. The amount of water flow (a function of rainfall and natural drainage systems) and the hardness of the rock are the two most important factors determining the rate of erosion.

As far as the erosion on the Sphinx and its enclosure is concerned, Egypt experienced three wet periods between 8000 and 2600 BCE, as previously mentioned. Yet the rainfall during these wet periods averaged just enough—12 to 24 inches annually—to turn the climate from arid to semiarid, resulting in a landscape similar to the southwest region of North America: dry, but wet enough to allow plant and animal life to flourish.

I argue that we can use geologists' knowledge of erosion to answer the question of the Sphinx's age. As would be expected, the softer limestone has eroded to a greater degree than the harder layers. However, the hard layers, especially at the top of the west enclosure wall, also show significant weathering. To explain this, Schoch postulates that the erosion occurred over many thousands of years, specifically from rainfall. Reader argues that it occurred relatively quickly, during Egypt's early dynastic times (2920–2650 BCE), because of sporadic and severe thunderstorms that resulted in sheet wash rolling across the plain and over the edge of the enclosure.

Given the known climate of Egypt for the past 10,000 years, it is highly probable the temperature and rainfall characteristics of the area fall into the region, noted in figure 2.9, where "very slight weathering of any kind" would be expected. The average rate of limestone erosion, drawn from table 2.2 found on page 56 (excluding the Giza plateau and Niagara Falls), is 3½ inches every 1,000 years. Using this average, it would take 10,000 years for the Sphinx's western enclosure wall to erode 3 feet, and 20,000 years for it to erode 6 feet. Although it would be incorrect to assume that this is actually the case, these figures support Schoch's conclusion that rock weathers slowly, and that the Great Sphinx of Egypt eroded in this manner.

If Reader is correct in his analysis that the erosion occurred at a faster pace, how many thunderstorms would be necessary to cause the observed degradation? What amount of water, and during what length of time, would be needed to flow down the plain and over the top of the enclosure wall? Although Giza did experience rainfall during early and predynastic times, the climatic evidence suggests that these rainy periods were moderate and not long-lived.[16]

The alternative to either Schoch or Reader's theory is that the conventional view is correct and the observed erosion occurred during the Fourth and Fifth dynasties, between about 2500 and 2350 BCE, a period of 150 years. This calls for an erosion rate of ¼ inch per year—nearly identical to the current erosion rate of Niagara's American Falls. If this is true, then the real mystery is not Schoch or Reader's geological analysis of the Sphinx and the Giza Plateau, but the unidentified forces that caused the limestone rock of the Sphinx enclosure to break down so rapidly.

Obviously, the weathering of the Sphinx is a scientific, geological matter, and there are no unidentified forces responsible for its erosion. Water is the primary source of weathering according to well-known geological principles. With this in mind, by surveying erosion rates in temperate, wet climates, it is possible to arrive at a general age of the Sphinx based on the erosion on the Sphinx enclosure walls.

Alaska's panhandle receives between 69 and 100 inches of rainfall per year, and according to erosion studies performed by Kevin Allred, published in the *Journal of Cave and Karst Studies,* bare limestone erosion ranges from 1 to 2.5 inches every 1,000 years, an average of 1.53 inches every 1,000 years.[17] Such data provide an estimate for when the Sphinx enclosure walls were exposed to the elements. Using an erosion rate of 1.53 inches every 1,000 years, it would require 11,750 years for limestone to erode 3 feet and 23,500 years to erode 6 feet. Given the moderate rainfall estimate between 10,000 and 3000 BCE for North Africa, it must be assumed that only a few inches of erosion occurred annually after 10,000 BCE and that the vast majority of erosion occurred during a period of substantial rainfall at some time in remote antiquity. The possibility exists, and the evidence points to, a Sphinx carving date sometime between 33,500 BCE and 21,750 BCE.

Although Schoch was the first to scientifically analyze the Sphinx and its enclosure, the hypothesis of a prehistoric Sphinx is nothing new. The renowned Egyptologist E. A. Wallis Budge, although conceding the

Sphinx belonged to the Fourth Dynasty, noted, "It is quite possible it may be much older."[18] Heinrich Brugsch thought so too. He believed that the Sphinx already existed in the time of Khafre. So did early twentieth-century Egyptologists Emmanuel de Rouge and Samuel Birch. Gaston Maspero believed that the Sphinx was already buried in sand at the time of Khufu and his predecessors, and that Khafre cleared sand from its enclosure.[19] These men, who were early icons of Egyptology, suspected that at one time there existed a Civilization X.

3

A MECHANICAL METHOD
OF CUTTING STONE

Painting a picture of the past, particularly the ancient past, is based more on speculation than on fact. Usually there is never enough evidence to state *anything* with total confidence, unless the evidence is conclusive and irrefutable. As a result, theories abound.

Today, the accepted theory is that the development of dynastic Egypt came about as the direct result of appreciable climate change. As the North African climate became increasingly more arid, pastoral tribes—seeking a new and reliable source of water—migrated to the Nile Valley. Within a few hundred years, or possibly a thousand years, the population reached a threshold where civil organization became a necessity. Initially two civilizations developed: one in the south, the other in the north. Around 3000 BCE these two civilizations were united under a single ruler named Narmer (or Menes). During the next five hundred years, the burgeoning Egyptian civilization developed techniques to build colossal structures and statues as far south as Thebes and as far north as Tanis. All these were religious in nature and deified the king as a living god.

Because there is never enough evidence to know when a stone temple was built or what the intention was of those who ordered an inscription carved, reconstructing an ancient civilization requires assumptions. Over time, through successive refinements, the history of this conceptually reconstructed civilization becomes a codified body of knowledge and, eventually, an established model with its own set of concepts, values, and practices. In effect, the theory becomes a paradigm, a particular way of viewing history. For some, this paradigm is, for all intents and purposes, effectively viewed as fact.

The unfortunate part of this process is that assumptions can be incorrect, even though at the time they were first conceived no doubt they were made with prudence. Another unfortunate part of this process is that once a theory has been established as a paradigm, its proponents become intellectual guardians and groom their successors to continue the tradition. Accordingly, any new evidence that calls for a significant modification of the paradigm, or evidence that contradicts it outright, is often viewed with an air of ridicule.

Take, for example, the cache of stone vessels discovered at Sakkara. According to modern Egyptology, these magnificent stone vessels were carved by hand using simple tools. Yet today, to achieve similar results, these vessels would require a manufacturing process.

According to twentieth-century Egyptologist Walter Emery, these vessels were fashioned in Egypt's archaic times before the First Dynasty and were the ancient Egyptians' greatest examples of artistic expression. *They were prehistoric.* Not only were they made in vast quantities, but their perfection was such that no culture or nation since has been able to equal their beauty. The hardest varieties of stone were used, including granite, diorite, schist, alabaster, volcanic ash, serpentine, steatite, breccia, marble, limestone, mottled black-and-white porphyritic rock, purple porphyry, red jasper, obsidian quartz, dolomite, rock crystal, and basalt.

Interestingly, Emery states, there is no satisfactory evidence to help explain the method of stonecutting used to manufacture these vessels.[1] Emery asks:

How did they achieve such accuracy, so that when we "swing" a shallow bowl or dish, no deviation from a perfect circle can be noted?

Emery also asks:

How did they cut rock-crystal tubular jars so that the jar's sides were not more than a millimeter thick?[2]

▲

Based on the condition of the vessels, Emery concluded that the crafts-men had a method of rotating the material against a fixed tool. To Emery's mind, it would have been impossible to obtain such accuracy through hand chiseling or grinding, regardless of how painstakingly it was done.

One clue as to how the crafters of these vessels accomplished their work is derived from the discovery of unfinished products. In the manu-facturing process the exterior shape of the vessel was finished first, and then the interior was hollowed out with a drill with a "curious eccen-tric handle, to which two oval stones were slung with ropes."[3] The stone weights spread outward when the drill was in use, providing extra power to the cutting blade, which was a flint blade shaped in the fashion of an arrowhead.

At the same archaeological sites that have yielded finished and unfin-ished vessels, numerous drills such as these have been found, as well as tubular drills that were probably used to craft smaller vessels. Although tubular drills may be effective in carving out the interior of a cylindrically shaped stone vessel such as an amphora-style vase, where the neck is slim-mer than the body, tubular drills, as a rule, are impractical to use. Again, Emery asks, "How, for example, was the upward pressure obtained to cut away the interior side of the shoulders?"

In my opinion, there is no doubt in Emery's mind that a sophisticated stonecutting technology had been employed by a lost, ancient Egyptian civilization. Although flint and copper tools account for some aspects of the evidence, copper that has a natural hardness of 87 cannot be improved to 135 (Brinell scale) by simple means. Nevertheless, according to Emery, copper saws and chisels were used in the cutting of schist and hard lime-stone. In the space between leaves of a schist bowl, the marks of a copper saw are clear.[4]

Other items that puzzled Emery were saw teeth and needles found at the same archaeological sites where the vessels had been discovered. With regard to the saws, missing portions of metal had been punched out, and in the case of the needles, typically the eye of the needle had been punched through and not drilled. But punched out by what? Whatever was used must have been harder than the metal it had punched out. Harder metals would include bronze or iron, but neither bronze nor iron came into use until many thousands of years after Egypt's predynastic period. Furthermore, grinding and polishing by hand, using stone, were employed to *finish* copper tools, but there is no evidence that these methods were used to *shape* vessels such as those found in Zer's tomb at Sakkara, which were made of hammered copper.

The crafters of these vessels also used the technique of copper riveting to attach spouts, handles, and rims. Wire binding was also used in the fixing of loop handles. This was of keen interest to Emery, because this technique was virtually unknown in early metalworking. All this could be explained as a result of the use of machine shops (places that specialize in the use of machine tools such as a lathe or planer), but this supposition has always been considered fringe or crazy.

ASPECTS OF EVIDENCE

Artifacts of an organic nature can be carbon dated, but structures of stone cannot. Inscriptions and documents tell of people, places, and events, as well as of a culture's philosophy. Tools can be classified by composition, function, and the quality of craftsmanship. But there is much uncertainty in the mix. How, for instance, do we know that the piece of coal (that was carbon dated) and the stone bench it was discovered next to are the same age? How do we know that we are interpreting an inscription correctly? How do we know what tools were used when and for what purpose?

We don't, really, so assumptions have to be made. It is worth noting that our assumptions are based on an underlying fundamental assumption: evolution is linear—that is, no culture with any advanced technical sophistication existed prior to our modern civilization. As a result, orthodox Egyptologists are opposed to the idea that the ancient Egyptians used anything but copper chisels and blunt-blade copper saws to quarry, cut, and shape granite. Nevertheless, while visiting Egypt it is difficult not to sense that the civilization that continually built on such an immense scale and with granite was as much of a mystery five thousand years ago as it is today.

For the last 150 years, researchers—both academic and independent—have been studying various engineering and construction methods to explain how the pyramids were built. Special interest groups have tried to move and raise a few courses of one-ton stone blocks, only to admit to the futility of their efforts. Still, I suspect that if enough determined people put their minds to it, they could build a pyramid that resembled one of the stone mountains on the Giza Plateau. But this is not really the point. The point is that building on such a huge scale, and with some of the hardest rock on the planet, is not a simple task regardless of the era in which construction took place.

How many chisels would it have taken to build a pyramid: a hundred thousand, a million? The issue is evidence, and there is no evidence that an army of men ever worked on the Giza Plateau hewing limestone and granite with copper implements. In fact, when it comes to the construction of the pyramids, there is no tool evidence of *any* kind. The only evidence that exists is the final product, the structures themselves. It is this "negative evidence" that generates the need for assumptions, which, in the past, created a need for written records to shed light on the subject.

Unfortunately, written records may not always exist, which happens to be the case with ancient Egypt. A third-century Egyptian priest under the reign of Ptolemy II was supposed to have written a detailed history of ancient Egypt, and from his works the chronology of Egypt was established. His name was Manetho. But his "detailed history" is misleading for two reasons. First, Manetho's original text does not exist. All that exists are quotations and synopses by later Roman historians.[5] Second, the writings referring to Manetho from other historians do not always agree. In some instances the names and dates are garbled "most horribly."[6] How much of the error is because of the copier and how much is Manetho's error is unknown and will likely never be determined. Nonetheless, Manetho's *Notes on Egypt* (the actual title) is the basis for Egyptian history, given that there is nothing to contradict him.[7] Insofar as his chronology was what the first Egyptologists used to lay out Egyptian history, Manetho is responsible for the creation of the dynasties that ruled Egypt.

Aside from Manetho, there is really nothing else to go by. So why rely on his record? Because, according to former Egyptologist Barbara Mertz, "Manetho's concept has been used for so long that it would be inconvenient to discard it."[8] Even so, Manetho does not describe how the pyramids were built, or who built them, or when they were built.

Another ancient historian, Herodotus, did describe a machine that supposedly was used to lift large blocks of stone, but his lifetime is very far removed from the actual event (more than two thousand years, according to accepted chronology). Even so, a single lever-based machine, possibly a real piece of technology from the pyramid builders handed down over many generations, does not account for the quarrying, roughing, and finishing of more than two million stone blocks. Neither does it explain the design of any given pyramid, internally or externally. So we are left with the final product as the sole evidence.

There are four aspects of the evidence that must be addressed in a logical and rational way. First, the *scale of construction was colossal,* as were the pieces to be assembled. Second, the materials used, *limestone and granite, are some of the most difficult building materials to handle,* even by today's standards. Third, the *manner in which the structures were built is extraordinarily precise,* which means the builders had a means to ensure that the cutting and assembly was, in fact, precise. With these three known facts, the assumption must be that machine tools were used, in part, in the construction process. The fourth consideration, and the most important one, is that *machine tool marks exist on a number of artifacts;* these marks cannot be explained by the use of simple tools.

These four tenets of evidence not only suggest that the tools the pyramid builders used were sufficiently sophisticated to quarry, cut, shape, transport, and place enormous amounts of granite and limestone, but also that, in all probability, the civilization that constructed the pyramids must have had a long period of technical development to be able to carry out such massive projects. This, of course, brings up a problem: Where are the machines? For whatever reason, they have not survived. Yet despite their absence, we are forced to assume by the objective analysis of the evidence that these machine tools did in fact exist, since machining techniques best explain the evidence. It is the most plausible answer in explaining how so many stones of such an enormous size were dressed for placement.

PETRIE AND PRECISION

Sir William Flinders Petrie is arguably the most famous of all Egyptologists, due in large part to his meticulous methods of excavation, measurement, and documentation. He was well liked by those who worked with him, and his legacy remained in Egypt for some time; the men he trained manned and directed expeditions for many years following his death.[9] During the late nineteenth century, Petrie was the first to publish detailed descriptions of the pyramids and temples, as well as detailed descriptions of associated artifacts discovered at Giza. Even today, Petrie's *Pyramids and Temples of Gizeh*, written in 1883, is a highly coveted book.[10]

Petrie was also the first to recognize that pottery was valuable to the archaeologist, particularly as a means of dating artifacts found in excavations. Most pottery has no intrinsic value, and as a result, researchers frequently discarded broken vessels. Likewise, given its lack of relative value, treasure hunters completely ignored almost everything ceramic; they were after gold and silver. Thus, pottery and potsherds almost always remained in the original place of discard. For Petrie, pottery was one of the most useful types of evidence, and in conjunction with cemetery excavations, it allowed him to date the development of Egyptian culture from earliest times. Pottery, however, was not all Petrie noticed.

By paying close attention to detail, Petrie was the first archaeologist to recognize that the ancient Egyptians used ingenious techniques for cutting and shaping stone, what he refers to as "mechanical methods." Petrie was convinced that he had solved the problem of the "methods employed" to cut and shape stone but also acknowledged that there was no proof that the tools existed or of how they were used. Still, from the artifacts he discovered and inspected closely, Petrie determined that whoever built the pyramids and temples on Giza were using tools with cutting points far harder than the granite, diorite, and basalt used to construct the pyramids.

Although neither Petrie nor anyone else at that time was able to determine what substances had been used as the cutting point, he logically assumed that the substance had to be beryl, topaz, chrysoberyl, corundum, sapphire, or diamond, because only these materials are hard enough to cut granite. Of these six types of material, Petrie favored uncrystallized corundum, although the quality of the finished product seemed to point to diamonds. Diamonds, however, are not indigenous to Egypt.

One way to cut hard stone is to use "powder sticks" of corundum, which are applied to implements made of copper or wood. By scraping the stone with the treated implements, the stone is gradually worn away. But according to Petrie, this is the case with softer stones such as alabaster, but not harder stones. Cutting hard stone requires jewel-tipped implements.[11]

Petrie claims that the evidence is clear on this point. Inscriptions on diorite bowls from the Fourth Dynasty that were discovered at Giza were not scraped or ground. Rather, whatever removed the rock to form the inscription easily plowed through the diorite. Some of the inscribed lines are only $1/150$ of an inch wide, and two parallel lines were carved with only $1/30$ of an inch between them. Thus, Petrie concluded that the tool to accomplish this had to be tough enough not to splinter yet must have had an edge only $1/200$ of an inch wide. He found the same type of tool evidence in saw marks that had been made in diorite: grooves as deep as $1/100$ inch that are regular and uniform in depth. The same is true for a granite core broken from a hole made from a tube drill. Grooves around this core form a regular spiral and are perfectly symmetrical with the axis of the core. For Petrie, this could only be accomplished by tools with fixed jewel points serving as the cutting surface of the drill tube.[12]

Petrie found numerous examples of tube drilling and described them in detail, in particular a granite box, which was hollowed out by making rows of holes with a tube drill and then breaking out the cores and intermediate pieces. In one box, two drill holes had clearly penetrated too deep into the sides of the box. At El Bersheh, there is a larger example where a platform of limestone rock was reduced with tube drills measuring about eighteen inches in diameter.[13]

Evidence also exists that demonstrates the use of straight saws, some of which must have been more than eight feet in length and varied from 0.03 to 0.2 inches thick. In the granite box of the Great Pyramid, the saw was pushed too deep into the material, twice over, and pulled back out again. A piece of syenite from Memphis, possibly waste material from a statue, exhibits cuts on four sides and a cut across its top by the breadth of the saw. Petrie also noticed marks on the basalt paving stones on the east side of the Great Pyramid. On one block the saw apparently ran askew; the block was abandoned. Another block shows regular and well-defined lines where the saw began to cut. And yet another was sawn on both sides and nearly cut into two pieces.[14]

One of the more unusual pieces, a piece of diorite, bears the regular grooves of circular arcs parallel to each other. Although the grooves are faint as a result of being polished out by crossed grinding, they are still visible. For Petrie, the only reasonable explanation for this piece is that it was produced by some type of circular saw.[15]

There is also evidence that items were turned on a lathe, given that numerous Old Kingdom diorite bowls and vases display great technical skill. According to Petrie, "The lathe appears to have been as familiar an instrument in the fourth dynasty, as it is in modern workshops."[16] One piece in particular, a bowl, clearly displays two surfaces where it had been knocked off its center, recentered, and cut again. The two surfaces on the bottom of the bowl meet in a cusp. For Petrie, "Such an appearance could not be produced by any grinding or rubbing process which pressed on the surface."[17] Another bowl is spherical, and therefore must have been cut by a tool sweeping an arc from a fixed point while the bowl rotated. Here the machinist recentered the tool near the mouth of the bowl to create a lip. According to Petrie, this bowl was certainly not created by hand. The bowl is exact in its circularity even at the cusp where the lip and the body of the bowl meet. "It is a clear proof of the rigidly mechanical method of striking the curves," according to Petrie.[18]

The mysterious part of Petrie's analysis is that for such tools to work properly and plow through granite and other hard stone, intense pressure is required. According to Petrie's calculations, the pressure required is at least two thousand pounds. For example, in Petrie's granite core No. 7, the tool sank one-tenth of an inch for every six inches of circumference, which is an astonishing rate for granite. Today, hydraulics applies the pressure needed to cut such hard material.[19]

Petrie also testified to the use of testing planes in working surfaces, drafted diagonals, the character of fine joints, and the accuracy of leveling, all of which demonstrated the experience and skill of the workers. One of the most astonishing feats of construction is the descending passageway in the Great Pyramid. The 350-foot-long, 3½-foot-square passageway descends 100 feet into the bedrock. Yet over the length of the tunnel, it varies by only ¼ inch. Despite such incredible perfection and Petrie's observation of that perfection, he acquiesced to the idea that such high precision was accomplished solely with the use of hand tools. He also believed that the pyramids were designed as tombs.

I am not sure how a saw or drill made from copper would fare under a stone weighing two thousand pounds, or even how the workers would turn the drill. In a world driven by the burgeoning dogma of Darwinism, perhaps it was better for Petrie to suspend construction logic a little bit rather than join the ranks of the "pyramidiots."

DUNN AND PRECISION

Petrie was not the only researcher to notice the fine cutting and crafting of granite. A hundred years later expert machinist and precision manufacturing executive Christopher Dunn revisited the same discussion. In 1995, armed with a machinist's measuring tools, Dunn traveled to Egypt to measure and gauge some artifacts that he had noticed on previous trips. With a precision straightedge, he determined that the proportions of many artifacts were much more precise than had previously been thought. One such example was the granite box in the bedrock chamber of the middle pyramid. In measuring the inside surfaces of the black granite box, Dunn found them to be perfectly flat.

He returned four years later and again checked the flatness of the wall. By sliding a straightedge along the interior wall of the granite box, while shining a flashlight behind the straightedge, any imperfections in the surface would allow light to pass underneath the ruler. Thus, the precision of its interior surface could be demonstrated. According to Dunn, the wall was precisely flat. He also slid his precision square along the top of the parallel, and it fit perfectly on the adjacent surface. The other corners were in the same condition, perfectly square, although one corner did reveal a small gap of about 0.001 of an inch. As for the corner radius, at one end of the box, one inside corner measured $3/32$ inch at the top and $7/16$ inch at the bottom.[20]

For the layman, square corners and flat surfaces may seem like nothing to get excited about. This is because today's manufacturing industry has perfected the production process, so we take it for granted. Have you ever tried to make a block of wood perfectly flat and square with a handheld planer, to within 0.001 of an inch? It's next to impossible. Yet, whoever built these stone boxes did so with granite.

To produce perfectly square and flat objects, a society has to develop systems of production as well as infallible methods of measurement to ensure that the item produced is of the highest quality. Even today, it is extremely difficult to achieve perfectly flat surfaces and square corners in granite. *Perfectly flat surfaces require machines.*

For Dunn, "Artifacts such as these fly in the face of any previous explanations of the ancient Egyptians stone cutting methods."[21] The more interesting question is not so much *how* boxes such as the one in the middle pyramid's chamber were manufactured, but *why* their builders required such precision and accuracy.

The obvious reason is that this was standard operating procedure.

There is another, subtler issue. A culture that had the vision and genius to design and erect structures of hard stone—such as temples and pyramids—would have been capable of fabricating tools to implement their grand vision for civilization. However, there are no tools known to the archaeological record that elicit the same awe that the colossal statues and structures of this ancient civilization do. No machine tools have been found to explain the precise contours of large granite ashlars found near the Valley Temple and the middle pyramid on the Giza Plateau, or the magnificent colossal granite statues of Ramses at Luxor. No measuring instruments have been uncovered to explain how ultraflat surfaces, finished to precision over large surface areas, were created. Indeed, the tools that have been introduced to explain the grandiose stone-working evidence are, in fact, incapable of doing the very work they are supposed to explain!

Given the facts and the evidence, it must be the case that there is a significant problem in our understanding of the past. Mainstream Egyptology maintains a logic that requires the tools used in the building process be present in the archaeological record to explain the existence of these granite marvels. If, by chance, future archaeologists ten thousand years from now uncovered a pickup truck next to an adjustable wrench and a screwdriver, does this mean that these were the sole tools used to create the truck? As the creators of the pickup truck, we know better. Would future archaeologists in the year 12,000 CE believe so too? If the same type of associative logic that we currently subscribe to is maintained over the next ten thousand years, they would indeed believe so too.

This modern-day example highlights a failure in associative logic and unfortunately allows the theorist to make up anything for an explanation, all under the guise of "direct evidence." However, it must be realized that when circumstantial evidence is explained only through vast leaps in logic, the direct evidence is really no evidence at all. In fact, accepting such vast leaps in logic is a suspension of reality, for the physics associated with construction and manufacturing are the same today as they were five thousand years ago, or a million years ago, for that matter.

As for the evidence, the ancient Egyptians created numerous artifacts from which methods of manufacture can be inferred. In 1883, Petrie remarked on the efficiency with which the ancient Egyptians cut hard igneous rock and concluded that on some artifacts, circular saws must have been used.[22]

However, to be effective, circular saws require some type of power.

GIZA'S BASALT PATIO

At the Great Pyramid's eastern face, a solitary granite slab sits next to the remains of large basalt patio. What type of granite structure or structures were next to the Great Pyramid, we will never know. The area has been picked clean. The only structure of significance that remains is the basalt patio that the local salesmen use as a rallying point in their daily routine. However, since whoever built the pyramids of Giza may have also built the pyramids and temple at Abu Sir, one of those structures was most likely a temple. The basalt patio and its orientation to the Great Pyramid at Giza is similar to the basalt patio and its relationship with the pyramid at Abu Sir.

For the tourist, there is nothing of special interest about these basalt patio blocks except that they are ancient and provide an anomalous charm to an otherwise barren area. (See plate 11 of the color insert.) Still, like everything else on the plateau, a number of stones have been removed from the edge of the patio. Although the patio area would be more appealing if it were intact, its pilfered state allows its builders' secrets to be exposed.

It is a riddle that an ancient civilization, believed to have been technically primitive, could not only build a single structure with the hardest rock known to man, but build an entire civilization out of it. To quarry and shape large quantities of granite to use in the construction process, they would have to have had an efficient and effective means of cutting.

But what is this method of cutting stone?

Fig. 3.1. A solitary slab of granite next to the Great Pyramid

The answer lies in a number of the Great Pyramid's basalt patio stones. These stones offer evidence that whoever built the pyramids, and the basalt patio, were experts in the technology of cutting and shaping stone.

When any material is manipulated to create a product—whether by a power tool, a milling machine, or a manual tool—the tool or process will leave its signature. It doesn't matter if the material is wood, metal, or stone. There will always be evidence on the object's surface detailing how it was created, unless it has been polished or sanded away. But that too leaves its mark.

For example, structures and statues that were carved by hand, such as the crypts and tombs in the area west of the Valley Temple just in front of the middle pyramid, are easily identifiable. The hand chisel left behind a slash mark or divot where it pushed its way through the rock. Such marks are easily identifiable on some of the Great Pyramid's core blocks. Objects created with stone hammers (round, fist-sized diorite stone-headed hammers), such as the granite box on display in the Memphis Museum courtyard, have a surface scarred with pockmarks or dimples. The surfaces of chiseled blocks are rough and uneven. The surface of highly polished rock is smooth, with an unmistakably reflective quality about it. Surfaces that have been cut in a high-speed process also display certain marks. The handyman who has spent a lifetime using radial saws, table saws, and other power tools, or the machinist whose career has focused on manufacturing precision products, knows this.

EVIDENCE OF POWERED SAWS

Although it is certain that chisels and hammers did play a role in the construction process—workers today still use hand tools—there was something else at work, something that makes the grand scale of the pyramids feasible and validates the existence of Civilization X. The telltale signs of the process that did the cutting are there if you know what to look for. This was what Christopher Dunn discovered, and what he brought me to Egypt to see.

The surface of the basalt paving stones is cracked in places and worn away, due to what appears to be water erosion. However, a number of peripheral stones that have been exposed by pilfering show little sign of erosion on their sides, and there are no chisel marks visible. Where they have been broken, they are rough and jagged. Otherwise they are smooth and lack any tool marks except for where mistakes may have been made. These mistakes are important clues to the manner in which the blocks were prepared.

The most obvious mistake appears of the north end of the basalt patio. Apparently, on one block the workman who was operating the saw started a cut that would have created a stone too short for its intended use. When he recognized the mistake he withdrew the blade and made the cut higher up. He did this not once but twice before making the final cut where it was supposed to be (figure 3.2). Since the block was originally an inner block of the patio no one would ever notice, until, that is, the site became derelict and some of the stones were stripped away. (See plates 12 and 13 of the color insert.)

On the basalt paving stones there are other mistakes made by ancient stonecutters; most of these mistakes appear as grooves or channels biting their way through the stone. The straight and even width of these grooves is beyond what could be accomplished by hand. However, if they had been cut by hand, what kind of tool would have been capable of making such a deep and precise cut? What would its teeth have to have been made from?

A second stone exhibiting saw marks sits on the northeast side of the

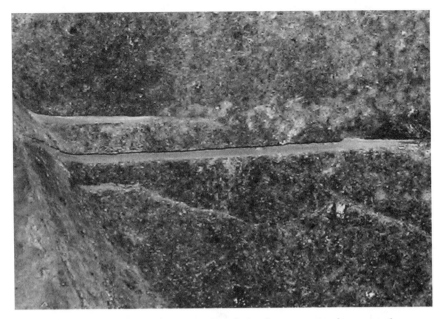

*Fig. 3.2. Close-up of saw marks where the cutter made a mistake
and started over*

Fig. 3.3. Second basalt block with saw marks

basalt patio. The cut originally knifes through a protrusion of rock, but at some time in the past this protrusion broke off, leaving what appear to be two separate cuts (figure 3.3). The second cut, although fainter, exists several inches to the right of the first cut.

A third stone exhibits ten saw marks (figure 3.4) where all the cuts are within one inch of each other. The cut marks might have been created before the block was placed, since the saw marks appear to continue past the visible portion of the stone.

Not far from the third stone exhibiting saw marks, at the far north end of the basalt patio, there is a fourth basalt stone with the same style of marks (figure 3.5). However, this stone also displays a flat, smooth surface where the stone was cut (figure 3.6), which is a distinct characteristic of a mechanized saw.

A fifth and a sixth stone (figures 3.7 and 3.8) suggest that the saw blade used to cut the basalt paving stones was circular. Both exhibit a rounded shape to the cut.

Fig. 3.4 (above left). Saw marks on the third stone
Fig. 3.5 (above right). Saw marks on the fourth stone

Fig. 3.6. Notice the flat, smooth surface on the fourth stone.

Fig. 3.7. Circular saw marks on the fifth stone

Fig. 3.8. Circular saw marks on the sixth stone

EVIDENCE OF MACHINING

A seventh paving stone exhibiting a saw mark rests on the east side of the basalt patio; this specific stone was featured in a recent documentary. According to the film, this stone was allegedly cut by an ox-driven saw with a large weight mounted on top of the saw to apply the cutting pressure.

What the documentary failed to mention was that this stone offers more evidence for the tool that made the cut. Below the cut the texture of the rock appears to be rough, but directly above its texture is smooth and displays minute lines that are evenly spaced and horizontal to the cut. These minuscule lines are similar to the machining marks that today's machinists refer to as feed lines.

Two other stones at the edge of the basalt patio also exhibit machinist feed lines.

There are other tool marks on other stones near the Great Pyramid. Interestingly, sophisticated technology (a large megapixel digital camera) led to the discovery by Christopher Dunn that the pyramid builders employed some type of advanced technology to custom-cut basalt blocks to create a paved patio.

Fig. 3.9. There are feed lines on this stone on the right-hand side, which can be seen in the close-up image in figure 3.11.

Fig. 3.10. Flat and smooth area of the seventh stone, where feed lines exist

Fig. 3.11. Up close, feed lines are visible on stone seven.

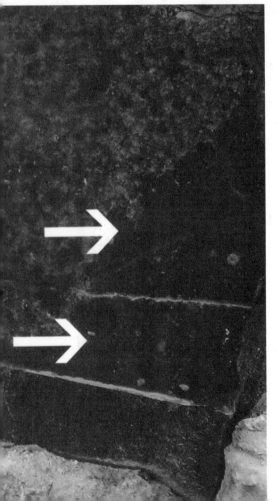

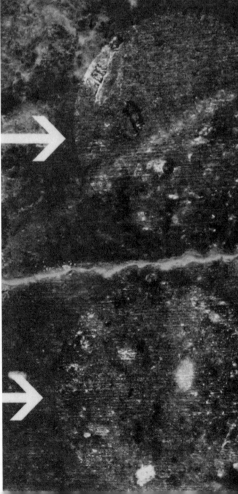

Fig. 3.12 (top). Second basalt stone exhibiting feed lines
Fig. 3.13 (bottom). Close-up of feed lines in figure 3.12

Fig. 3.14 (top). Third basalt stone exhibiting feed lines
Fig. 3.15 (bottom). Close-up of feed lines in figure 3.14

What the evidence indicates is that the pyramid builders mass-produced stone blocks to create their structures, and then, when necessary, further shaped the stone by hand once the stone was ready to be placed in its final position. As a result, it is evident that both simple and sophisticated tools were used in constructing the pyramids and other structures on the Giza Plateau.

However, the most astounding discovery is located at a restricted site called Abu Rawash.

4

A NEW ROSETTA STONE

Giza is always congested with buses, vans, and taxis carrying tourists between the hotels and nearby sites and workers from their homes to their jobs. There are no stop lights; the traffic is so heavy that they would only make matters worse. Policemen wearing white officer caps and navy blue vests stamped "Giza Traffic" on the back direct throngs of cars, buses, trucks, and an occasional mule-driven cart. Their sleeves striped in neon green provide easy visibility for impatient drivers.

Compared with the bustling nonstop Giza traffic, the short ride heading out of town north on the Alexandria highway is a pleasure. Traffic is less dense, and the view is magnificent. Unlike the streets of Giza, where the tightly packed buildings block every view, the road to Alex, as local residents refer to it, is a vista of yellow-and-white dunes under a bright blue sky. No more than ten minutes away, still within Giza's city limits, is a hidden treasure—the ancient ruins of Abu Rawash.

No roads exist leading to Abu Rawash; there is only a beaten trail in the sand where cars and trucks occasionally have made their way. Of course, Farahat, our veteran driver, knows the way. Climbing the trail up the plateau is slow going, but the ancient ruins aren't very far, and the desert is a refreshing change from the speeding cars of Giza and their honking horns.

Few tourists visit the ruins at Abu Rawash, and you won't find it on most maps. Officially, going there is forbidden, but that doesn't seem to bother the drivers and guides who earn their living from tourism. As such, there are no Tourism Police to provide security, but on the bright side, there are no sellers hawking their goods or asking for a picture, either.

A quarter mile or so up the trail stands a shack where two men patiently wait and watch for visitors. They guard the way. They are guides, so to speak, eagerly awaiting adventuresome tourists in order to earn a few pounds Egyptian. In Egypt, it seems as if everyone wants a piece of the tourist trade. I don't mind. It's part of their culture and a necessary cordiality. "Baksheesh," the Egyptians call it. Although this Arab term effectively means money, it really means forgiveness, I am told.

One of the Abu Rawash guardians, a short man wearing a long, flowing blue tunic and a white turban, waves us down. Farahat and the guardian chat for a minute. "He wants to go with us," Farahat says. We don't have much of a choice, so "our guide" gets in the back seat with me, then it's on to Egypt's northernmost pyramid.

Abu Rawash's pyramid complex rests atop a small plateau nearly five hundred feet above the surrounding terrain. (See plate 14 of the color insert.)

This is unusual placement for the typical pyramid; all other pyramids were built much closer to sea level. The view to the south is dazzling. Giza, the city, lies below; in the distance Giza's trio of pyramids stretches into the sky, truly an amazing scene.

On the plateau it's still and quiet. The ancient complex doesn't look like much. The pyramid, such as it is, is built around an outcropping of natural rock; there are a few courses of limestone blocks, approximately fifteen in all. The official story behind the pyramid is that it was built by an early Fourth Dynasty pharaoh, Djedefre, who was the son of Khufu. According to the story, Djedefre, whose mother was a Libyan queen, murdered his older half-brother, Kauab, in order to become pharaoh, since Kauab had a stronger claim to the throne. In the end, Djedefre, by the hand of his younger half-brother, Khafre, met the same fate he had dished out to Kauab. Djedefre's successor then demolished the site, reducing it to a shell of a building in a field of rubble.[1] That was before thousands of years of weathering and scavenging. Compared to the grandeur and beauty of the Sphinx poised at the east gate to the Giza pyramids, Abu Rawash's pyramid doesn't look like much of a pyramid.

However, looks are deceiving. On the north side of the pyramid, the area for the descending passageway had been cut into the bedrock. (See plate 15 of the color insert.) Essentially, it is a channel nearly twenty feet wide that empties into a rectangular pit. Egyptologists believe this rectangular pit was supposed to be the burial chamber and its antechamber for King Djedefre. Even in its dilapidated state, the pyramid's megalithic blocks and the excavation into the bedrock are a remarkable sight.

Alone, I descended into the cool shadows of the pyramid and wondered about the men who had worked here so long ago. Who were they really? How could they accomplish such a colossal engineering feat with the simplest of tools? Seeing the pyramid in person was beyond compare. How the pyramid builders accomplished the task of quarrying and cutting such large blocks of stone and assembling them into a gigantic structure is, to this day, one of the deepest mysteries of history.

Even though nearly all the granite casing stones have long since been removed, on the first course of limestone blocks, next to where the descending passageway begins, there are two pink granite blocks, witnesses to the splendor of what was. Both these stones are enormous beyond belief.

Our driver, Farahat, helped Chris Dunn measure the easternmost stone. After some calculations, Chris said each must weigh close to sixty tons. (See plate 16 of the color insert.) Over the millennia, whoever scavenged the granite from Abu Rawash was unable to move these two pieces. I assume they were left untouched because they were (and are) nearly impossible to move even using heavy equipment. Getting a sixty-ton block of granite in the air even a few inches cannot be accomplished by brute manpower alone. The number of men required to lift the block would not be able to fit around the stone. Besides, why try and move such large stones, since Abu Rawash's pyramid, like so many others, was cased in granite? There were plenty more granite stones to choose from that required much less force, as numerous piles of pink granite on the plateau attest to.

Not far from the two granite witnesses stands an enigma: a three-and-a-half-foot-tall granite pin or pillar. (See plate 17 of the color insert.) At least, that's what it looks like. What it really was when first made may never be known.

In contrast to the khaki-colored limestone blocks that make up the core of the pyramid, the pink granite is beautiful, even though almost all of it exists as heaps and piles scattered around. Rubble at other areas is covered with the fine yellow powder deposited by the desert wind. The granite at Abu Rawash is clean and displays bright speckles of quartzite laced in black-and-pink rock that sparkle in the sun; it is beautiful despite the destruction and demolition that occurred here. (See plate 18 of the color insert.)

According to another driver and tour guide, Naroz Aziz, during the mid-1990s French and German archaeologists camped at Abu Rawash one winter and cleaned everything up. Before this, he stated, Abu Rawash had been a mound of rubble and dirt. Now it was clean and the pyramid clearly visible. He was likely referring to the Swiss-French excavations led by Michel Valloggia. Evidently all rubble, except the granite, had been pulled away from the base of the pyramid and disposed of. Remarkably, there may be enough granite strewn about to case most of the existing pyramid.

Although most of the granite is broken, a few pieces have retained some of their original form. In one pile there is a square block. In another there is what looks to be a casing stone, triangular in form. (See plate

Fig. 4.1. Remnants of a granite stone with carrying lobe

19 of the color insert.) If the amount of granite strewn about is only a fraction of the granite used, what scavengers could not use, the original quantity of granite had to have been enormous.

Perhaps the biggest mystery of all is the long trench cut into the bedrock on the east side of the pyramid, several hundred feet from its base. (See plate 20 of the color insert.) According to Egyptologists, this long, deep trench (approximately forty feet wide and sixty feet deep) was a "boat pit" where the solar boat, which the king would use on his journey in the afterlife, would be placed. However, no remains of a boat have ever been found at Abu Rawash. What was discovered were fragments of statues carved from red quartzite. Sometime long ago they had been tossed into the trench. According to Egyptologists, more than 120 statues once adorned the site, most of which were of the ruler sitting on his throne.

Although Egyptologists attribute the pyramid at Abu Rawash to the early Fourth Dynasty, why the site was chosen and why it was never finished is an unsolved puzzle. Not only is it built high on a plateau and a mile away from where the Nile was at that time, it was also later used as a cemetery, even though it was believed to have been abandoned. The core on which the pyramid was built is honeycombed with more than thirty rock-cut tombs attributed to the Fifth and Sixth Dynasties.[2]

Abu Rawash is a very important site, not so much because it offers a view of a pyramid in progress, which is certainly unique and valuable, but because it contains irrefutable evidence of what was used to cut rock. To this day, the evidence is still there. Since I have never read about this evidence in any journal or seen it addressed in a film documentary, or even seen a picture of it on the Internet, apparently it is an unmentionable artifact, and possibly a secret—indeed, a secret that should be confiscated, hauled away, crated, and hidden, locked away in the basement of the Cairo Museum forever, an artifact that no orthodox archaeologist or Egyptologist would want to mention publicly.

I first learned about this stone in Kempton, Illinois, on May 6, 2006, at a conference hosted by Adventures Unlimited Press. Christopher Dunn had returned that day from Egypt and driven straight to the conference from Chicago's O'Hare Airport. In his keynote address, in which he presented many photographs, a photograph of the stone at Abu Rawash was

Fig. 4.2. The stone at Abu Rawash (view from the southeast side of the pyramid)

the final one. Staring at the photo projected on the giant screen, I could hardly believe my eyes. Nine months later, Dunn and I visited Egypt on a research trip.

If "seeing is believing," then being at Abu Rawash myself, touching the most significant find in the history of civilization was the experience of a lifetime. This incredible stone is located on the east side of the Abu Rawash pyramid about a third of the way south of the structure's northeast corner. It is approximately four feet wide, six feet long, and ten inches thick. Workers from one of the past excavation teams must have pulled it from the rubble and placed it atop seven softball-sized stones. In pristine condition, a result most likely of being buried for thousands of years, it now rests about thirty feet from the base of the pyramid. Someday, this granite slab may be as important as the Rosetta Stone, and for good reason.

It has long been speculated by those intrigued with history's mysteries that an ancient technical civilization existed during remote times. Such speculation, popularly referred to as the Atlantis Syndrome by skeptics and cynics alike, has created resentment of sorts between so-called independent

Fig. 4.3 (top). Another view of the stone at Abu Rawash
Fig. 4.4 (bottom). Smooth, flat surface of the stone

Fig. 4.5. The stone at Abu Rawash (view from the north)
Fig. 4.6. The stone at Abu Rawash (view from the west)

and academic researchers, what have been termed in the press the New Age and Orthodox camps.

New Age aficionados are alleged (by the orthodoxy) to believe unfounded theories, while orthodox folk are alleged (by the New Age) to ignore important evidence in their historical paradigms. For the New Age or alternative historians who claim that civilization is far older than the orthodoxy puts forth, the problem has always been the evidence, which for the most part is circumstantial and some of which is highly suspect.

For the orthodoxy, the problem has always been how to explain the more mysterious aspects of ancient history, such as the widespread use of granite as a building material—not to mention the existence of unique large and ornate granite carvings. Like the skeleton that tells a story to the forensics expert, so does the granite stone at Abu Rawash, particularly to the experienced machinist.

There is no mistake that a sophisticated technology was responsible for this stone's existence. The stone measures approximately 56.75 inches long by 47 inches wide by 9 inches high. Its face or upright surface is smooth to the touch but not flat. Its surface is concave. At one end of the stone there is an arc separating the smooth surface from the rough surface. Dunn determined that the radius was accurate over approximately 93 percent of the arc, and using the dimensions of the chord (56.75 in) and the sagitta (1.42 in), he also determined that the radius the arc belonged to was 23.684 feet (7.218 m).*[3]

Upon close inspection of the smooth portion of the stone, tiny lines—nearly microscopic—are visible across the width of the stone, in the same direction as the arc. You can't feel them with your hand, but you can see them if you look really closely. Whatever device did the cutting on this stone, it left grooves approximately 0.05 inch wide, which would normally be associated with the feed rate of the saw, but could also indicate a blade with multiple cutting teeth.[4]

I talked with a granite expert at a local custom stone shop about ancient Egypt and methods of cutting stone. He insisted everything in ancient times was carved by hand. But when he viewed the photos of the stone at Abu Rawash, all he could say was, "That's crazy!" He said it three times and then finally exclaimed, "That had to have been done by a milling machine or something to make that type of cut."

There are five facts of great interest about this stone. First, whatever tool cut this slab of granite did so with relative ease, since the quartz crystals in the rock were cut as smooth and flat as the feldspar. Second, the tool that made the cut left an abrupt, exact terminating line in the shape of an arc between the smooth and rough portions of the stone. (See plate 21 of

---

*A chord is a line segment that joins two points on a curve. A sagitta is the perpendicular distance from an arc's midpoint to the chord across it, equal to the radius (R) minus the apothem (r). (The apothem is the perpendicular distance from a center to any of its sides.)

Fig. 4.7. Horizontal feed lines from the device that cut the stone

Fig. 4.8. Slice mark near the top of the stone

Fig. 4.9. Slice mark near the bottom of the stone

the color insert.) Third, whatever tool made the cut also rendered the stone concave along its width. Fourth, there are two slice marks (or steps) exhibited on the stone's smooth surface. One is near the termination arc and the other on the opposite end. And fifth, there are machinist "feed lines" in the smooth part of the stone along its breadth the length of the stone. (See plate 22 of the color insert.)

Explaining these five features of the stone at Abu Rawash is difficult to do by claiming that simple hand tools were responsible. And when taking into account the feed lines, it is impossible. If an ox-driven saw was the tool used, why would there be an arc-shaped termination line?

It could be a hoax, but if it were, who would have the funds and the tools to accomplish such a feat? A granite slab would have to be purchased (very expensive), then cut and transported to Abu Rawash. The hoaxer would have to be a granite worker with access to expensive machinery or a very rich person with good connections.

What makes a hoax highly unlikely is the way the stone was cut. Whatever tool cut the stone left not one but two concave surfaces. (See plate 23 of the color insert.) One concave surface has already been discussed, the arc that separates the smooth surface from the rough at the end of the block. The second radius, or concave surface, is in the depth of the stone's smooth area. So the middle of the stone is thinner than its sides. How these two concave features of the stone—technically two radii—were created is the key to determining which tool made the cut. It may also explain what the stone was probably used for.

It is difficult to imagine why anyone would cut any stone into this shape today, one hundred years ago, or five thousand years ago. After contemplating how a material could be shaped by a single cut, Dunn came up with a plausible answer. The slab might have been waste material discarded in the process of cutting a triangular casing stone.

According to Dunn, the stone has two radii on two axes, which indicates that a popular machinist's technique might have been used to achieve a cut larger than the diameter of the saw being used. Such a technique, in theory, would result in waste material the same shape as the stone at Abu Rawash. Using a milling cutter, Dunn tested the theory. The result was waste material in the shape of a rectangle, as well as a wedge-shaped object, two sides of which formed a right triangle. As is true of the stone at Abu Rawash, the hard plastic waste material contained two radii, one along its face and the other along its depth. Although much smaller than its granite inspiration, the rectangular piece of plastic was an exact duplicate.

The cutting technique Dunn used explains the concave shape of the stone and the termination arc at its end, and also the feed lines, as well as the single rough end. As the saw neared the end of the block, the waste material broke away, like a half-sawn tree branch breaking under its own

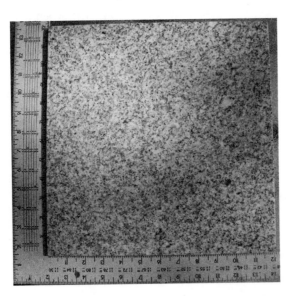

Fig. 4.10. Granite tile purchased at a local building supply store in the United States

weight. It also explains the slice or step marks in the surface. Whoever was operating the cutting device changed the angle. All the evidence about this stone suggests that the granite slab was cut with some type of saw.

What convinced me even more that the stone had been mechanically cut was when I compared it to the machining marks in a gray granite tile I purchased from a local building supply store. Like the stone at Abu Rawash, the unpolished side of the granite tile exhibited the same machine feed lines, and without doubt the granite from the building supply store had been cut with a machine. (See plates 24, 25, and 26 of the color insert.)

Perhaps the most interesting question is, what size saw would make a cut on a block of granite 47 inches wide and 56 inches long?

According to Dunn, in his article "The Mega Saws of the Pyramid Builders,"[5] the diameter of the saw can be determined with a few calculations. Since the surface of the granite is concave, the saw must have been at an angle, or perhaps the granite block was fed into the saw at an angle. So by knowing the dimensions of both radii, an accurate calculation of the saw diameter can be made.

The radius of the saw, based on the arc across the face of the slab, was 22.134 feet (6.746 m). And since the saw must have been on an angle, a simple formula can be used to determine with reasonable certainty the diameter of the saw and the saw's tilt. Thus, according to Dunn's calculations, the saw had to have a diameter of 35.9 feet and an angle of 46.5 degrees to produce both radii present in the granite slab. He tested these calculations with a 1:61 scale model and found the results to be comparable to the photograph of the granite.

In Dunn's opinion, there are other features at Abu Rawash and Giza that might shed further light on the mysteries there. As previously mentioned, not far from the stone at Abu Rawash there is a deep trench cut into the bedrock. Similar trenches exist at Giza on the east side of the Great Pyramid. Although these trenches have been labeled boat-pits because of their shape, the trench at Abu Rawash is narrow and deep, so it does not accurately represent the shape of a boat. For Dunn, it is plausible that these trenches were originally used to mount a saw, with the bottom half of the blade resting in the trench.

A large saw such as this would obviously require power of some kind.

This, of course, creates a paradox according to the standard model of history. The ancient Egyptians did not—*could not*—have any kind of power other than what can be provided by man or beast. Yet the stone at Abu Rawash testifies that power was somehow being generated to cut granite.

For Dunn, "Any craftsperson of substantial skill, wielding only the tools that remain in the archaeological record, would be incapable of recreating this stonework [at Abu Rawash]."[6] Furthermore, he states, "The accepted conventional theory that all the remarkable finely crafted stonework in the pyramids and temple in Egypt was produced by hand, using copper tools, stone pounders, wooden hammers, wooden squares and pieces of string is absurd."[7]

In 1883, Sir William Flinders Petrie believed that circular saws must have been in use when he noted parallel arcs existing in artifact No. 6. Although they had been polished out, the grooves were still visible. For Petrie, "The only feasible explanation of this piece is that it was produced by a circular saw."

It takes extraordinary evidence to support extraordinary claims, the saying goes. At Abu Rawash, this single slab of granite does just that. It's irrefutable evidence for the existence of Civilization X, and its historical significance is that it is paradigm changing. The stone at Abu Rawash is a new Rosetta Stone.

5

A PHILOSOPHY IN STONE

Memphis is a small village today, but more than three thousand years ago it was the center of Egyptian civilization. A few miles south of Giza little remains of the ancient capital, but what has survived offers extraordinary insight into the past. Like the granite boxes of the Serapeum and Abu Sir, several artifacts and one in particular defy explanation.

One of Memphis's most impressive monuments is a colossal statue of what is believed to be Pharaoh Ramses II. Made of limestone, and now sheltered in a concrete structure, the statue is so large that its protective building had to be two stories high, and that's with the statue lying down. Placed upright, the statue would be close to forty feet tall. On its back it is nearly ten feet tall.

Viewing the face and chest of this monstrosity from ground level is nearly impossible, unless you are close to seven feet tall. The balcony, however, offers a unique view that spans the width and length of the building. It's impossible to capture the entire statue in a single frame of film except with a wide-angle lens. (See plates 27 and 28 of the color insert.)

The detail of this stone giant is incredible. In perfect proportion, the face of Ramses is not only convincing but convincingly alive. His chest gleams in the sun; smooth, rounded pectoral muscles complete with nipples top a trim waist above a ribbed apron, finely carved. His belt and buckle carved in relief boast the sacred writing of the hieroglyphic style. The statue looks as if it was finished yesterday. But it is his face that is so captivating. His countenance smiles; it shines with the kindness of a benevolent and merciful ruler.

Fig. 5.1. Two colossal granite Ramses statues at Memphis

There are two other giant statues in the museum's northern court-yard, although not as impressive as the covered statue of Ramses. A fourth colossal statue discovered at Memphis was moved to Cairo during the 1950s and placed in a park by the Bab Al-Hadid train station. In the summer of 2006, this eighty-three-ton statue was moved to Giza. There it will become one of the main attractions for the Grand Egyptian Museum, scheduled to open in 2010.

At Thebes, at the Ramesseum,* rest the remains of another giant statue. Toppled over and broken, it lies next to the temple ruins. (See figure 5.3 and plate 29 of the color insert.)

---

*The Ramesseum is a memorial temple for Pharaoh Ramses II.

Fig. 5.2. Upper portion of a sixty-foot-tall granite Ramses statue from the Ramesseum, housed at the British Museum

Fig. 5.3. The Ramesseum

The puzzling part of these statues is not just their size, although that is an incredible feat in itself, but that three of them were carved in granite. This means that blocks of granite at least forty feet tall (one statue was close to seventy feet tall) and twenty feet wide had to be quarried, transported, carved to specification, and then erected—a difficult task even today. With modern technology, stone blocks the size of these Ramses statues are cut with extraordinarily large machines, some as big as a bus, and are typically used as raw materials scheduled to be further reduced for countertops, pillar facings, patio tiles, and cemetery headstones.

Despite the high level of technology our civilization has achieved, very few people alive today have the skills required to re-create the exquisitely precise colossal granite Ramses. Such a project would require a special team of artists and workers such as Gutzon Borglum and the men and women who designed and carved the presidential heads of Mount Rushmore.

RAMSES' LEGACY

Colossal statues have not only been found at Memphis and Luxor. Among the ruins at Tanis, eighty miles northeast of Cairo, are two broken colossal sandstone statues of Ramses II and a third statue, still intact, next to the temple pylon. Like the majority of ancient sites, this entire temple area is littered with granite blocks, some of which are elegantly inscribed. Five hundred miles to the south, at the ancient city of Thebes, are the Temple of Karnak, the Temple of Amun-Mut-Khonsu (see plate 30 of the color insert), the Temple of Amenhotep III, and the Ramesseum. Each boasts mammoth statues of Ramses. Although nothing remains of Amenhotep's temple, the seated Colossi of Memnon reach sixty feet into the sky (figure 5.4).

On the west bank of the Nile at the Ramesseum, the largest granite statues ever carved once stood. One statue still lies where it was toppled next to the remaining columns of the temple. According to estimates, the statue was nearly seventy feet tall when completed and weighed twelve hundred tons. The bust of another colossal Ramses from the Ramesseum now takes center stage in the Egyptian wing of the British Museum (see figure 5.2), originally one of the seated versions of the colossal Ramses.

A pair of seated Ramseses was erected in the temple. Amazingly, the Ramses bust in the British Museum was made from granite containing two colors. According to the British Museum placard, the stoneworkers who designed and carved the statue used the change in colors to draw a distinction between the body and head of the statue.

Another colossal but broken Ramses statue discovered in 1962 was restored in 1986 and loaned to Memphis, Tennessee, as the centerpiece of an exhibition on Ramses II. Although this twenty-four-foot, forty-seven-ton statue is one of the smaller statues of Ramses, lifting and transporting the statue proved to be a difficult task.[1] Amazingly, we are again led to believe that the ancient Egyptians used only hand tools, copper saws (with later saws made of bronze) and drills, chisels, hammer stones, and sheer manpower to manipulate and move these statues!

At Luxor, in the Temple of Amun-Mut-Khonsu, there are four more statues of Ramses, seated and wearing the Hedjet, the white, bulbous crown of Upper Egypt. Two statues guard the entranceway to the temple, and two more greet visitors as they enter. Like their upright versions, these seated statues of granite are also giants approaching a height of forty feet.

Perhaps the most interesting aspect of these colossal statues is that it

Fig. 5.4. Colossi of Memnon

appears the craftspeople who carved them were using a pattern, or at least a standard ideal, of what the statues' faces should look like. Whether in Memphis or in Luxor, Ramses' face has a distinct and familiar appearance: large almond-shaped eyes, rounded cheeks, full lips, and a loving smile. Ramses' countenance is unique in that its soft, almost youthful smile is accompanied by the wisdom and experience of an older man, strapped on through an honorary beard. The tender look the artists gave to Ramses lends the statues a feeling of warmth, almost as if they were in some way alive. The faces are carved with such purity and beauty that one cannot be sure if the posing model was male or female, or if there was a model. With such delicate features, only the beard suggests that the image depicted is male.

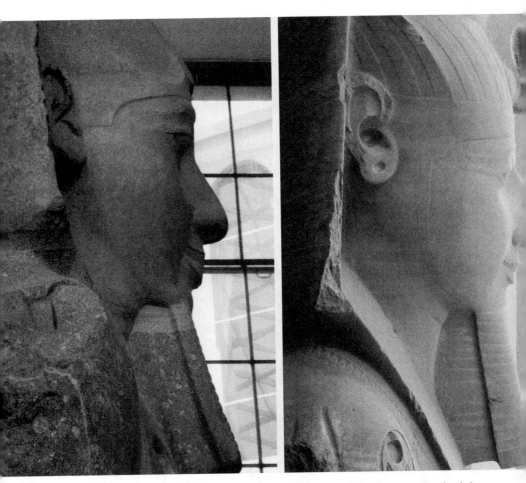

Fig. 5.5. Profiles of Ramses statues, Thebes (left) and Memphis (right)

Fig. 5.6. Ramses' countenance
in the British Museum

Fig. 5.7. Ramses' head at the
temple entrance

How does the warm feeling radiating from these statues' faces relate to perfect geometry? All the features of Ramses' face are symmetrical. So two left halves of Ramses' face put together would reconstitute the original face, unlike the typical human face, which, although it appears symmetrical, is almost always asymmetrical to various degrees.[2] To the human mind and eye, symmetry defines beauty. The more asymmetrical a face, the less attractive it is.

Such an analysis of ancient Egyptian statues is nothing new. Art historians have long known and documented the idealistic and geometric style of ancient Egypt's artists. According to Samuel Mercer, "The Egyptians had a strong sense of balance and symmetry in art, where a fidelity of proportion and a counterpoising of elements are used to secure a harmonious balance."[3] Furthermore, Mercer adds that Egypt's most delicate craftsmanship in art came early in its history.

The Egyptian artist favored standardized types as opposed to true portraits, according to Mercer, so as to convey a dignity of appearance. Art historians Ernst Kjellberg and Gosta Saflund refer to this idealized geometric style typical of Old Kingdom art as "the static unchanging element in the Egyptian portrayal of the male."[4] John Wilson calls it "the ideal of god-like majesty."[5] Why they chose this look is not thoroughly understood, although the traditional approach is that the pharaoh was portraying himself as God as well as man.

THE SYMBOLISM OF RAMSES' COUNTENANCE

Artists paint, draw, or carve their materials to achieve a specific look and feel in their work. For example, Michelangelo's sixteenth-century sculpture of David depicts a perfect yet lifelike figure of a man, right down to the detail found in its sinuous muscles. The same is true for the Venus de Milo, which depicts the beauty of women. Both statues were carved as if models posed for the artist. In abstract art, such as the untitled steel statue in front of Chicago's Richard J. Daley Center, viewers are left to their own interpretations. However, the statues discovered at Luxor and Memphis are neither lifelike nor abstract. They are geometric, carved into near-perfect proportion.

The Greeks are well known for their hand-carved lifelike statues. Side by side, the Ramses statue from Luxor compares poorly with a Greek statue from the British Museum. The Ramses head appears cartoonlike in contrast to the Greek carving, and the Greek statue certainly appears lifelike. (See plate 31 of the color insert.) As art historians have suggested, it is fair to conclude that the Ramses statues were not patterned after Ramses, but were representations symbolic of an ideal.

Since art is typically a social commentary or an expression of someone's inner vision of social conditions, and Ramses did not carve his own image into stone, then what might the Ramses statues reflect or symbolize? The answer to this question, I believe, is more philosophical than religious. According to traditionalists, by erecting his colossal statues, Ramses was "providing his people with a simple, accessible focus for their religious feelings which official religion denied them . . . a means of expressing— most publicly—their loyalty to the crown."[6]

Although, according to Mercer, this is true in a superficial way, there is deeper meaning. "The spirit of Egyptian art is a spirit of truth . . . the art of perspective, representing things according to their reality."[7] For philosopher and Egyptologist René Schwaller de Lubicz, "The ancient Egyptians used images whose concrete aspect evokes abstract ideas. In our languages, based as they are on a conventional alphabet, words evoke the abstract idea of their function by fixing concepts in a definitive manner; thus, to the contrary of the Egyptian image, they invite a concrete understanding of the ideas that are expressed." In essence, Egyptian art was designed to transcribe thinking.[8] Even the choice of material for these statues held a philosophical value:

> Granite, coming from fire, is also employed for certain doors or for colossi. At Luxor, for example, the colossi standing or walking in the name of Ramses (birth of the Sun) which surround the first court of the temple are of red granite. Black granite was chosen for carving the seated colossi in front of the pylon: "that of the west is carved from a block of black granite chosen in the quarry so that the red crown is found to be carved in a vein of red traversing the block." On the sides of each throne seating the other two black granite colossi at the second entrance to the temple is the representation of the Nile gods uniting the Two-Lands, as well as the black cubit, identical in measure to the cubit of the Rodah Nilometer and to the two basalt cubits of Dendera. Black granite was also chosen for sculpting the splendid statue of Thothmes III bearing, in the manner of a Nile god, offerings of plants.[9]

Art and science are reflected in modern society's structures. Statues held a special place thousands of years ago, much as they do today. For example, dressed in his 1917 U.S. Army uniform and regalia, the "doughboy" statue of a World War I veteran does not represent an individual, but the sacrifice of thousands of men and their families. Philosophically, it may also represent the courage and dedication which that generation of people exemplified. On the other hand, the seated statue of Abraham Lincoln in Washington's National Mall represents the man.

Yet the Lincoln statute also represents the concepts that Lincoln himself stood for. In fact, the Lincoln Memorial is a temple dedicated to concepts such as emancipation, preservation, inspiration, hope, and union. Lincoln sits majestically, his arms resting on each side of his throne. A dignified look assures us he was a great man. But his throne is not the throne of a king. It is the throne of a nation, a civilization. The statue of Lincoln itself was specially designed by artists to evoke feelings of patriotism and altruism in honoring the civil rights of all people. Likewise, the megalithic granite Ramses in the Temple of Amun-Mut-Khonsu evokes similar feelings, as does the Ramses temple with its own perfect geometric proportions. It too not only demonstrates technical precision, but also makes a philosophical statement in concordance with the temple's theme. (See plate 32 of the color insert.)

As is true of our civilization today, every civilization or culture that has existed was propelled by an underlying ideology or philosophy. The ideology and philosophy of Western civilization is one of democracy, the scientific method, a free-market economy, and beliefs associated with the Christian tradition. Civil organization and technical advancement are the result. Important and sacred structures and public buildings and churches reflect this. In many cases today's architecture is aesthetically pleasing yet plain, its beauty achieved through simple geometric measures.

During the Middle Ages, the great European cathedrals commissioned by the church were designed to evoke emotions of awe and reverence. Aside from the science and technology involved in the construction process, these magnificent structures were also built with an underlying philosophy, a philosophy that embraced the message of Christ, skillfully explained in the seminal 1926 book *Mystery of the Cathedrals* by Fulcanelli. Just as in our modern civilization, past and present, the art and science that went into the construction of the ancient Egyptian temple reflects the ideals and skills of the civilization that created it, ideas that run deep into a philosophy of Nature.

Luxor's Temple of Amun-Mut-Khonsu is not about the piety of a man. Rather, it is a tribute to the technical know-how of the civilization that built it and a testament to the philosophy that made Egyptian civilization great. Amun, Mut, and Khonsu are not "gods" but principles that form and explain the human nature as coherently as such an abstract subject can be explained. In fact, this theme of Man is seen throughout ancient Egypt. The enormous granite statues at Memphis, Tanis, and Luxor were

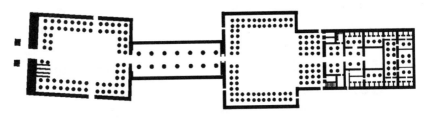

Fig. 5.8. Layout of the Temple of Amun-Mut-Khonsu

the celebration of civilization and mankind as the essence and culmination of Nature's principles. Just as the ancient historians declared that the temple was an institution of higher education, the temple was (and is) a form of communication, a lesson—and at its core was the builder's philosophy carved in stone.

The definition of Man and the story of the human experience was built into the temple architecture. Physically, the temple describes the structure of the human form, from the importance of the femur in the creation of blood cells to the role of the pineal gland in the brain. Spiritually, the temple conveys life's cosmic drama and Man's spiritual immortality.

Amun was the Hidden One or the Invisible One. Today Amun is best described as the Western concept of God: omnipotent and omnipresent. He was self-created, the creative power and source for all life, in the heavens and on earth, as well as the Underworld (the spiritual world for the deceased). Mut, which means "mother," was the cosmic wife of Amun and the mother of "the son," named Khonsu, who represented the king.

However, the kingship of Khonsu is not a physical kingship but refers to a cosmic (or spiritual) ruler who was made flesh through the forces of Nature. Khonsu as the king represents the essence of mankind, the archetypal "Man" essence of all who have ever lived, are alive now, and will live in the future. Khonsu, by being associated with Re and Thoth, represented the essence of life's energy, wisdom, and knowledge wherein mankind is a consequence of the universe's evolution that culminates in the physical endowment of the universe's self-perception as human. In myth, Khonsu was a lover of games, but also represented the principles of healing, conception, and childbirth. Literally, Khonsu was "the king's placenta."

These three gods (or neters)—Amun, Mut, and Khonsu—were known as the Triad of Thebes, but they were never meant to be worshipped as god(s). They represented a teaching, a lecture carved into the temple wall having to do with the philosophy of the archetypal Man and the mystery of mankind's origin. This was the underlying theme behind Luxor's Temple of Amun-Mut-Khonsu as well as the essence of pharaonic office —the Anthropocosm, or Man Cosmos.

The concept "Man as the Cosmos" explains why the designers of the temple's statues carved the diminutive female figure into nearly every

Ramses statue (figure 5.9). The smaller female statue at the feet of Ramses represents the *manifestation* of mankind. The figure is female because it is only through the female that mankind, as well as all of Nature, reproduces. In essence, the female form is the quintessential man, embodying the creative and nurturing forces that exist in all biological forms. *She represents mankind,* since she is responsible for mankind's creation in the womb and his nurturing as a boy.

The colossal Ramses statue represents the androgynous archetypal Man, the cosmic principle of Man (which includes both male and female natures) as the ultimate expression of the universe. The scene carved into the side of Pharaoh's chair offers the explanation in the uniting of cosmic and natural principles described by the litany of the bulrush and the lotus. The scene represents the lower and the upper realms, the microcosm and the macrocosm, coming together or being tied together as a single existence (figure 5.10). This is in the Hermetic sense of "as above, so below."

Understanding the concept of Man as the Cosmos allows a more accurate and more appropriate view of ancient Egypt, for it provides a

*Fig. 5.9. Seated Ramses with diminutive female figure
next to right calf*

Fig. 5.10 (left). Old Kingdom diorite statue of the Pharaoh Khafre, discovered in Giza's Valley Temple

Fig. 5.11 (below left). Old Kingdom litany of upper and lower realms carved into Khafre's chair

Fig. 5.12 (below right). Litany of upper and lower realms carved into Ramses' chair

valid explanation for the androgynous and perfectly geometric statues that adorn the temples. Thus do the colossal statues themselves hold the key to their interpretation. Their perfect geometric and androgynous shapes, clearly visible in the faces, reference the abstract and cosmic principles of Mankind.

Thus was the pharaoh as much a symbol as he was a king, and a pretext for embodying the mythical and the mystical nature of Man. Literally, the mythology declares that the birth of Ra (the sun) is a cosmic expression wherein the pharaoh represented the view that our physical lives are dependent on the dynamics of the universe and, primarily, the sun. In other words, the life of mankind cannot be separated from that of the universe. Accordingly, there is little wonder that Ramses is the widest and most encompassing expression of the king found throughout ancient Egypt.

Although the temple does not offer the literal explanation that Westerners are accustomed to, in its totality the Temple of Amun-Mut-Khonsu was a symbol that could be intuitively understood regardless of language. In every room and corridor, the esotericism of symbol is bonded with the exotericism of science, with the purpose of addressing the eternal question of cause and effect.

The concept built into the temple was also remembered as a story. In myth, Seth represents the creative principle that puts the human being into physical form. He represents the active principle of the abstract becoming form, or Ptah, the "fire in earth." So it is Seth's nemesis, Horus, who animates the king. However, Horus must be delivered from his bodily prison in the same way the mortal's soul must be saved, and in the end becomes the divine and perfect being. Thus, Horus represents all phases of creation, from the becoming to the resurrection and the return to the source. In this way, the universal Horus is the divine presence in all that exists.[10] Temple inscriptions explain this as a ritual where the royal fulfillment of Horus goes through phases in becoming a glorified body. In the end, Horus becomes the "King of divine origin, almighty in things of created Nature."[11]

The Temple of Amun-Mut-Khonsu anthropomorphizes Horus's becoming and return, which is really man's state of existence. In the "theogamy chamber" (the marriage of the gods), the spiritual birth of

Amun-Ra is depicted as the royal infant who is baptized and named through celestial forces. The terrestrial father, the god, assumed the form of Thothmes IV, and Queen Mut-m-uia (Mut in the barque), the spiritual mother, became pregnant by him. Then, Amun announces that this future child-king will be Amun-hotep heq-uas, the hotep of Amun, as leaven of the rising flax. Khnemu, the divine potter from Elephantine, announces the child's conception and fashions his form so that it is more beautiful than that of all the neters. With the assistance of celestial principles, the child is then brought into the world to be nourished with the milk of the "heavenly cow" (Hathor) from which all beings have life.

This story of the king's birth is symbolic and esoteric, and does not refer to any specific individual, but symbolizes mankind as a totality. It is the "becoming" of mankind as the physical universe, and ultimately as human beings. From a Christian perspective it is the same concept as the biblical Logos, where the divine Word of the beginning is the All, or the undifferentiated state of existence that is the nature of the Self. It is the same philosophical view as the Christian revelation of divine incarnation, but in the Egyptian Mysteries it was called the reconciliation of Seth and Horus.

According to Schwaller de Lubicz, such an insight helps explain why the pharaonic sages considered the precessional transition from the Age of Aries to the Age of Pisces a natural progression toward Christianity as foreseen by the Egyptian temple, and why the first Christians chose the sign of the fish as their standard.

Life is spiritual, and this understanding of Mankind's "becoming" creates unity and harmony for the individual as well as society. Thus, the return to the source is not only the aim for the king but for all men. In ancient Egypt this philosophical view of life was represented in mythology by the resurrected Osiris—the true King—who becomes enlightened (understanding the true anthropocosmic state of existence) and returns to the source.

Today, we separate science and philosophy. Yet it is a reality that science and philosophy are different aspects of a single body of knowledge. So wherever there is advanced technology, there is also advanced philosophy. Indeed, there is no more superior philosophy, which is really a view of Nature, than what has been articulated by the ancient Egyptians. Such a philosophy had to have been based on advanced knowledge of the natural world and an intuitive understanding of human nature. Ironically, it is the same philosophy that is emerging out of today's "New Science." For me, it is further evidence of the existence of Civilization X.

6

A PYRAMID OF
ASSUMPTIONS

Egyptology claims that Egypt's large pyramids were built as tombs for the Old Kingdom pharaohs. Yet with tens of millions of stone blocks used in their construction, from Meidum in the south to Abu Rawash in the north, in no place is the name of their builders inscribed, except for a single quarry mark of red ochre paint in the Great Pyramid. However, this was possibly forged by Richard Howard-Vyse under the pressure of competition with another archaeologist, the Italian Count Caviglia.

The assignment of pyramids as tombs for the pharaohs is one of the greatest assumptions in modern archaeology. There is actually no evidence that the pyramids *were* tombs. In some instances the decision to attribute ownership was made on the basis of tombs in nearby cemeteries, since it was assumed to be customary that the king's servants and courtiers were buried near him.[1]

Despite the claim that the pyramid was a tomb, a number of Egyptologists do recognize that the intent of the pyramid remains a mystery. According to Egyptologist Dr. Miroslav Verner, director of the Egyptology Institute at Charles University in Prague, "They [pyramids] still challenge us to explain why and how they were built. And in many respects they remain a great secret of the past."[2] Even Dr. Zahi Hawass, the secretary general of Egypt's Supreme Council of Antiquities, seems to agree on this point, stating that the "pyramids have magic and mystery. Its magic touches your heart, and when it touches your heart, you think about how they were built." Interestingly, Hawass also asks, "Who built them?"[3] (See plate 33 of the color insert.)

TOMB THEORY TROUBLES

According to tomb theory, the earliest kings of Egypt were buried beneath a rectangular structure made of mud brick. This tomb consisted of a large open pit dug deep into the ground and partitioned into rooms, the center room being the burial chamber. Over the pit, a roof was built using timbers as the supporting structure. At the pit's edge, a thick mud-brick retaining wall was built that extended above the ground, creating a hollow space above the roof. This hollow space was filled in with rubble, sand, and gravel. As a result, it formed a low, benchlike building; this was called a mastaba.[4]

Effectively, the mastaba was a large, rectangular headstone. (See plate 34 of the color insert.) Mastabas were common during the Old Kingdom's first dynasties. However, according to tomb theory, construction technology suddenly expanded, and the mastaba evolved into a step pyramid. A century later technology again expanded, and the step pyramid became the spectacular stone pyramid.

The origin of the tomb theory dates back to the beginning of Egyptology. During the late nineteenth century, British archaeologist Sir William Flinders Petrie (1853–1942) excavated eleven royal tombs. These included the tomb of the first dynastic king, Narmer, who ruled ca. 3100 BCE during Dynasty 0, eight other First Dynasty tombs, and two Second Dynasty tombs. Also at that time, at Giza, George Reisner (1867–1942)

Fig. 6.1. Mastaba No. 17 at Meidum

charted the development of royal burials through the Fourth Dynasty. What Petrie and Reisner discovered drove them to believe that the pyramids were tombs. Although the pyramids were empty, Egyptian nobility and their families were systematically buried underneath mastabas in fields surrounding the pyramids.[5] Thus, because of their proximity to these cemeteries, the pyramids were assumed to be tombs.

Later, proof for the tomb theory was found in Nubia (modern-day Sudan), Egypt's southern neighbor. During the sixth and seventh centuries BCE, Nubian kings were entombed in small, steep-sided pyramids; painted on the walls of the burial chambers are Egyptian-style scenes of burial rites. Accordingly, Egyptologists believed that the Nubians borrowed this tradition of burying the dead in pyramids from their northern neighbors, the Egyptians.

With this understanding of African history in mind, there had to be a logical, linear sequence to pyramid building. So Egyptologists considered it a likely scenario that during the Third Dynasty (ca. 2600 BCE), the Pharaoh Djoser decided that the standard mastaba did not constitute enough of a tomb. Under the guidance of the architect Imhotep, Djoser built the first pyramid at Sakkara, the Step Pyramid. The Step Pyramid

Fig. 6.2. The Great Pyramid at Giza

Fig. 6.3. The Third Pyramid at Giza

started out as a mastaba, but through three phases of construction was transformed into a pyramid.

Later, in subsequent dynasties, each pharaoh had to outdo his predecessor, which resulted in more pyramids being built at Sakkara and the three massive ones on the Giza Plateau. As a result, Giza became a necropolis and "the site of the dead pharaoh's mystical transfiguration, re-birth, and ascent into heaven." (See plate 35 of the color insert.) It was also "his residence in the beyond, from which he ruled over all the people of his time."[6]

In conjunction with the tomb theory, Egyptologists also developed a secondary political motive for the pharaoh's tomb-building desire. The state's theocratic ideology behind pyramid construction was that the people needed a project to bring them together as a nation. Accordingly, every household throughout Egypt sent men and food on a seasonal basis in dedication to the king and the building of his tomb.

The pyramid-tomb was so important because it served as a "resurrection machine." Without it, the kings could not attain eternal life and continue to rule. But exactly how a pyramid worked as a vehicle for transfiguration, and how the king ruled his people in the afterlife, has never been fully explained.

Pyramid Economics

Aside from the tools used and the techniques of construction, one of the more important questions concerning the construction of a large pyramid is that of economics. Abundant resources are required to build any large structure. This was as true thousands of years ago as it is today. How much does a large pyramid consisting of 2.5 million blocks, each weighing between ten and fifty tons, cost?

According to engineer Markus Schulte of the global design and business consulting firm Arup, the 5.9 million tons of limestone required for the Great Pyramid at Giza would cost $18 billion today. Add to that fifty thousand laborers working for ten years at a cost of $255 billion, plus 30 percent for general contracting costs. The total bill for the pyramid would be $380 billion. However, using modern techniques and substituted materials, great savings could be obtained, lowering the cost to somewhere between $30 billion and $35 billion.[7] Whatever the case, such high costs for any construction project, tomb or not, requires justification. In my opinion, why any society would devote such a huge amount of resources to a tomb is a very important question, a question that has never been seriously considered.

One possible answer is that the desire to build the tombs originated solely with the pharaohs, and the constituent Egyptian had no choice in the matter. They also had little input into the management of public projects. However, without foremen and managers, no large project would ever be built. So the middle managers as well as upper management (those who oversaw the project's design and construction) were also willing to follow the king's wishes or, again, probably had no choice. As a result, the Egyptians spent a vast amount of resources during the Old Kingdom's five-hundred-year existence, and in return, received nothing of utility for their service or their society.

Aside from the incredibly large price tag on pyramid building, there are other logical problems. If the king was willing to spend his vast wealth on a tomb, wouldn't it make more sense to order a palace residence to be constructed during his lifetime, one that he could enjoy while alive? A royal residence for any of the Old Kingdom pharaohs has never been found.

Pyramid location is also a problem. Egyptologists have not ascertained why one king built at Giza and another king somewhere else, such as Sakkara or Dashur.[8]

Fig. 6.4. The main pyramid at Abu Sir

Consequently, the tomb theory does a poor job of explaining Old Kingdom pyramids. It also fails to explain anything pertinent about these pyramids as they relate to ancient Egyptian society outside of Osiris resurrection mythology. More importantly, in my opinion, if a civilization—any civilization—has the technical expertise to build structures on a massive scale, such as what occurred at Giza, then it is certain that civilization had to operate in a rational, realistic, and efficient manner. Both the Rhind and the Moscow papyri show that the ancient Egyptians "possessed sound practical knowledge and knew how to make the fullest use"[9] of that knowledge.

That repertoire of knowledge included a decimal system, the use of fractions, and the calculation of geometric areas for the rectangle and circle, as well as the surface of a hemisphere; and volumes for pyramids, cylinders, and cones. Most importantly, they were aware of the relationship between the sides of a 3:4:5 (right) triangle—known to modern mathematics as the Pythagorean theorem.[10] Although there is no evidence to suggest that they theorized about *pi,* the evidence indicates that in practice, it was used.[11]

Pyramid projects were not haphazardly planned. They were designed and built to preordained specifications to serve a specific purpose, particularly the Great Pyramid. According to German engineer Rudolf Gantenbrink, who pioneered the exploration of the shafts in the Queen's Chamber:

> They did not embark on a reckless building spree but that the structure was already carefully planned before work commenced, with the consistent application of expertise that was still relatively simple for the period.[12]

Indeed, for the native African author and intellectual Cheikh Anta Diop, the Great Pyramid did not represent the "groping beginnings of Egyptian civilization and science, but rather the crowning of a culture that had attained its apogee and, before disappearing, probably wished to leave future generations a proud testimonial of its superiority."[13]

How can a civilization carry out advanced construction projects with such genius yet remain primitive in its thinking?

Holding fanciful beliefs while having proficient knowledge of mathematics, as the Rhind and Moscow papyri indicate, is inconsistent, since philosophy and science are really different aspects of the same concept. The cumulative cultural evidence of history does not support, and is entirely inconsistent with, such a stupendous farce as a $35 billion tomb! Furthermore, no other culture before or since has constructed tombs of such an immense size. So why is the tomb theory adamantly maintained?

Tomb Theory Origins

The short answer is that it has been a tradition for a very long time with an entire discipline resting on its prevalence. Sir William Flinders Petrie, the earliest authority on the pyramids of Giza, could not find a reason to believe the pyramids were anything but tombs. Why? Because, given the knowledge of history at that time, there was no other reasonable explanation. Also at that time, the theory of evolution had become prevalent in academic circles, so any proper explanation would have to fit the linear pace of history. Even Petrie could not offer any alternative explanation. As a result, he concluded that since all Egypt's pyramids were tombs, then the Great Pyramid, which he found to be unique, also had to be a tomb:

> In the first place, all the other Pyramids were built for tombs; and this at once throws the burden of proof upon those who claim a different purpose for the Great Pyramid. In the second place, the Great Pyramid contains a coffer, exactly like the ordinary Egyptian burial coffers of early times; like them both in its general form, and also in having grooves for a lid, and pin holes for fastening that lid on. Very strong evidence is therefore required if we would establish any other purpose for it than that of receiving and safe-guarding a body.[14]

Yet inasmuch as Petrie accepted the tomb theory, he had his reservations about the Great Pyramid: "It will be well, while discussing theories, to consider how the Tombic theory of the Great Pyramid stands affected by the results of accurate measurement and examination. What evidence, then, has been produced?"[15] He puts forth thirteen inconsistencies from his observations and measurements with the tomb theory.

1. Khufu was not buried in the Great Pyramid, according to Strabo.
2. The passages are well defined and would lead explorers straight to the chambers, instead of concealing them.
3. The coffer could not be taken in with its lid [it couldn't be taken into the pyramid with the lid on it].
4. The coffer is unusually deep.
5. The grooves are not dovetailed to hold a lid on [since retracted].
6. No lid has ever been seen.
7. In no other case is a coffer devoid of ornament or inscription.
8. In no other case are the neighbouring walls and passages of the Pyramid so devoid of hieratic and every other emblem.

9. The upper passages are unique, and also the above-ground place of the coffer.
10. The coffer is not built around to protect it, as others were.
11. The chamber has ventilating channels.
12. The lid might be a later addition to the coffer.
13. The coffer has certain cubic proportions, which show a care and design beyond what could be expected in any burial-coffer.[16]

Petrie was able to explain away most of the thirteen points he cited, and in the end he decided that "the damaged remains of this theory of accurate proportions, and the fact of the upper passages and air-channels not being known in other Pyramids, are then the only evidences which are left to reverse the universal rule of Pyramids being tombs, and coffers being intended for coffins."[17] In essence, no one, even Petrie, had any idea for what purpose the Great Pyramid was built.

Before Petrie was born, the tomb theory was the dominant explanation. In the ninth century the Arab historian al-Mas'udi, the "Herodotus of the Arabs," wrote that in 873 BCE an aged Copt insisted that the pyramids were the tombs of ancient kings and that the king's body was placed in a sarcophagus of stone and then the pyramid was completed around the sarcophagus. The entranceway to the pyramid was placed beneath the pyramid itself. According to the Copt, the pyramid was built in stages and then polished from the top down.[18]

Even further back, during the height of the Roman Empire, the Greek and Roman historians Diodorus (ca. 90–ca. 30 BCE) and Strabo (64 BCE–24 CE) also believed that the pyramids were tombs. Other ancient historians, such as Pliny, claimed that the pyramids were generally understood to be a treasure vault and a way to give the people something to do. The first Western historian, Herodotus (ca. 490–ca. 425 BCE), had also written that the purpose for the pyramid was a tomb.[19]

However, the writings put forth by ancient historians have always been suspect, particularly in the case of ancient Egypt. Some scholars such as Thomas Africa believe that "nationalist priests idealized their roles in antiquity and in the Saite era and provided Diodorus with an account of Egyptian society which was a blend of Ptolemaic reality and sacerdotal wishful imagery."[20] Aristotle, in his *Poetics,* leaves it unclear whether he believes Herodotus but states that his *Histories* were actual histories as opposed to poetry, since "it is not the function of the poet to relate what has happened, but what may happen—what is possible according to the law of probability or necessity," and added that "the work of Herodotus might be put into verse." But in the same sentence he states that Herodotus's works "would still be a species of history."[21]

What the truth is about Herodotus's writings we may never know. I don't think there is reason to doubt Herodotus, or any other ancient historian, since it was probable that he was recording what the ancient Egyptians told him, even if they were relating an inaccuracy. What *can* be said with confidence is that the pyramid tomb theory has been in existence for at least two thousand years, and may even reach back to early dynastic times.

The pyramid tomb theory is tied to Western history and its view of the ancient world. The origin of the tomb theory, it seems, rests in the hands of Herodotus. However, there is ample evidence to demonstrate that the pyramid was never designed to be a tomb.

ANCIENT EGYPT'S ROYAL TOMBS

Egypt was governed as a theocracy. However, if we examine Egyptian society through the lens of the Western concept of theocracy, it appears to be a confusing amalgamation of primitive mythology that is not consistent with the civil greatness that Egyptian society achieved. Nor does it explain the ancient Egyptian understanding of *theurgia*, or "works of the divine."

As for the pharaoh being a god, such an interpretation of Egyptian culture is too simplistic, given the vast amount of knowledge and the complex way in which their beliefs were expressed and disseminated. Nor does the pyramid-tomb match their social structure, technically or artistically; their social traditions of art and art in the funerary rituals were flamboyant, but the pyramids have no art in them at all. And the word *pharaoh* does not translate literally into English or any other language as "lord" or "king." The word *pharaoh* is from *per aa,* which means "great house."[22]

The Egyptians built a vast number of royal tombs over their three-thousand-year history. Most of them had been looted long before excavations of the nineteenth and twentieth centuries. Nonetheless, there is a long history of what a royal Egyptian tomb looked like; many of them are in the Valley of the Kings, as well as the aforementioned mastaba fields of Giza. What can be ascertained from these examples is that the tomb was designed as a houselike structure and decorated par excellence. The royal tomb had hallways and chambers with level floors and steps for ease of use, in the same way that the earlier mastabas were sectioned off in houselike fashion. As is the case with King Tutankhamen's tomb (the only unlooted royal burial so far discovered), the Egyptians filled the burial chamber with the deceased's possessions. For that reason, the tomb really was designed to be the "house" of the deceased. Why the Egyptian tomb had to be a house and not a pyramid rests in their beliefs.

The ancient Egyptian ritual of mummification and burial has long been a subject of fascination for the Western world. With the 1922 discovery of King Tutankhamen's tomb, it became apparent that the ancient Egyptians spent a great deal of effort in preparing not only the body, but the inside of the tomb as well. They filled it with numerous items of beauty and personal possessions of the deceased.

For us, it makes little sense to bury so much wealth instead of passing it along to the next generation. The common interpretation of the ancient Egyptian burial practice is that the deceased needed all those things in the afterlife. Such a rationale, however, is based on a superficial understanding of ancient Egyptian philosophy and beliefs. Ancient mortuary texts provide more of the answer. It was the hope of the ancient Egyptian not only to transcend terrestrial life, but to achieve immortality as a heavenly star. Their fear was that the deceased's Ba would not be able to join with his or her Ka in the afterlife, and if the body was allowed to disintegrate, the person's essence would disappear and be absorbed into the energy field that is the fabric of Nature. To prevent this unfortunate event, the deceased's body was mummified.

For the ancient Egyptians, the two most important concepts concerning the afterlife were the Ka and the Ba. Although not an exact analogy, the Ka and the Ba are what the Western religious tradition might refer to as spirit and soul. A third factor, *ankh,* represented immortality. The Ka was believed to be the part of the person's consciousness (personality and inner qualities) that related to the immediate world. The Ka was that part of the person connected to the physical body: where the person lived, his or her possessions, and those with whom he or she associated. The Ka was the energy or spirit that emanated from the person. The Ba represented the part of consciousness that was immortal, the eternal force that caused all Nature to exist.

For the Ka to be reunited with the Ba upon burial, the possessions of the deceased were gathered together by the family and placed in the tomb along with the body. Food offerings to the Ka of the deceased were also interred. When the Ba and Ka were joined in the afterlife, ankh would result as the fully resurrected and glorified essence of the deceased, reaching beyond the limits of the earthly realm and thereby achieving immortality. For this reason, the tomb was referred to as the Per Ka (house of the Ka); the priests, who were in charge of it, were the "priests of the Ka"; and the temple was called Per Ba (house of the Ba).

Upon death, the Ka separated from the body and naturally sought a means to take form again. However, if the deceased person harbored regrets or violent desires, the Ka would, according to Schwaller de Lubicz, seek "any substance whatsoever, psychic in particular, borrowed from a living being, in order to return to a ghostlike shadow-existence."[23] Only if the Ka were able to unite with its Ba would the individual person have a continued existence through the unity or "oneness" with its Ba. For this unity to continue into the next life, the Ka would have to be transformed in the tradition of Osiris, whose essence was reincarnated as his son, Horus.

With this understanding of the Egyptian tomb's purpose throughout dynastic history—that it was designed to be a house for the deceased—it is easy to see that the Giza pyramids, and in particular the Great Pyramid, certainly do not qualify as tombs. Their passageways and chambers were not constructed for human use, nor to accommodate the burial rites that occurred at the time of burial.

MORE TOMB THEORY TROUBLES

According to the tomb theory, pyramid construction began during the First Dynasty in Sakkara, ten miles south of Giza, when Djoser converted his mastaba into the Step Pyramid. A number of years later at Dashur, five miles south of Sakkara, pyramid development continued with limited success in the "Bent" Pyramid, and finally with complete success in the Red Pyramid. The Red Pyramid, two-thirds the size of the Great Pyramid, so-named because of its reddish color, was the first true pyramid, according to Egyptologists. With construction techniques now fully developed, during the Fourth Dynasty (roughly 2500 BCE) a new site was chosen at Abu Rawash for pyramid building. But a third of the way into its construction, the decision was made to abandon it in favor of the Giza Plateau.

There are, however, a number of inconsistencies and questions with this logic and chronology of tomb theory:

> After the Step Pyramid, other Old Kingdom pyramids built at Sakkara were adorned with hieroglyphic inscriptions, the Pyramid Texts, but the other pyramids, from Abu Rawash to Meidum, contain no inscriptions of any kind.
>
> The interior design of the Great Pyramid has no precedent or antecedent in Egyptian civilization, or any other civilization.
>
> During the millennium following the Fourth Dynasty, the Egyptians built nearly one hundred smaller pyramids. However, they used a different method of construction, resulting in structures of substandard quality when compared to the Giza pyramids. Today, these later pyramids are in a state of severe deterioration.

The most difficult of problems with Egypt's pyramids is an engineering riddle. How did the ancient builders create such a massive structure "so finely dressed," as Verner puts it, "that it is barely possible to insert a playing card between adjacent stones?"[24] According to Columbia University Research Scholar of Middle Eastern Studies Ogden Goelet:

> If we assume that Khufu reigned for fifty years and that his builders worked at a breakneck pace ten hours a day, one enormous block had to be added to the pyramid every four minutes or so—every day for fifty years, inexorably. Only the precision scheduling, rigorous planning, and careful organization of an efficient, honest, and clear-thinking bureaucracy could complete a project like this.[25]

Although the seventy-ton slabs of granite that were used to build the walls and ceiling of the King's Chamber are often cited as mysteries of ancient technology, some of the heaviest pieces of stone come from the third (Mycerinus) pyramid's mortuary temple. George Reisner, the principal archaeologist at Giza, estimates that these blocks weigh about two hundred tons. In comparison with the Great Pyramid's casing stones, which average between two and three tons, or the granite slabs of the King's Chamber, the foundation stones at Mycerinus's temple are extraordinarily large.[26] Furthermore, existing ancient Egyptian records offer no information on the methods employed by the builders of the pyramids in either planning or constructing their monumental works,[27] discounting several murals that show men pulling a single stone block on a sled.

The prevailing theory is that pyramid building was accomplished with a combination of ramps, sleds, and lifting devices, using an unknown technique in conjunction with a highly effective system of labor.[28] However, if ramps were used to move stones up and into the pyramid, the ramp itself would have to have had a volume of 1,560,000 cubic meters (55,090,880 feet) and a height of 146.6 meters (481 feet). The ramp would have been as large a project as the pyramid and a marvel in and of itself.[29]

In recent years there have been attempts to establish as fact that multiton stone blocks could be moved with sleds using sheer muscle power. All these attempts have failed, however, which is an important piece of evidence in itself, leading to a suspicion that Fourth Dynasty Egyptians did *not* build the three Giza pyramids.

The most recent theory describing how the pyramids were built comes from Jean-Pierre Houdin, a French architect, and his father, Henri. According to the Houdins, ramps were used, but not in the way Egyptologists have typically theorized. Instead, external ramps were used to raise blocks for the first third of the pyramid. Then, to raise blocks further, an internal ramp was built into the pyramid itself, just inside its outer edge. Logical in its approach, this theory is likely the best one, since it is also supported by evidence.

During the 1980s a French team performed a microgravimetry survey of the Great Pyramid, searching for possible hidden chambers. Although they found none, what they *did* discover is a less-dense region of blocks spiraling around the pyramid at its outer edge. During the twenty years

Fig. 6.5. The Red Pyramid at Dahshur

since the survey was performed, this less-dense area has remained a mystery. Now, with the Houdin theory of pyramid construction, such an area should exist if, in fact, inner ramps were used to move blocks into higher areas of the pyramid.[30]

Yet even if we know the process used to build the pyramids, there remains the problem of how its builders quarried, shaped, and shipped millions of tons of stone to the construction site. According to Merle Booker, the technical director of the Indiana Limestone Institution of America, if a company were to build the Great Pyramid today, it would take twenty-seven years to fill the order for 131,467,940 cubic feet of stone, assuming that thirty-three limestone quarries operated three shifts per day and there were no work stoppages. This is, of course, using the most modern quarrying equipment available for cutting, lifting, and transporting stone.[31]

Another construction theory, put forth by materials scientist Joseph Davidovits in 1988, and one backed by "concrete" evidence, is that the outer core blocks of the pyramid were poured with reconstituted limestone. In support of Davidovits, after five years of research, Michel W. Barsoum, professor of materials science at Drexel University, agrees and has gone on record stating, "I cannot come to you with more convincing evidence of casting. After that, I'd need to get a video tape of them doing it." He and his team have concluded that the inner and outer casing stones were cast, and that the backing blocks and the top halves of the Great Pyramid and the middle pyramid were also probably cast.

That this artificial aggregate stone has survived for thousands of years and has been believed by Egyptologists and archaeologists to be cut stone is a measure of the genius of the Great Pyramid's builders. They were outstanding architects—civil and mechanical engineers—as much as they were talented chemists and materials scientists.

The real mystery for Barsoum is the fact that the pyramid builders were able to lift seventy-ton granite beams two-thirds of the way up the Great Pyramid, and they were able to carve the giant granite slabs with nothing harder than copper. Referring to the third pyramid's granite casing stones and how its builders had begun surfacing the north side, for Barsoum, "how that was accomplished, with nothing harder than copper, is simply stunning and astounding."[32]

There are even larger engineering scenarios that are difficult to explain. In the past, scientists have studied the issues surrounding the construction of very large pyramids. One of the most interesting facts is that the labor involved in cutting the amount of stone in the Great Pyramid equals half the labor required to cut *all* the stone for *all* the monuments and temples that were built during the New Kingdom, Late period, and Ptolemaic period combined. For the Great Pyramid, two million cubic meters (seventy million cubic feet) of limestone were cut. The New Kingdom, Late period, and Ptolemaic period combined used four million cubic meters (141.3 million cubic feet) of sandstone for all their monuments.[33] More stone was cut building the pyramids of Giza than was used from 1550 BCE to 30 BCE.

From a materials perspective, to make matters worse, during the Old Kingdom, structures were built from limestone and granite. However, during the New Kingdom, psammite sandstone was used, which is so soft that in its softest spot it can be scratched with a fingernail. Even temples built during the Ptolemaic period are composed of extremely soft stone.[34] So the trend in stonecutting technology makes little sense. During the Old Kingdom, when only copper tools were available, the ancient Egyptians were cutting fossil-shell limestone, a heterogeneous material very difficult to cut precisely. Moreover, later, soft white limestone was used, even in areas where granite was plentiful, such as southern Egypt. Finally, by the Eighteenth Dynasty, soft limestone gave way to sandstone. All the while the hardness of tools improved as a switch was made to bronze tools and then to iron ones.[35] This chronology of tools and materials, however, does not make sense.

Perhaps the most perplexing construction problems involve the Great Pyramid. The ascending passageway, the tunnel that leads to the Grand Gallery, was plugged with three enormous granite blocks each four feet thick, three-and-a-half feet wide, and fourteen feet long. Curiously, the granite plugs were an inch wider than the passageway's opening, so they could *not* have been introduced externally. The builders of the Great Pyramid had to have placed them in the passageway during construction, which, of course, means a funeral never took place in the Great Pyramid,[36] since the passageways were blocked from the beginning of construction.

THE PYRAMIDS ALREADY EXISTED

Given all the problems associated with the tomb theory, I believe it makes more sense to assume that the large pyramids built along the western banks of the Nile River already existed when the earliest predynastic peoples began settling in the Nile Valley. Not knowing what the pyramids were, and recognizing that they were closed structures, they assumed they were tombs. As such, they settled in the areas where pyramids were built and turned pyramid complexes into cemeteries. At Giza, they buried their dead underneath mastabas to the east and west of the northernmost pyramid, as well as between the Valley Temple and the middle pyramid and to the south.

This area west of the Valley Temple and east of the middle pyramid is best described as small rolling limestone bluffs buried in a field of yellow sand. Throughout this area, numerous tombs have been cut into the natural limestone formations. The evidence of chisel marks is clearly visible within the tunnels that lead to the crypts, as well as in the crypts themselves. Although there are some finely carved tomb entranceways, the dominating character of workmanship is crude but effective. In contrast to the workmanship of the structures and structural ruins on the plateau, the workers here certainly used hand tools.

The hypothesis that the pyramids and temples already existed prior to dynastic Egypt solves a number of inconsistencies. It provides a motive

Fig. 6.6. Rock-cut tombs at Giza between the Valley Temple
and the middle pyramid

*Fig. 6.7. Rock-cut tombs at Giza between the Valley Temple
and the middle pyramid*

for Djoser to modify his mastaba into a step pyramid, and for the early dynastic kings to inscribe their religious convictions into the Sakkara pyramids. The reason: *They were patterning their tombs after what they thought to be tombs at Giza, which they believed to be the tombs of their ancestors.* It explains why pyramids built before and after the Third and Fourth Dynasties were of a lesser quality. Old Kingdom pharaohs were copying the Giza pyramids, but they had no choice about using simpler methods and tools.

In comparison with Fourth Dynasty pyramids, the pyramids of the Fifth Dynasty are inferior, even shoddy. All were smaller than Giza's third pyramid, except for one at Abu Sir. Fifth Dynasty pyramids were built of stone rubble and sand sandwiched between stone walls, a type of construction that rapidly deteriorates once its casing stones have been removed. Today, unlike the pyramids of Giza, these structures are in ruin.

There have been attempts to "prove" that the simplest of techniques were used to build the pyramids. In all cases, heavy equipment eventually had to be used. Thus, it is logical to assume that it is not possible to build a large Egyptian-style pyramid using simple methods and without heavy equipment. There is really no other logical conclusion except that the ancient Egyptians of 2500 BCE did *not* possess the technology required to build large pyramids. There has to be a much deeper history to Egyptian civilization, a history that predicates the existence of a Civilization X.

7

A BETTER
INTERPRETATION
OF THE EVIDENCE

Despite the prevailing orthodox view, there have always been research-ers who have questioned the evidence for tomb theory in a critical but logical manner. During the thirteenth century, Abd al-Latif al-Baghdadi observed that the pyramids "illustrate man's intelligence, and the pure genius that has been expended on their construction, and that the sci-ences, geometry and engineering have been brought to the highest pitch in them." More importantly, according to al-Baghdadi, they tell us about the people who built them and "their science."[1] During more recent times, the most important critical view of tomb theory came from one of Napoleon's surveyors, the French cartographer and engineer Edmé-François Jomard (1777–1862).

Jomard, who was a member of Napoleon's team of scientists in his 1798 expedition to Egypt, devoted most of his life and his work to understanding ancient Egypt. In 1803, he helped establish a catalog of hieroglyphs and during the next five years helped draft the famous French publication of *Description de L'Égypte*. He was also the first man to deduce the geodetic (mathematics- and measurement-based) origin of the Greek linear scale. Furthermore, from classical texts he was able to determine that the ancient Greek unit of measure called the stadium (600 feet) was equivalent to 185 meters, a distance that surveyors later discovered was a repeating distance between important ancient sites.

Jomard also deduced that the stadium was one-tenth of a minute of the meridian degree, and since ancient authors believed that the apothem (again, the perpendicular distance from the center to any of its sides) of the Great Pyramid was intended to represent this length, this proportion must have been deliberate. He also understood from ancient texts that the base of the Great Pyramid was half a minute of a degree of longitude, so 480 times the length of the base equaled one degree.

Ultimately, in Jomard's eyes, the Great Pyramid was a structure based on geodetics. In other words, the pyramid's builders had the necessary astronomical, geographical, and geodetic skills to accurately measure the meridian degree, and since they had that knowledge they could also measure the dimensions of Earth. According to historian Martin Bernal, "He became convinced that the Ancient Egyptians must have had an accurate knowledge of the earth's circumference and based their units of linear measurement upon it."[2] For Jomard, the Great Pyramid was a repository of measure, a testament to a civilization. It was not a tomb but a shrine of advanced skill and knowledge.

However, there was a serious problem with Jomard's findings. If his insights were correct, then the Greek linear scale was not Greek at all, but Egyptian and very old. This implies that the Egyptians held a superior knowledge, one that the Greeks were unable to learn and preserve. His findings were also in conflict with the current paradigm and amounted to academic heresy. Bernal notes, "Differences between this heterodox school and academic Egyptology became sharp after the discipline's establishment in the 1860s, and acute in the 1880s after it accepted the dominance of Classics."

Academic Egyptologists focused mainly on linguistics and ancient Egyptian written material. According to Bernal, they were primarily philologists. However, their competition, the alternative researchers, were "mathematicians, surveyors and astronomers."[3] These two groups of researchers, both with interests in ancient Egypt, would never mix, and with the backing of the university system in their favor, the Egyptologists would never have to refute technical arguments that they were unable to follow anyway. Yet the heart of the struggle between these historical paradigms was even darker, according to Bernal:

The struggle was unequal from the start, for the heretics were fighting against the two principal paradigms of the nineteenth century—"progress" and racism. If they were right, an ancient African or semi-African people had had better mathematics than any European until the nineteenth century itself.[4]

A major problem of the dissenting researchers was that they lacked organization (and this is just as true today as it was one hundred years ago). Legitimate, methodical approaches—even though valid in their application and conclusions—were dismissed because of this lack of organization; the independent researchers were categorized as fanatics. Another factor was that classics studies and linguistics are more prestigious than other disciplines, notably mathematics. With the help of renowned science historian Otto Neugebauer, who demonstrated significant Mesopotamian influence on Greek mathematics and astronomy and insisted that the Egyptians had no original or abstract ideas themselves, the orthodoxy had all the "scientific" weight it needed.[5]

Anyone claiming that the Great Pyramid was anything other than a tomb was a "pyramidiot," although, interestingly, Neugebauer shied away from articulating any theories about pyramids specifically. Opposing theories, regardless of their merits, were effectively debunked with very little effort. Precision and other uses of *pi* or *phi* were practical knacks (processes that were discovered by accident but worked technically) and not representative of profound thought. Over time, although a more politically correct word—*pseudoscience*—came into use, it carried the same insult.[6]

Nonetheless, a few scholars, such as astronomer Sir Norman Lockyer, risked their careers by confronting the evidence. Lockyer, whose mind was boggled by the mathematical elegance of Egyptian structures, claimed that they had been very carefully built for astronomical purposes.[7]

Since Lockyer's day others have joined the ranks of the scientific heterodoxy, most notably the French philosopher René Schwaller de Lubicz. Although Schwaller de Lubicz was never officially part of the academic establishment, his exhaustive research during the 1940s of the Temple of Amun-Mut-Khonsu, its measures and its geometry, was seminal. Although

Schwaller de Lubicz's work—which depicts a sophisticated philosophy of science and the application of that science to architecture—was rhetorically abused for more than sixty years, it has never been refuted.

And then there is Harvard academic Livio Catullo Stecchini, who, during the 1950s and 1960s, showed in a plausible fashion that the ancient Egyptians had a precise knowledge of global measurement that was applied with precision in other countries besides Egypt. More recently, in 1969, one of the great Renaissance historians, Giorgio de Santillana, along with Hertha Von Dechend, bucked the system with *Hamlet's Mill,* a seminal and scholarly book loaded with historical evidence that ancient myth was nothing less than a scientific language whose origins dated to sometime before 6000 BCE.[8]

Today, valid scientific attempts at understanding why the Giza pyramids, and particularly the Great Pyramid, were built and what they may have been used for are generally ignored, particularly when they contradict archaeological and Egyptological interpretations of history. This is the case because any serious scientific effort to examine the possible function of the pyramids delivers evidence contradictory to the orthodox explanation. Furthermore, by engaging in intellectual discussion with members of the opposition, orthodox arguers begin to resemble them, since many alternative arguments are based on logical deduction and mathematics.

For example, French architect and archaeologist Jean-Philippe Lauer (1902–2001), who spent many years studying the Sakkara pyramid complex, engaged in nontomb pyramid theories. Although, as Bernal points out, he denounced any idea that suggested the pyramids were anything but tombs, "he admitted that the measurements do have some remarkable properties; that one can find such relations as pi, phi, the 'golden number' and Pythagoras' triangle from them; and that these generally correspond to what Herodotos and other ancient writers claimed for them."[9] Lauer believed that the Greeks were the first true mathematicians, but some ancient texts and traditions, such as Iamblichus's *Life of Pythagoras,* contradicted this, stating that a large number of Greek philosophers, astronomers, and mathematicians studied in Egypt. In dealing with this contradiction, Lauer wrote:

Even though up to now no esoteric Egyptian mathematical document has been discovered, we know, if we can believe the Greeks, that the Egyptian priests were very jealous of the secrets of their science and that they occupied themselves, Aristotle tells us, in mathematics. It seems, then, reasonably probable that they had been in possession of an esoteric science erected, little by little, in the secrecy of the temples during the long centuries that separate the construction of the pyramids, towards the year 2800, to the eve of Greek mathematical thought in the 6th century BCE. As far as geometry is concerned, the analysis of buildings as famous as the Great Pyramid would take a notable place in the researches of these priests; and it is perfectly conceivable that they could have succeeded in discovering in it, perhaps long after their erection, chance qualities that had remained totally unsuspected to the constructors.[10]

And . . .

For the whole length of the 3,000 years of her history, Egypt thus, little by little, prepared the way for the Greek scholars who—like Thales, Pythagoras, and Plato—came to study then even to teach, like Euclid, at the school in Alexandria. But it was in their philosophic spirit, which knew how to draw from the treasure amassed by the technical Positivism of the Egyptians, that geometry came to the stage of a genuine science.[11]

In the face of contradiction, Bernal finds it difficult to see "why he [Lauer] should then baulk at the simplest solution, believe the Greeks and accept, with the German Egyptologist Professor Brunner, that there was an 'axial age' around 3000 BCE"—this "axial age" of sophisticated knowledge of mathematics being consistent with the traditions of later Egyptians that were told to visiting Greeks. Bernal believes there is nothing to back the hypothesis that the Greeks achieved a qualitative intellectual breakthrough (the so-called Greek Miracle) during the fourth century BCE that approximated the actual achievements of the pyramids. He agrees with the ancient model of history, that ancient Egyptians had a tradition of superior mathematics.[12]

Bernal, with his three-volume work *Black Athena,* has finally raised this issue with the academic world, focusing in particular on how this relates to ancient Egypt. However, despite the brilliance of daring scholars who have challenged orthodox views, the most important questions concerning early dynastic Egypt are yet to be answered.

THE PROBLEM OF THE DYNASTIC RACE

Although the dynastic race theory has lost its flavor with modern-day, academic Egyptologists, the reasons why nineteenth- and twentieth-century Egyptologists favored an extra-African origin for dynastic Egypt was based on evidence. Petrie found few artifacts that could be dated to a period before the Fourth Dynasty. In his memoir, *Ten Years Digging in Egypt,* Petrie noted, "The civilization that we find before us in the earliest known history appears elaborate and perfect."[13] After that he commented that changes in taste and custom occurred slowly after the first few dynasties. For Petrie, the people of this earlier culture were not just masters of the arts but "also of combined labor, of masonry, of sculpture, of metal working, of turning, of carpentry, of pottery, of weaving, of dyeing, and other elements of a highly organized social life."[14]

However, at Meidum, twenty miles south of Giza, Petrie found burials of what he regarded as two separate predynastic cultures. The more recent culture buried its dead with the body at full length; Petrie believed that these deceased individuals were members of the nobility. The older culture buried its dead with the knees curled up to the nose and lying on one side facing east with heads to the north. Petrie interpreted the Meidum cemetery as being a place where not only two separate occupations were interred but also two separate races. He assumed that the earlier culture had provided the leadership for the Fourth Dynasty and was the driving force behind it. Egyptologists refer to this unknown culture as the "dynastic race" and assumed that it could not have been from Africa, due to the fact that it was so in synch with the social and political thinking of the day.

At Naqada, Petrie found the same dual-culture scenario and unearthed 2,100 graves containing an assortment of clay pots, palettes, and various amulets made of stone, bone, and ivory, attributing them to a period between 4000 and 3100 BCE. Petrie concluded that life before the pharaohs was primitive, and that in the years preceding dynastic times, Egyptian culture suddenly evolved. For Petrie, the best explanation of the evidence was that "a great European confederacy" invaded the Nile Valley multiple times—"Greece, Asia Minor, Italy, and Libya, all leagued together." Thus, the grand Egyptian civilization of monuments, obelisks, and temples was the result of an "incoming race" that found a native population with beliefs and customs very different from its own. For Petrie, at Meidum these two races—one aboriginal and the other from abroad— had not yet mingled.[15]

At that time, diffusionist theories of superior cultures and the spread of civilization to indigenous peoples were popular among Western Europe's colonial powers. During the early part of the twentieth century, fascism was fashionable, so diffusionist theories of a superior race were appealing. Africa, however, was known as the Dark Continent and was thought to be incapable of producing such an advanced culture.

Later, the dynastic race theory shifted to the Mesopotamian Valley and invaders from the East. In this modified version, culturally and politically superior Mesopotamians quickly established themselves as rulers over the primitive Egyptians. Continuing excavations appeared to bear out this theory. Skeletons more robust than the typical ancient Egyptian, exhibiting dolichocephalous (oblong) skulls, were discovered and believed to be the evidence that a dynastic race had existed. Late predynastic graves of Upper Egypt's northern part also produced skeletal remains of an unusually large size.

According to Walter B. Emery (1903–1971), who specialized in archaic and predynastic Egypt, the differences between these skeletons and the typical ancient Egyptian skeleton are so distinct that the suggestion these people were derived from earlier peoples was impossible.[16] One dolichocephalous skull from a Third Dynasty ruler, found in 1902 in a mastaba in Beith Khallaf, belonged to a man whose height was six feet, two inches. It may have been the remains of King Sanakht, whose name was found in the tomb.[17]

According to this Mesopotamian dynastic race theory, Egypt's pharaonic class entered the Nile Valley from the east; royal art from the First Dynasty was similar to that found in Mesopotamia. During the 1930s, the German explorer Hans Winkler advanced this theory by discovering ancient rock art in the eastern desert. Between the Nile Valley and the Red Sea, Winkler found numerous images of boats similar to those found in early Mesopotamian art. He argued that Mesopotamian invaders used the Red Sea to access Egypt, and as they made their way to the Nile River, they left their marks on the rocks. Other evidence also seemed to support such an idea. Carvings on an ivory knife handle from Gebel-el-Arak in Egypt were believed to be Mesopotamian or Syrian, and paintings on the walls of a late predynastic tomb at Hierakonpolis (the ancient capital of Upper Egypt) also suggested invasion. Hierakonpolis's tomb and the knife handle displayed Egypt's native ships and strange vessels with a high prow and stern, unmistakably Mesopotamian in origin.[18]

However, there were problems with a Mesopotamian invasion by sea. Winkler's "Egyptian boat" rock art was dated to be older than its Mesopotamian counterparts by many centuries. And in 1969, archaeologists from the American Museum of Natural History discovered a settlement that closed the book on the dynastic race invasion theory.

While excavating outside Hierakonpolis near the ancient city of Nekhen, the American archaeologists discovered the remains of an entire Amratian* village along an ancient dried-up creek bed, which led to a reconstructed view of predynastic daily life. The Amratian village was composed of farmers and craftsmen whose leaders managed the manufacture and trade of their goods. It was also evident that these predynastic Egyptians began to build simple irrigation systems and were developing a written language. As time went on their tombs became larger and more sophisticated, eventually becoming similar to the tombs of the early pharaohs. For Egyptologists, the excavations at Hierakonpolis proved that a dynastic race did not invade the Nile Valley. It was more likely that the dynastic race evolved slowly over time from these early Amratians and others like them.

Despite this critical blow to the dynastic race theory, the evidence for Egypt and Mesopotamia remains, and it is not trivial. It is exten-

---

*Amratian is an archaeological term referring to an ancient culture of Egygt named for the place it was first identified.

sive and cannot be explained by casual trade, such as cylinder seals of Mesopotamian origin found in Egypt dated to between 3500 and 2900 BCE. According to Pennsylvania State University Professor of Classics and Ancient Mediterranean Studies Donald Redford, "It would seem that besides trade items, a human component of alien origin is to be sought in the Gerzean (prehistoric) demography of Egypt. This is not to resurrect the moribound 'dynastic race' theory, but we should be careful not to misread the evidence or ignore its real weight."[19] For Redford, this ethnic duality of ancient Egypt existed long before 3600 BCE.[20] Although little is said today concerning what this "ethnic duality" was, prior to 1965, and particularly during the first half of the twentieth century, it was carefully studied in the shape and size of human skeletons and in particular the shape of skulls. In 1905, Egyptologists Douglas Derry and Elliot Smith systematically examined and measured numerous skeletal remains unearthed on the Giza Plateau cemetery by George Reisner in graves consisting of "pits of varying depth hewn in the limestone and with a side chamber."[21] Today, there is little left in the way of human remains in the cemetery around Giza's pyramids, but when first excavated, the graves proved to be a valuable source of predynastic and early dynastic Egyptian corpses.

According to Derry, predynastic and early dynastic burials were performed with the deceased in a contracted, fetal position—just as Petrie noted. But around and after the Fourth Dynasty, burials were performed with the body in an extended position. There was also a significant difference in skeletal types suggesting, in conjunction with burial practices, that over the years a new population began mixing with an older population.

In 1909, Nubian excavations provided numerous human remains from the southern regions of ancient Egypt that could be compared with the remains from northern Egypt. After comparing the two sets of data—skeletal measurements from Giza and Nubia—it was clear to Derry "that the pyramid builders were a different race from the people whose descendants they had hitherto been supposed to be,"[22] assuming that the early dynastic individuals entombed at Giza did in fact build the pyramids, and that "quite definitely they [predynastic and early dynastic peoples] had not come from the south as the Dynastic people were far removed from any negroid element."[23]

What Derry and other Egyptologists such as Cicely Fawcett, Geoffrey Morant, Arthur Thomson, and David Randall-MacIver had determined through the comparison of human remains was that there were essential differences between the crania of predynastic and early dynastic Egyptians, a distinction that gradually disappeared later on as the two peoples mixed. The predynastic people had narrow skulls with a height measurement exceeding the breadth, a condition common in native Africans. However, the reverse was the case for the dynastic race. They not only had broader skulls, but the height of their skulls, while exceeding that in the predynastic race, was still less than the breadth.[24] In other words, the dynastic race had larger heads, which, for Derry meant larger brains.

For both sets of human remains, there is little difference in the length of the skull, but a significant difference in the breadth, 132 millimeters for the predynastic peoples as opposed to 139 millimeters in the dynastic race. Derry viewed this as significant and regarded these measurements as "characteristic" of the two different races. He also drew attention to the work of Hermann Junker during his 1909 to 1910 excavation at a cemetery called Turah, a few miles from Cairo on the east side of the Nile. The Turah cemetery consisted of late predynastic and First Dynasty graves. But there were also burials from the Third Dynasty. According to Derry, "These skulls exhibited very clearly the inherent differences as between the Predynastic and Dynastic races."[25]

According to Derry's findings, the people first buried at Turah were dolichocephalic (long headed), but over the years and by the Third Dynasty they had become mesocephalic (round headed). The cephalic index* for men grew from 72.3 to 76.2, while the women went from 74.6 to 79.1, almost brachycephalic (broad headed).

By lumping these figures together and taking the means of the three dynastic measurements (length, breadth, and height), the result, according to Derry, is so far removed from the mean of predynastic people that

---

*The cephalic index is a rating scale used to measure the size of the head. The rating is obtained by multiplying the maximum width of the head by 100 and dividing that number by the maximum length of the head. Numbers between 75 and 80 are considered normal; 75 and below is considered dolichocephalic; between 75 and 80 is mesocephalic; and above 80 is brachycephalic.

"under no circumstances could they be considered the same race." Derry also believed that the data indicated the presence of a dominant race or aristocracy, albeit few in number.

Although the data were correct, Derry erroneously concluded that a more intelligent race, one with mesocephalic skulls, brought a sophisticated knowledge of building in stone, of sculpture, of carving relief painting, and of writing to Egypt. It was the only way to explain the enormous jump from the primitive predynastic Egypt to the advanced civilization of the Old Kingdom.

One of the last distinguished Egyptologists to argue in favor of the idea that a dynastic race had invaded Egypt was Emery, the chair of the University of London's Egyptology department. Emery felt, however, that this dynastic race was not composed of invading Mesopotamians. After weighing the evidence gleaned over years of excavations and the subsequent analysis of same, he believed it was possible that a more advanced community from an undiscovered area was at least partially responsible for the birth of dynastic Egypt. He believed that another culture whose achievements were passed on to Egypt and Mesopotamia best explained the common features of and differences between both Egyptian and Mesopotamian civilizations.

According to Emery, the dynastic race ruled as the elite and performed the dual roles of priests and governmental officials. This leadership mixed socially only with the Egyptian aristocracy. Precisely who this dynastic race was is still a matter of speculation. However, some scholars associate them with a people referred to by the ancient Egyptians as the Shemsu Hor, the Disciples of Horus or the Followers of Horus. The Shemsu Hor were recognized as the dominant sacerdotal caste in predynastic Egypt until approximately 3000 BCE.

At the end of the fourth millennium BCE, the people known as the Followers of Horus apparently formed a civilized aristocracy and ruled over the whole of Egypt.[26] And while the blending of these two races did occur, it was not a sudden event. Throughout Egypt's Archaic period, the distinction between the civilized aristocracy and the masses, according to Emery, was very marked, particularly in regard to their burial customs. Not until the beginning of the Second Dynasty is there evidence of the lower classes adopting the funerary architecture and mode of burial of the aristocracy.[27]

Still, the difficulty in deducing precisely who the first Egyptians were stems from a lack of evidence. Mesopotamia certainly shows a background of development. Egypt does not.[28] However, it's really a broader philosophical question that historians of all disciplines have debated for centuries. Does a heightened civilization naturally form in primitive cultures because a critical stage of development is reached after slow growth, or does some external stimulus from another culture serve as a catalyst?

On one hand, a steady progression in culture toward a heightened civilization is really indisputable. Knowledge that is gained by one generation is passed on to the next, and after many generations the culture will most assuredly reach a threshold where it can be considered a "civilization." Yet trade and exploration have always been traits of the human experience, so it is also likely that cultures from different regions had contact with each other. However, to what extent one culture influences another is sometimes difficult to ascertain. What can be said about Egypt and Mesopotamia is that a sharing of knowledge and certain practices did occur. The real nut of the question is, was Mesopotamia responsible for the birth of dynastic Egypt?

Although Mesopotamian and Egyptian cultures are treated as separate, diverse civilizations, there are indications that Mesopotamia influenced Egypt just before the beginning of the First Dynasty. The use of cylinder seals to stamp a letter was typical of Sumer and not of Egypt. But as mentioned previously, cylinder seals have been found in late predynastic graves. In Sumer, mud brick was used to erect ziggurats,* and in the earliest large structures in Egypt, mud brick was also used. Moreover, the mud-brick buildings of the Egyptians appear to be of the same recessed-niche style found in Mesopotamia, which appears suddenly and fully formed in the Nile Valley. But in Mesopotamia, archaeologists have traced development through various stages.[29]

According to Emery, just because Mesopotamia was not the source of the dynastic race doesn't mean that the dynastic race didn't exist. The rapid advance of civilization in the Nile Valley prior to Egypt's

---

*Ziggurats are pyramidal temples that have the form of a terraced step pyramid of successively receding stories or levels.

unification had to be explained somehow, and the best explanation was that a core group of people served as an organizing and governing body. Furthermore, a dynastic race did not have to take the "the form of a horde invasion."[30] For Emery, although the evidence is clear that Egypt and Mesopotamia had predynastic relations, as in the case of shared architectural concepts, the Egyptians were clearly superior in their construction practices.[31]

What is believed to be certain is that at the beginning of Egypt's historic period, the country was divided into two rival kingdoms, one in the north and the other in the south. Both were governed by a royal house and aristocracy of the same race that was traditionally referred to as the Followers of Horus, which the third-century historian Manetho referred to as the demigods. Although scholars still debate how the southern and northern kingdoms were united, records of the unification found at the ancient capital of Upper Egypt, Hierakonpolis, demonstrate that unification did take place.

On two large ceremonial limestone mace heads and on both sides of a large palette carved from green schist, the unification is recorded. Both monuments belonged to different kings, yet they commemorate the same event. The ceremonial mace heads sing the praises of a king known as the Scorpion King, and the palette boasts of a conquest led by Narmer, whom Egyptologists identify as the first dynastic ruler, Menes. It is possible, though, that the unification might refer to something else, a philosophical concept uniting the abstract and the concrete, the spiritual and the physical.

UPON CLOSER EXAMINATION

Given the evidence of a grand civilization built in granite, and the differences in early and predynastic burials recorded by Petrie and Derry, the idea that migrating cattle herders were responsible for dynastic Egypt is unreasonable. So is an invading culture from either Europe or Mesopotamia. Neither of these scenarios explains the evidence, because the evidence has been masked by orthodox Egyptologists, whose conservative views have dominated and monopolized the published literature on the subject.

The dynastic race theory grew out of conflicts in evidence in an attempt to explain the vast differences in excavated artifacts. In *Naqada and Ballas,* Petrie states that the artifacts he discovered, such as flints and pottery, belonged to a large population that occupied all of Upper Egypt, and that in his opinion, there was no connection between this "dynastic race" civilization and the Egyptian civilization. So different were their burials and artifacts that he was convinced they were a completely different race, and thereby labeled them "the New Race."[32]

According to Petrie, this New Race intruded on Egyptian tombs of the Old Kingdom, and later the Twelfth Dynasty Egyptians superposed their burials on those of the New Race. With that evidence, Petrie concluded that the New Race lived in Egypt *after* the Fourth Dynasty but *before* the Twelfth Dynasty.

For Petrie, the evidence was obvious. "The earthenware tables, bowls, and other artifacts which are found in the later style of the 'New Race' tombs," he wrote, "appear to be copied from the well-known forms of the Early Empire." Nor did the New Race use the potter's wheel in crafting their earthenware. Even in later periods of the New Race, Egyptian objects are absent.[33] The absolute exclusion of remains, one from the other, in both tombs and towns, "makes it impossible to regard them as dwelling in the country together," according to Petrie. Thus, he concluded that they were "invaders [who] destroyed or expelled the whole Egyptian population, and occupied the Thebaid alone!"[34]

Petrie attributed the New Race to migrating Libyans. In shape, form, and decoration, their pottery resembled that of the Kabyle people of modern Libya. So did their hunting habits, as well as their tattooing practices, ascertained by the Libyans found in the tomb of Seti I (ca. 1370 BCE). Petrie wrote, "In the New Race we see a branch of the same Libyan race that founded the Amorite power; we have in their remains the example of the civilization of the southern Mediterranean at the beginning of the use of metal, about 3200 BCE. . . . In short, we have revealed a section of the Mediterranean civilization, preserved and dated for us by the soil of Egypt."[35]

According to Budge, however, there was no consensus among early Egyptologists concerning the interpretation of the evidence. A geologist by the name of Jean-Jacques De Morgan (1857–1924) put to rest many questions, Budge wrote, since his expertise as a geologist and mining engineer was "outside the competence of Egyptologists."[36]

De Morgan showed that the remains of the New Race were in a continuous chain of sites extending from Cairo in the north to Wadi Haifa in the south. So Petrie's New Race occupied the entire Nile Valley for nearly 1,000 years. De Morgan also reiterated that it was clear that the New Race was at a lower stage in the scale of civilization and that the manners, customs, industries, and abilities of the two peoples were entirely different. Furthermore, artifacts discovered in New Race graves did not show the slightest trace of Egyptian influence. Nor did their graves contain any objects made by Egyptians, but there was considerable evidence to show that the *historical Egyptians* (3000 to 2000 BCE) borrowed largely from the traditions of the New Race.[37]

Like Petrie, De Morgan concluded that the Egyptians and the New Race did not live side by side and did not occupy the Nile Valley at the same time. If they did, surely the inferior civilization would have adopted the manners, customs, arts, and industry of the more advanced civilization. "This being so," he wrote, "one of the two peoples must have preceded the other in the country of Egypt, and the first occupant could be none other than Professor Petrie's 'New Race,' because, in spite of its less advanced degree of civilization, it had borrowed nothing from the more advanced Egyptians." With that, De Morgan concluded that the New Race was aboriginal, or perhaps more correctly, the inhabitants of Egypt, whom the Egyptians found there when they entered or invaded the country, were aboriginal: "They could be nothing else."[38]

After proving the great antiquity of the New Race, De Morgan went on to challenge Petrie on his dating of the New Race. Petrie dated the New Race to have existed between the Fourth and Twelfth Dynasties, but according to De Morgan this was impossible. "How could a semi-barbarous people," he asked, "like those which formed the 'New Race,' who were armed with flint weapons only, invade Egypt, and expel or massacre the whole of the population of the country without leaving any trace of it behind?"[39]

The authority of De Morgan prevailed, and to further rationalize and interpret the evidence, a "dynastic race" was created by later Egyptologists (Petrie included), and they were labeled as invaders.

Despite the peer influence and pressure from De Morgan, Petrie was correct in his analysis of the evidence. The New Race did live from great antiquity and up through the Twelfth Dynasty. The New Race was, in fact, the dynastic race that reclaimed its ancestors' lands. The great monuments and other structures and artifacts were already there. That's what confused Petrie. The New Race and those who built the Old Kingdom lived many thousands of years apart, but they were, culturally, originally from the same group of people. In this, one Egyptologist was right.

Emile-Clément Amélineau claimed that the artifacts he found at Abydos—those that resembled the artifacts found by Petrie at Tiikh— dated from the time of the "divine" kings of Egypt.[40] With this thinking, the problem of the dynastic race is solved, with the benefit of the assumption that *the ancient Egyptians were correct in recording the chronology of their kings*. The dynastic race that Emery, Derry, Petrie, Winkler, Fawcett, Morant, Thomson, and Randall-MacIver banked their careers on did exist, but its people were not invaders or from any other country. They were themselves native Egyptians who had maintained their culture for thousands of years. Although their level of civil sophistication had suffered in some catastrophe so that they did not have the tools or techniques to build as their ancestors did, they did retain their religious and philosophical principles.

In predynastic times there were three methods of burial. The grave received the disseminated and incomplete bones, or the skeleton was placed in the fetal position, or the body was burned in a monumental tomb. According to Budge, Alfred Wiedemann viewed these three types of burial as being not so different than the classical customs of the Egyptians. According to Wiedemann, "It may be shown that they are intimately united with the Egyptian religion and with the worship of Osiris and Horus, as learnt from the Book of the Dead and the ritual formulae of the Egyptians and that the vestiges of this very ancient custom [dismemberment] have never completely disappeared, and are preserved not only in the texts but also in actual practices. Even in later Egyptian periods, the lower part of the foot of the mummy was dislocated. In other cases the phallus of the corpse was removed, embalmed separately, and buried near the mummy."[41]

Wiedemann explains further that "this dismemberment and disorder of the bodies in the graves discovered by Petrie, [was] a custom which was symbolically preserved down to the latest epoch of Egyptian history."[42]

The same problem early Egyptologists encountered with evidence interpretation can be applied to Egypt's most treasured monuments, pyramids, and temples. Almost as suddenly as ancient Egypt's engineering genius arose, it disappeared. A few hundred years later, construction efforts by the Fifth Dynasty were at best feeble. In that dynasty, structures were erected by piling stone rubble between a building's outer and inner shells. Ancient Egypt was never again to see the majesty of true pyramid building. Egyptologist John Wilson of the University of Chicago wrote:

> The several pyramids of the Third and Fourth Dynasties far surpass later pyramids in technical craftsmanship. Viewed as the supreme efforts of the state, they show that the earliest historical Egypt was once capable of scrupulous intellectual honesty. For a short time she was activated by what we call the "scientific spirit," experimental and conscientious. After she had thus discovered her powers and the forms which suited her, the spirit was limited to conservative repetition, subject to change only within known and tested forms.[43]

This sudden burst of engineering genius that existed for the few centuries of the Third and Fourth Dynasties makes little sense. What makes more sense is that *the pyramids already existed*. Such a scenario best explains all the evidence. As Petrie noted, the royal tombs were already there when the indigenous New Race came to occupy the Nile Valley. It's a very good assumption to make that those who ventured into the Nile Valley between 4000 and 3000 BCE assumed the pyramids were tombs (what else could they be?) and started a tradition of burying their dead in the fields where their ancestors, "the gods," buried their deceased. This, of course, means that at one time in the remote past a technically sophisticated civilization existed.

Such a concept is not extraordinary. Not only does the evidence presented so far point in that direction, the Egyptians themselves claim that their tradition reached far into antiquity to the civilization I refer to as Civilization X.

According to the Turin Papyrus kings' list, prior to Narmer, the first king of the First Dynasty, the Shemsu-Hor ruled for 13,420 years, and before them the gods ruled for 23,200 years.[44] This provides the possibility that the pyramids were constructed sometime after 39,620 BCE but before 3000 BCE.

8

A PULSE GENERATOR
INSIDE THE GREAT
PYRAMID

In a recent documentary entitled *Engineering an Empire: Ancient Egypt,* hosted by Peter Weller, several renowned Egyptologists appeared and presented their admiration for the skill and technical prowess of the ancient Egyptians, with regard to the construction of pyramid tombs for the king. I found the title somewhat misleading, however, since the methodology used by the ancient Egyptians to carve out tunnels and chambers from bedrock was never discussed. Nonetheless, the first hour of the two-hour program focused on Sakkara's Step Pyramid in a unique and fascinating way. Weller and his camera crew descended into the depths of the pyramid's underground tunnels for a rare look at "Djoser's chambers," a truly groundbreaking section of film. Next the narrator addressed the Red Pyramid at Dashur, supposedly the first true pyramid ever built by the Egyptians.

Anticipating what would be said about the Great Pyramid's interior, I was disappointed when the narrator glossed over the Giza pyramids in a matter of seconds. The documentary producer's decision to skip the Great Pyramid is unfortunate, because its interior design with its multiple chambers and mixture of shafts is as mysterious as it gets for any structure built at any time. Whoever can decipher not only *how* the Great Pyramid was engineered, but also *why* it was engineered, will surely make history.

Despite boards attached to the floor to prevent slipping, walking up the ascending passageway of the Great Pyramid is a quite a task. One really has to crawl up, since hunching over is mandatory. It's hot and the air is stale from the constant line of tourists moving in and out of the pyramid, and the taller you are the worse it is.

In February 2007 when I toured the Great Pyramid, arriving at the base of the Grand Gallery, I could see that the Queen's Chamber was closed. A yellow iron gate barred admission. Entering the Grand Gallery was a fantastic yet eerie experience. After this, one has to crawl through a short tunnel from the Grand Gallery into the antechamber before progressing into the King's Chamber. Being in the Great Pyramid is an experience of a lifetime.

When I entered the King's Chamber, a small group of people were performing an initiation or ritual of some kind around the granite box at the chamber's far end. The hum of their chant filled the air and was amplified by the acoustics of the chamber. Even with low lighting, the red hue of the granite walls was visible. Running my hand across the north wall next to the mouth of the north shaft, I could feel that the granite slabs, which make up the wall, were flat but not polished. On the southern wall, whatever had been attached to the shaft had been removed. A huge piece of the granite wall in the shape of an oval was missing. Whatever was used to remove the inlaid object must have been powerful. It appeared that the granite and whatever was attached to the wall had been ripped away.

THE GREAT PYRAMID'S INTERNAL DESIGN

With its bizarre configuration of internal chambers, passageways, and shafts, the Great Pyramid's internal design is perhaps the biggest ancient mystery to be solved. Egyptologist John Romer, in considering the Great Pyramid's design, says it is

> an alien thing, so foreign that some of our most basic modern points of reference—the theoretical point, for example, where the pyramid's central axis bisects its baseline—are but abstractions in themselves. . . . From the very beginning of the work, therefore, the pyramid-makers had need of much of the information that a modern building plan

provides: a plan that described the harmonics of the Pyramid's interior architecture and linked them to the Pyramid's exterior; to its height and width, to the level of its baselines and the position of its central axis. A subtle plan as well, that set a maze of mathematics behind the Pyramid's smooth exterior.[1]

Other Egyptologists seem to agree, such as Bob Briar, who stated in an interview, "If we didn't know that they actually built the pyramids, if we didn't have the pyramids there on the Giza Plateau, I think we would say they couldn't have done it."[2]

There is little reason to suspect that so much work was devoted to the creation of three separate chambers—one of which was built with granite—for the sole purpose of entombing the king. On this point the German engineer Rudolph Gantenbrink, whose robot crawled up the Queen's Chamber shafts, agrees, adding, "It is also clear that they did not embark on a reckless building spree but that the structure was already carefully planned before work commenced, with the consistent application of expertise that was still relatively simple for the period." According to Gantenbrink, the pyramid builders worked from a plan, in the form of a grid, which was created in a scale of 1:40.[3]

It is in the careful examination of the Great Pyramid's interior design that the tomb theory is exposed for what it is: an outdated theory based on ancient hearsay, and a very poorly assembled theory at that, contrived and completely unscientific. How the strange arrangement of the Great Pyramid's internal chambers and shafts is rationalized as being a tomb complex is even less credible than tomb theory itself.

According to tomb theory, when the pyramid was being constructed, the king's burial chamber was originally the subterranean chamber that was cut into the bedrock below the pyramid. However, as construction progressed, the king or his architect decided that it should be moved to another location midway within the height of the pyramid. Later, it was moved again to a third location above the second location, and that second location was then to become the queen's burial chamber.

Even if this were true, the logic in this explanation fails to account for the original intent of the large passageway, called the Grand Gallery, that forms a magnificent seven-layered corbel-vault ceiling built from

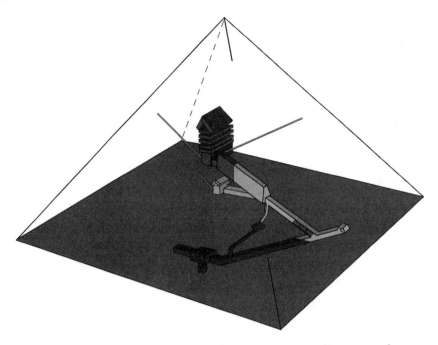

Fig. 8.1. Three-dimensional view of the Great Pyramid's interior design

enormous limestone blocks. The gallery joins the upper chamber to the middle chamber directly beneath it. Interestingly, on both sides of the Grand Gallery are low ramps that run the length of the passageway. Cut into these ramps are twenty-seven square openings, alternating from large to small, at regular intervals that correspond to right-angled niches in the gallery walls. Their function has been debated ever since their discovery.

The prevailing theory is that a wooden structure was anchored in these openings (slots) in order to move construction materials or support blocks while the corbeled ceiling was under construction. Admittedly, academic Egyptologists recognize that, so far, no theory accurately explains the curious slots built into the Grand Gallery's ramps.

At the lower end of the Great Gallery, a narrow passageway leads to a corridor that descends into the bedrock underneath the pyramid. When discovered, this shaft was filled with rock and sand.

Petrie believed that this shaft was an exit route for those who lowered the granite blocks into the ascending corridor after the king was entombed. However, if that were true, the shaft could not have been filled from the top. Another theory explains that it provided fresh air to the men who were excavating the underground chamber, but that would mean that the underground chamber as well as the shaft were built after the Great Gallery.[4] Common-sense construction, ancient or modern, dictates that foundation and excavation work are performed first.

Near the entrance of the middle chamber, the connecting passageway steps down and slopes, overall sixty centimeters, to meet the floor of the chamber. Why it was constructed like this is unknown. According to some theorists, the original floor was granite and was removed by thieves or confiscated and used in the upper (King's) chamber.[5]

The middle chamber itself is an enigma as well. Situated precisely on the pyramid's east–west axis, the room is built out of limestone blocks with a corbeled ceiling and sports a niche 4.5 meters (14.75 feet) tall in its east wall. The purpose of this niche is unknown, but it is assumed to be the spot where a statue of Khufu was placed. More bizarre are the narrow shafts built within the north and south walls of the chamber, which were originally tapered (and sealed) to a small hole where the shaft meets the chamber wall.[6]

One explanation for these shafts is that the middle chamber was a backup burial chamber for the pharaoh in the event of the pharaoh's sudden death while the pyramid was still under construction. (The upper chamber also contains shafts.) After the upper chamber was completed, the shafts in the middle chamber were sealed.

Finally, there are the upper chamber and its antechamber. More baffling than the main chamber, both are constructed from red granite. The walls, floor, and ceiling are made of granite. In all, the ceiling of the upper chamber is composed of nine slabs of granite weighing a total of four hundred tons.[7] Above the ceiling are forty-three beams of granite stacked in five rows, whose purpose has remained a mystery. It has been suggested that the extra granite was applied to support the weight of the pyramid. However, the middle chamber, being lower in the body of the pyramid, supports more weight than the upper chamber, and it was not built with reinforcement slabs.

Although the prevailing theory is that the shafts were constructed for the purpose of air circulation, in the context of the concept of a resurrection machine, the shafts find another meaning. The soul of the king would ascend one of the shafts, believed to be astronomically aligned to the constellation of Orion, on his way to becoming a star.

Such ideas concerning the purpose of the Great Pyramid, so speculative in nature, leave much to be desired. A more pragmatic approach, such as a project manager might undertake and backed by engineering principles, provides a better understanding of the design and function of the Great Pyramid.

AN ENGINEERING MODEL

Giza's Great Pyramid tells a story, but not the story of a pharaoh, or king, or anyone in particular. It is the story of an ancient technical civilization whispered through the evidence of design, material, and function. In every passageway, chamber, and wall there is the unmistakable fingerprint of refined craftsmanship and superb engineering design. Giza's Great Pyramid tells the story of Civilization X.

Despite its enormous size, at first glance the Great Pyramid looks simple enough. One stone is stacked on another. But to assume that it is a simple structure designed for a simple purpose because there are no steel girders or elevators is a deliberate discounting of the evidence. With three chambers, eight passageways, and a Grand Gallery, the Great Pyramid is internally complex and may be, for modern researchers, the largest puzzle box ever built.

The original entrance opens to a narrow passage 4 feet tall by 3.5 feet wide, which descends 100 feet into the bedrock, ending in a subterranean room. Although large (46 by 27 feet), the subterranean chamber appears to be crude and unfinished, and is void of any inscriptions. An ascending passage joins with the descending passage near the ground level; it is very narrow, also 4 feet high by 3.5 feet wide, and rises at an angle of 26.5 degrees for 129 feet, then levels off into another very small corridor that leads to the pyramid's middle chamber. Another very large corbeled chamber off the ascending passage leads to the upper chamber, which has been built from slabs of solid granite.

Although its casing stones and outer retaining wall have been removed, as well as any interior equipment, if it ever existed, this giant puzzle box remains relatively intact. Explaining what the pyramid was used for—

Fig. 8.2. Western area of the subterranean chamber (square pit in foreground) (courtesy of John Cadman)

which means explaining every chamber and passageway in a holistic, integrated manner—is more than just the Holy Grail of Egyptology. It may be the key to understanding our own history and civilization.

Since there are four chambers designed into the Great Pyramid, there are also four keys to analyzing what its function may have been. Each chamber has its own unique character. First, the upper chamber's walls and ceiling are made of granite slabs with two built-in shafts on the north and south walls that exit to the pyramid's exterior.

In addition, as mentioned earlier, forty-three granite beams were placed in a hidden chamber above this chamber's ceiling. Second, the Grand Gallery chamber is the largest room in the pyramid and leads to the upper chamber. Third, the middle chamber, which is made of limestone, also attaches to two shafts. And fourth, the subterranean chamber is located 100 feet into the bedrock, and when compared to the rest of the chambers, appears to be crude or possibly unfinished.

Of all the chambers in the Great Pyramid, the subterranean chamber is the largest, as well as the most mysterious. It is 46 feet long, 27 feet wide, hewn into the limestone bedrock, and difficult to describe. The

*Fig. 8.3 (top). Eastern area of the subterranean chamber
(courtesy of John Cadman)*
*Fig. 8.4 (bottom). Entrance tunnel (left) and "dead end
shaft" of the subterranean chamber*

descending passageway's entrance to the subterranean chamber is near the floor at the northeast corner. A six-foot-wide square pit shaped like a funnel has been tunneled in the middle of the floor, near the east wall. This square-shaped pit is actually the mouth of a shaft that is eleven feet deep, although in 1816 the Italian explorer Count Caviglia drilled into the pit another thirty feet.

Today, a handrail has been installed around the pit to keep visitors from accidentally falling into it. The western half of the chamber has been carved nearly six feet higher than the eastern half and sculpted into several large finlike protrusions. All these finlike protrusions are situated east to west and are nearly as tall as the ceiling. Between the large protrusions, a stepped channel starts at the floor and flows toward the back of the chamber. In its center there is a channel leading to the western wall. In the southeastern corner, a tunnel known as the "dead end shaft," thirty inches in height and width, runs south fifty-seven feet, then ends at a wall. There are two other features in the design of the Great Pyramid that appear to be part of the work performed in the bedrock, the well shaft and the "grotto."

If the subterranean chamber was nothing more than a mistake, and was originally designed to be a burial vault, an enormous amount of resources was wasted. On the other hand, if the chamber was an integral part of the overall design of the Great Pyramid and performed a function, then what could that function possibly be? One engineer who has studied it claims that its design is similar to an old-fashioned pump.

In the latter part of the twentieth century, Edward Kunkel, in his book *The Pharaoh's Pump,* put forth the theory that the subterranean chamber was a hydraulic ram pump that forced water up through the pyramid and out through the shafts in the upper chamber. Kunkel also believed that water was used to build the pyramid. Stone was carried down the Nile on barges and then through a series of locks built between the river and the construction site. This canal led to an artificial moat that surrounded the Great Pyramid and was retained by a wall. The subterranean water pump pulled water from the moat into an open, inner area of the pyramid. The casing stones of the pyramid retained the water. (In this theory, the casing stones were set in place before the core limestone blocks.) So the subterranean pump had a dual purpose. First, it was used in building the pyramid by flooding a series of locks so that stone blocks could be transported to the site, and when the pyramid was completed, the pump served the greater purpose of pumping water into the surrounding fields to irrigate their crops.

How Kunkel's pump worked is that air in the subterranean chamber became compressed by water flowing down the descending passage. When the air in the chamber could be compressed no more, a check valve at the top of the descending passage closed. The compressed air then forced water up through the well shaft and into the Grand Gallery. To assist this process, a vacuum was created in the hidden chamber above the upper chamber though a yet-to-be-determined method of combustion.

The reduction in air pressure above the water then pulled water up through the pyramid into the Grand Gallery. A release valve at the top of the Grand Gallery opened and released the vacuum, allowing fresh air in. This caused the water to move down the Grand Gallery. Furthermore, a valve in the antechamber opened, while a valve below the Grand Gallery closed. This moved water into the middle chamber. The air in the middle chamber was then compressed and forced water into the upper chamber, where compressed air in the antechamber forced water to the outside through two shafts on the north and south walls.

Although parts of Kunkel's theory have their problems, such as the placement of casing stones before the inner limestone core stones, he was the first person to recognize that the Great Pyramid might be a device, and specifically, to determine a possible hydraulic function for the subterranean chamber. It would be close to fifty years before another mechanically inclined researcher picked up where Kunkel left off.

JOHN CADMAN'S PULSE GENERATOR

In 1999, John Cadman, the former chief engineer of a king-crab boat and now a breeder of Black Russian terriers, was inspired by Kunkel's work. According to Cadman, Kunkel's theory that all chambers in the pyramid constituted a water pump was incorrect. Only the subterranean chamber and its associated shafts were likely a water pump—specifically, a type of pump that needs no electricity to operate, which is called a ram pump.

To test his hypothesis, Cadman obtained a number of photographs displaying the features of the subterranean chamber. What he noticed in these pictures is that water had eroded a significant part of the chamber. The most obvious area of erosion was the ceiling, suggesting to him that the pump, at one time, must have been operational. For Cadman, the patterns of erosion also confirm that a tunnel from the subterranean chamber's pit to the Nile River must have existed when the pyramid was complete, although it is now filled in with sand and debris.

There is also significant erosion on the subterranean chamber's floor. In the step channel, the erosion pattern suggests that the flow of water ran along the face of the step. As the water entered the step channel it was diverted, which would cause erosion. On the subterranean chamber floor, the pattern of erosion is matched exactly by water flowing through the stepped channel. There is also significant erosion on the floor, walls, and ceiling that match the step and primary water flows, as well as chipping of the subterranean chamber's ceiling, a feature that resulted from cavitation. (Cavitation is the creation of gas bubbles in water because of violent churning.)

According to Cadman, the rarefaction wave from the pump's action creates extreme negative pressure, equal and opposite to the compression wave, in the wastegate line. This negative pressure resulted in cavitation inside the subterranean chamber. The layering of limestone on the Giza Plateau would result in the leading edges of the layers being chipped by the cavitation, and for Cadman the ceiling damage is exactly what you would expect from a compression wave striking the ceiling.

The subterranean chamber's antechamber also displays erosion on the ceiling. Here, trapped air likely provided space for turbulence. According

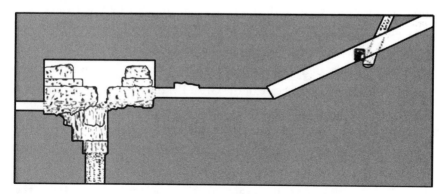

Fig. 8.5. Cross section of the subterranean chamber and passageways

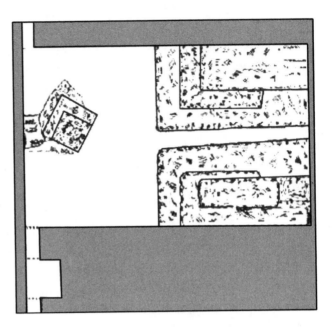

Fig. 8.6. Overhead view of the subterranean chamber

to Cadman, the ceiling erosion, which is extensive, is also indicative of flowing water, and also includes damage from cavitation as a result of an extremely low-pressure rarefaction wave created by the moving water.

Ram-pump technology is not new. Modern civilization developed ram-pump technology more than two hundred years ago, prior to the invention of electric-powered water pumps. This style of pump functions through the force of gravity. The ram pump pulls water from a reservoir and moves it to a higher level. As noted earlier, from the reservoir, water flows down the input (drive) pipe into the compression (pump) chamber, then out the discharge pipe located at a higher ground level. Some of the water moves out through the waste valve until the velocity of the moving water forces the valve shut. With the waste valve closed, water can no longer freely flow into the system. As a consequence, physics demands that the water must compress, which results in a shock wave (or compression wave) originating from the area of the valve. In the case of the Great Pyramid, the compression wave would have been at the minimum 3,300 pounds per square inch (psi).

At the same time that the water is compressing in the chamber, the water in the input line reverses direction until the shock wave reaches air (which is enhanced by a standpipe), while a high-pressure surge moves through the output line's check-valve. As the shock wave moves out of the compression chamber, low pressure is created in the system that is equal to

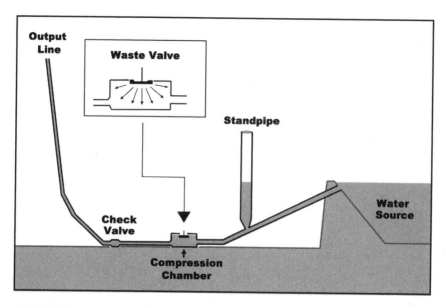

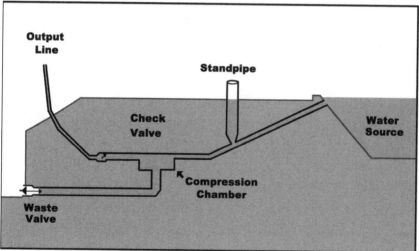

Fig. 8.7 (top). Standard hydraulic ram pump (courtesy of John Cadman)
Fig. 8.8 (bottom). Underground hydraulic ram pump with compression
chamber (courtesy of John Cadman)

and opposite the shock wave. This opposing pressure immediately reopens the waste valve, and the cycle begins again. Unlike a standard ram pump that emits a steady "thumping" sound, when this system is operating its thumping is like a heartbeat rhythm or pulse.

Although the typical eighteenth-century ram pump was situated above the ground, placing the system underground, as is the case in the Great Pyramid, is a unique application of ram-pump technology. According to Cadman, an underground ram pump requires a longer compression chamber to allow for wastewater output. And the output line needs to be placed near the compression chamber's ceiling to automatically remove air from the chamber. Furthermore, the standpipe and output pipe require an exit above ground. Although it might seem unnecessary to build the pump underground, according to Cadman, it has its advantages.

CADMAN MODELS THE GREAT PYRAMID'S SUBTERRANEAN CHAMBER

Cadman began modeling the Great Pyramid's subterranean chamber in June 1999. His first model leaked, and then cracked. Nor would it function. Several months later he began work on a second model and connected a new line to the bottom of the pit shaft, believing this new line had to be the pressurized output. On New Year's Eve 1999 he had another breakthrough in the theoretical understanding of the correct pump layout. With renewed excitement, he continued model construction with a third model.

On April 3, 2000, his third model was finished, and this pump model worked without a hitch. He added a straight pipe to compare the pumping action with and without a subterranean chamber. What he discovered was that the subterranean chamber absorbed much of the reverse pulse. He also observed that without the subterranean chamber, the reverse pulse was large and the output flow was more erratic, confirming for him that the output in the Great Pyramid's subterranean chamber traveled through what is called the dead end shaft.

For Cadman, it also confirmed his suspicion that the ancient oral tradition is correct. There had to be a tunnel running from the subterranean chamber's pit to the Nile River. To the best of my knowledge, through experimentation or modeling, no one has ever proved anything like this about the Great Pyramid. On that day in April, John Cadman did.

With this success, a few weeks later Cadman decided to move the model to a seasonal creek with a pond serving as a reservoir, and he began to experiment further.

Cadman also proved that water could be elevated to any part of the pyramid. But what was more of a surprise was when he encased the pump assembly in cement to simulate the effect of being underground. The shock wave from the pumping action formed a vertical compression wave! So the subterranean chamber must have also created a vertical compression wave. For Cadman, this meant that the subterranean ram pump also had an acoustical element.

To study the acoustics and fluid dynamics of the system, Cadman built a second and a third model. The third model, an acoustic model, weighed five hundred pounds and was placed, as the previous model had been, along the seasonal creek with the small pond as a reservoir. Made of fiberglass and epoxy, it was set in a mold, then reinforced with cement and rebar to withstand the water pressure created by the pump. From this third model, the Great Pyramid pump got its name. When operating, the characteristic heartbeat-like thump of the pump could be felt through the ground twenty feet away and heard nearly a hundred feet away. Because of the powerful pulses it generated, Cadman named it the "pulse generator."

The fourth model was constructed to study how water moved through the subterranean chamber and could operate in two different modes. This model was fitted with twenty-five individual ink injection locations and a glass top. It had a glass wall on its east side to view water flow, although Cadman discovered that the glass top quickly shattered when the model was operating in pump/pulse mode. Nevertheless, when not in pump/pulse mode, it was clear by studying the movement of water within the modeled subterranean chamber that the flow was complex and precise.

What he discovered was that the sound wave striking the perpendicular surface reflects the majority of the pulse back toward the source. He also discovered that when the fluid jet strikes a perpendicular surface, it spreads in a 360° pattern perpendicular to the jet. Thus, he concluded that the design of the subterranean chamber incorporated fluid dynamics as well as acoustical dynamics. In his own words, "The dynamics are on par with that of computerized storm analysis: somewhere between hurricane dynamics and tornado dynamics."

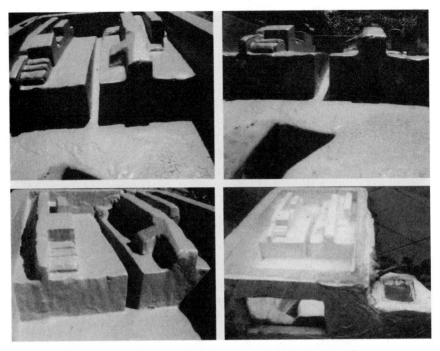

Fig. 8.9. Cadman's model of the subterranean chamber

Fig. 8.10. Ink jets in the "flow" model

Fig. 8.11 (top). Water flow around the subterranean chamber's pit
Fig. 8.12 (bottom). Water flow around the step and channel

Cadman's model also revealed some performance issues that were built into the Great Pyramid's subterranean pump. An additional "assist" line, from the compression chamber to a secondary location, speeds the movement of water through the output pipe. It also focuses the shock wave in the line leading to the compression chamber. The result is that a pulse is transmitted through the ceiling of the compression chamber. Thus, the line that connects the waste valve to the compression chamber acts as a waveguide, forcing the shock wave into a pulse. Therefore, the pulse is transmitted vertically (through the ceiling) as well as down the waste-valve line.

For the historian, what this model means is that a better understanding of the Great Pyramid, as well as the Giza Plateau, is now attainable. In its completed state the Great Pyramid required a moat, which was fed by a system of aqueducts from the Western Nile (the Ur Nile). This was an ideal source for a gravity-fed water system, since the Western Nile was at a higher elevation than the plateau. It explains the remains of a retaining wall that once surrounded the pyramid. The wall served as an embankment for on onsite reservoir, which in appearance was a moat. Tunnels, such as the "well" at the pyramid's entrance, connected the Great Pyramid complex to an ancient lake, Lake Moeris, and the Western Nile.

Lake Moeris (Egyptian *Mer-Wer,* meaning "Great Lake") was an ancient lake fifty miles southwest of Cairo. At one time it was very large and occupied the entire Faiyum depression. It was also called the Pure Lake and the Lake of Osiris by the ancient Egyptians.

During prehistoric times the waters of Lake Moeris stood nearly 120 feet above sea level, but by 10,000 BCE they had dropped to nearly twenty-five feet below sea level, possibly as a result of the Nile channel being naturally diverted. With increases from rain, between 9000 BCE and 4000 BCE the lake rose again, but gradually subsided. And as the climate became increasingly more arid, a canal connected Lake Moeris to the Nile; over the years it slowly silted. During the Middle Kingdom, 2000 BCE to 1600 BCE, dynastic Egyptians widened and deepened the channel, thereby restoring its flow. At that time the lake was believed to be fifty-five feet above sea level.

There is little doubt that the lake served as a means of flood control as well as a reservoir for irrigation. Egypt's Ptolemaic kings of the third century BCE partially drained Lake Moeris to make available 450 square miles of rich alluvial soil, which was irrigated by canals and extensive cultivation. Since then the water level of Lake Moeris has continually declined, and it is now the small, shallow saltwater Lake Qārūn.[8]

LORD OF THE UNDERGROUND TUNNELS

Tunnels beneath the Giza Plateau have always been a source of contention and speculation. According to ancient oral traditions, tunnels linked the pyramids and may have linked Giza to Sakkara. Although there is no proof to validate the extensiveness of these tunnels, shafts leading into the bedrock (now filled with sand) are a common sight on the plateau (figure 8.15). Yet, given that the subterranean chamber was most likely a water pump, the existence of tunnels makes sense and should be investigated further.

It would have to be through tunnels that water was forced into the Great Pyramid's onsite reservoir. As water filled the reservoir, the subterranean area of the pyramid was flooded by water rushing through the entranceway and down the descending passage. When the pump was functioning, any excess water flowed down the causeway and into the Nile River. This type of configuration was necessary, since a constant level of moat water was required to sustain a regular and consistent pulse, which Cadman determined was the primary function of the subterranean assembly of chambers and shafts.

According to the ancient oral tradition, a buried tunnel exists that connects the bottom of the pit in the subterranean chamber to the ancient Nile River. Cadman believes that this tunnel was a drain with a sliding stone plug at its end, the opening and closing of which caused a pulsating action. Where the dead end shaft terminates is the backside of a closed check-valve, and the tunnel continues beyond.

It is interesting to note that, according to Zahi Hawass, the Giza Plateau was known during New Kingdom times by the hieroglyphic inscription *pr osr nb rstw. Pr* means "place" or "house," and *osr* means

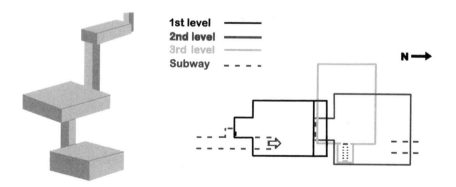

Fig. 8.13. 3-D configuration of the Osiris tomb (left); overhead view of the Osiris tomb (right) (courtesy of John Cadman)

"Osiris," so together *pr osr* means "the place of Osiris." *Nb* means "Lord" and *rstw* means "cemetery." However, *rstw* literally means "the underground tunnel," so during the New Kingdom the Giza Plateau was "House of Osiris and Lord of the Underground Tunnels." This inscription was found carved into the floor of an underground chamber down the so-called Osiris shaft, located under the causeway that links the middle pyramid to the Sphinx. A tunnel west of this shaft runs about twelve feet toward the Great Pyramid, and at that point narrows significantly.[9]

It is also interesting to note that on the second level of the Osiris shaft, Hawass and his team discovered four pillars, and between these pillars were two large granite boxes with their lids removed. Although Hawass dates this level of the shaft to the Twenty-Sixth Dynasty based on the pottery found there,[10] it is likely the case that the shaft was part of the pyramid complex's original design.

THE GIZA PULSE PUMP GENERATOR

When the pyramid was functioning, the descending passage, subterranean chamber, dead end shaft, pit, well shaft, and grotto made up the components of the Giza pulse pump generator. According to Cadman, it could be operational today if all the tunnels associated with the pyramid could be cleared. Besides the well shaft that connects the descending passage to the middle chamber of the pyramid, there are two other tunnels that would need to be cleared. Clearing the pit associated with the dead end shaft (where the check-valve exists) would expose the horizontal shaft. If these shafts were cleared, the moat reservoir was in place, and the well in front of the pyramid connected to a Lake Moeris substitute, the pump could be operational.

One of the most important results from Cadman's experiments was discovering the significance of the well shaft and its effect on the pump's pulse rate. This specific design issue leads to the intent of the Great Pyramid's designer.

The well shaft begins near the bottom of the descending passageway and extends upward 170 feet. In the water-pump assembly, the well shaft functions as a standpipe, providing a shortcut for the reverse shock wave to reach air. In essence, it maximizes the pulse rate of the pump.

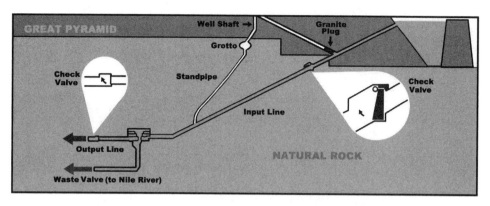

Fig.8.14. The Great Pyramid's subterranean pulse pump

*Fig. 8.15. Shafts carved into the bedrock on the south side
of the middle pyramid*

Although standpipes are typically twice the diameter of the input (drive) pipe, in the Giza assembly the standpipe (well shaft) is actually 25 percent smaller than the input pipe (descending passageway), which has a peculiar effect on the system. It lowers the elevation of the pulsing water below the water level of the moat reservoir. Interestingly, this specific elevation correlates to the height of the grotto, which serves as a reservoir, allowing for stabilization and regulation of the reverse pulse. A block of granite, existing within the grotto that fits within the pipe, is believed to function as some type of choke or regulator.

According to Cadman, the well shaft was part of the original design of the pyramid, and as a standpipe in the pump assembly, it served to maximize the pulse rate of the pump. The standpipe also reduced the reverse surge out of the descending passage, as well as reduced pumping efficiency and pulse intensity.

Pump Efficiency

Cadman tested four different pump configurations, two circulating and two elevating, to gauge the well shaft's affect efficiency. When in a circulating-pump mode, the well shaft reduced the efficiency by 29 percent. And, in an elevating-pump mode, the well shaft reduced the efficiency by 68 percent. The increase in efficiency of the well shaft provided an extra twenty pulses per minute, from sixty to eighty. Since the

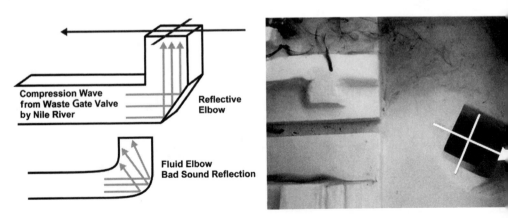

Fig. 8.16. The subterranean chamber pit is offset by 45 degrees. (courtesy of John Cadman)

Giza configuration of the subterranean chamber included a well shaft, for the builders of the pyramid, pumping efficiency did not appear to be of primary importance. So if pumping efficiency was not of primary importance then what was?

One way to approach this question is to review the general layout of the subterranean chamber. The subterranean chamber pit is offset by 45° in relation to the general configuration of the chamber and is aligned northwest to southeast. According to Cadman, this is so because a plane placed at a 45° angle will maintain the unidirectionality and consistency of the compression wave. In other words, this reflective elbow ensures the consistency of the compression wave. Any other type of elbow at the pit's bottom would diffract (scatter) the compression wave. So the pit's alignment is strictly for acoustical dynamics and for creating a standing wave in the waste line and subterranean chamber.

To create the standing wave in the waste gate line and subterranean chamber, it would be imperative to have the reflective elbow. The pit's offset is exactly aligned with the tunnel (figure 8.16, right; the white arrow is aligned with the exit tunnel). Not only does the reflective elbow completely explain the pit's diagonal offset, but it also confirms that the compression wave is a major design consideration. The designers thoroughly understood complex fluid dynamics as well as complex acoustics (see figure 8.16, right; the white arrow shows the direction of the tunnel at the bottom of the pit; the ink injection photo shows some of the flows in the step area).

Another way to approach the question is to review the engineering significance of the dead end shaft. It allows for a pressure change, which in turn changes the frequency of the compression wave. A gate valve at the end of the dead end shaft provides a means for accomplishing this. Adjusting the back pressure by adjusting the gate valve allows for changes

Operation Type	Destination	Δ Elevation	Valve Status	Ratio
Circulating Pump	GP Moat Level	(+0')	(well shaft "on")	1:3.5
			(well shaft "off")	1:2.5
Elevating Pump	Chephron Moat Level	(+100')	(well shaft "on")	1:9.25
			(well shaft "off")	1:3

Fig. 8.17. The results of Cadman's experiment

in timing. In essence, this is a simple method to compensate for different water temperatures and atmospheric pressure, which are factors that affect the velocity of the compression wave.

Cadman's testing demonstrated that the pulse rate can be altered by at least 30 percent, between sixty and eighty pulses per minute. He also discovered that adjusting the back pressure changed the water's density and, as a consequence, altered the compression wave's velocity and frequency. In essence, such an assembly allows for easy fine tuning of the lower portion of the Great Pyramid to create the standing wave in the subterranean chamber and waste gate shaft.

These experimental results confirm that the compression wave was a major design consideration. Also, according to Cadman, the square pit carved into the subterranean chamber created a whirlpool as water moved through the system of tunnels—apparently another design feature to efficiently move water to the chamber and out the waste line.

If pump efficiency—in other words, pumping water—was not of prime importance to the ancient Egyptians, then what was? According to the experimental evidence, the answer is a compression wave, which, of course, creates another question. Why was a compression wave of primary interest to the Great Pyramid's builders?

Plate 2. Curved granite object displaying three surfaces

Plate 1. A granite trough emerging from the sand on the east side of the second pyramid

Plate 3. The Valley Temple (left of the Sphinx)
and the Sphinx Temple (to the right)

Plate 4. Granite pillars and lintels of the Valley Temple

Plate 5. One would expect a corner to be created by the staggering of two different sizes of blocks, much in the same way bricklayers make a corner today. Instead, the corners of the Valley Temple are built into the blocks themselves and alternated between the adjoining walls.

Plate 6. Rock-cut tombs of the Sphinx "Museum"

Plate 7. A stone box deep in the Giza cemetery

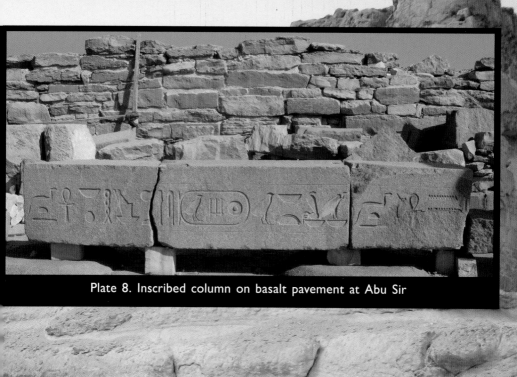

Plate 8. Inscribed column on basalt pavement at Abu Sir

Plate 9. A water basin at Abu Sir

Plate 10. An example of precision corners carved from granite

Plate 11. Basalt paving next to the Great Pyramid

Plate 12. Saw marks on basalt stone at the northern edge of the patio

Plate 13. Close-up of basalt block exhibiting saw marks

Plate 14. The west side of the pyramid at Abu Rawash

Plate 15. Looking down Abu Rawash's descending passageway

Plate 16. Colossal granite stones of Abu Rawash

Plate 17. Unknown granite
(pin or pillar?) carving at
Abu Rawash

Plate 18. Square block of granite

Plate 20. Deep trench (boat pit?) cut into rock on the east side of the pyramid

Plate 19. Possible granite casing stone

Plate 21. Arc separating rough stone from smooth stone

Plate 22. Horizontal feed lines from the device that cut the stone

Plate 23. Concave shape of the stone

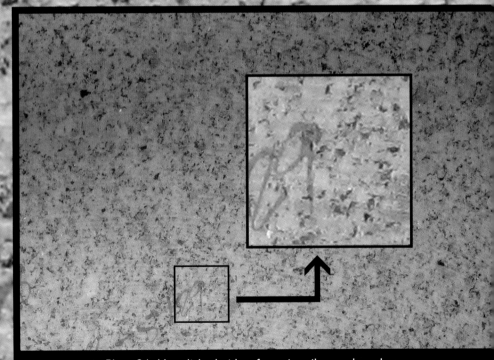

Plate 24. Unpolished side of granite tile purchased at a
local building supply store

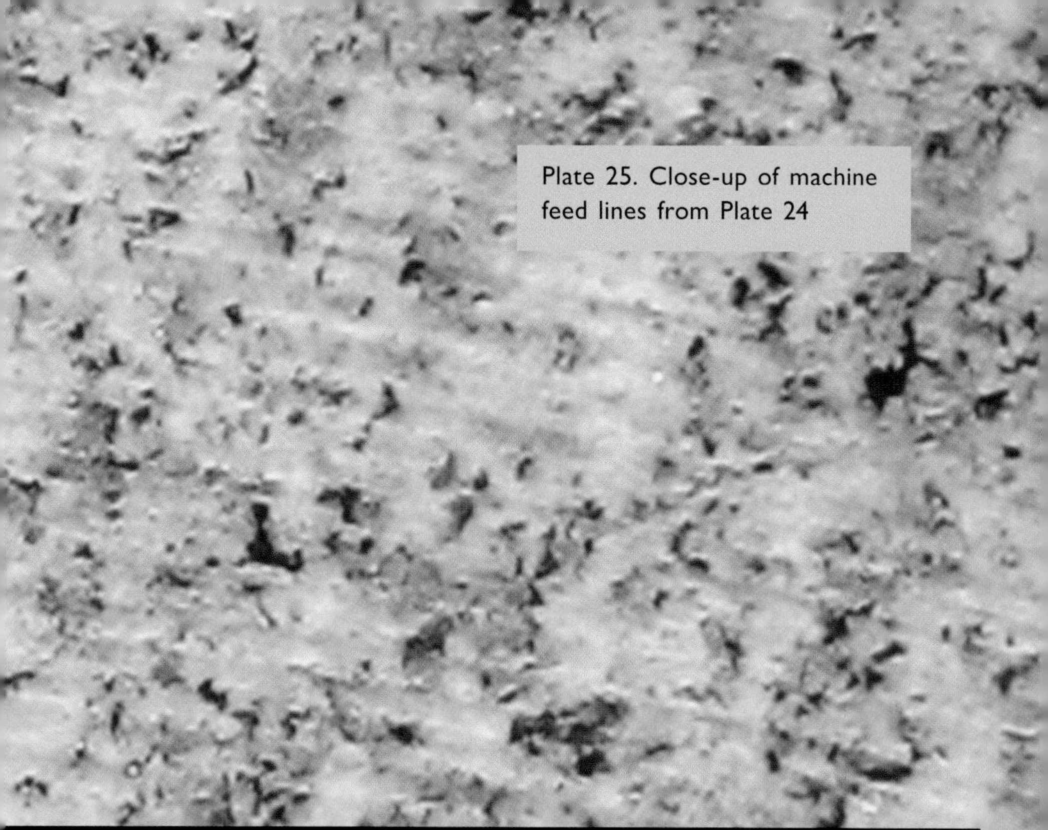

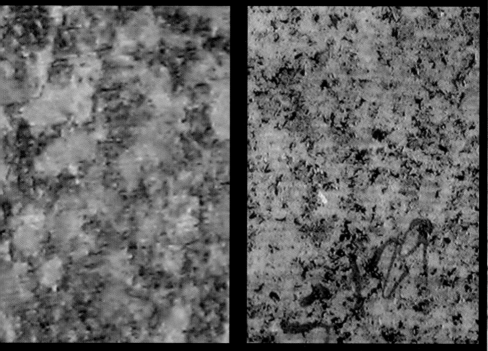

Plate 25. Close-up of machine feed lines from Plate 24

Plate 26. Comparison of machine lines from Abu Rawash (left) and a modern-day, purchased tile

Plate 27. Ground level view of the colossal Ramses at Memphis

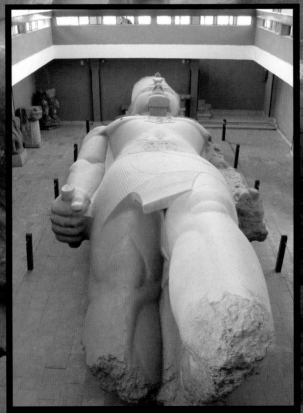

Plate 28. Colossal limestone statue of
Ramses at Memphis

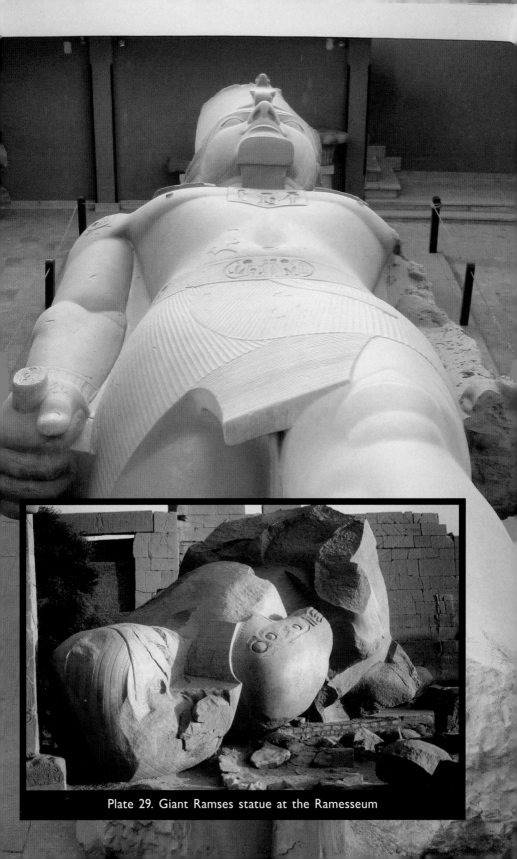

Plate 29. Giant Ramses statue at the Ramesseum

Plate 30. The Temple of Amun-Mut-Khonsu

Plate 31. Egyptian statue compared with Greek hand-carved statue

Plate 32. Enormous scale of statues at the
Temple of Amun-Mut Khonsu

Plate 33. Could these monuments really be the world's largest tombs?

Plate 34. Mud brick was used to form Mastaba No. 17

Plate 35. Giza's Middle Pyramid

Plate 36. The pyramid core at Meidum

Plate 37. Builders of the Great Pyramid used extraordinarily large-size blocks

Plate 38. The Bent Pyramid at Dahshur

Plate 39. One of Ireland's stone towers. It is speculated that these towers were, in effect, antennas designed to direct low-frequency electromagnetic waves into surrounding fields to enhance crop yield.

Plate 40. Columns at Denderah's Temple of Hathor

Plate 41. Artist's rendition of a supernova burst close to Earth (NASA)

9

A NETWORK OF
PYRAMIDS

As demonstrated by John Cadman, a pulse-pump compression-wave generator was at the core of the builder's design for the Great Pyramid. Since the compression wave was intentionally directed upward, toward the upper areas of the pyramid, it must be the case that either the middle or upper chamber was designed to react with this compression wave.

Although both the lower and upper chambers of the pyramid were exposed to the compression wave emanating from the bedrock chamber, there is little to suggest in the way of materials that the lower chamber would bring forth any type of phenomenon in its reaction to such vibrations. With its rough-cut walls and ceiling, the middle chamber would muffle or absorb the wave's vibrations. However, the uppermost chamber is uniquely and completely made of granite. As mentioned earlier, above its ceiling there are five rows of granite beams stacked one atop another—forty-three granite beams. Furthermore, the rows of granite above the upper chamber are separated by granite blocks that act as spacers. So it seems that by design, the builders wanted, at the top of the pyramid, as much surface of the granite exposed to the air as possible.

THE PURPOSE OF GRANITE

If the Great Pyramid were designed as a tomb, it could be argued that granite, since it is more difficult to work with than any other rock, was chosen for its value as well as its sparkling beauty. However, in the theory proposed here, there would have to have been a functionally motivating factor in the builders' choice of granite.

Granite is a very hard rock and erosion resistant. However, since the upper chamber is already protected by the core of the pyramid, what function would require that the chamber be made of granite? More importantly, what properties of granite would react in some way with a compression wave?

The high-fidelity stereo industry uses granite not only to provide a stable base for equipment but also because of its resonance qualities. All materials have a natural resonance frequency. In other words, all materials will vibrate at certain frequencies. In the world of stereo aficionados, the resonance of other materials in the soundstage (a room) distorts the stereo's sound, which means that other sounds are made that you do not want. This includes the rack where components of the sound system are housed. However, selecting granite, with a clear and pure sound, as a base for components will not only dampen extraneous sounds (rack vibration), it will also help produce a full sound through its resonance.

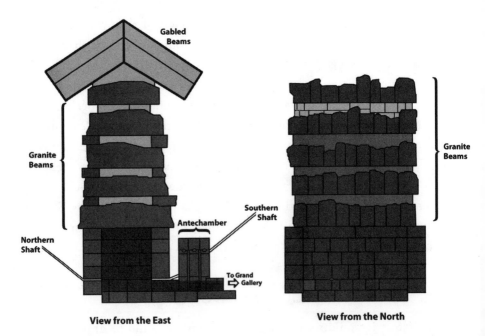

Fig. 9.1. Cross-section and overview of the Great Pyramid's upper chamber

Granite, simply put, has a sound of its own. And, by further isolating the granite base from the rack with rubber washers or other polymer fixtures, the granite's resonance properties can be further controlled. With this in mind, it might be the case that the purpose of building a granite chamber was to create resonance.

Although at first this may be difficult to believe, the evidence for resonance in the upper chamber is compelling. As previously mentioned, above this chamber there is even more granite in an enclosed area accessible only through a hole about two feet wide at the top of the Grand Gallery. In this "hidden" chamber, commonly known as Davidson's Chamber, there are five vertical rows of granite beams. In all, there are forty-three granite slabs above the chamber, weighing up to seventy tons each. Every layer of granite is cut square on three sides, but rough on top, and separated by spaces large enough for a person to crawl into.

If the granite was purposely placed here in order to react to the subterranean chamber's compression wave, each granite beam would vibrate in its own space when subjected to a suitable amount of force. Furthermore, according to Dunn, if each slab of granite were tuned to the same frequency, when one began to vibrate all others would, too, in harmony with the first beam. In effect, all granite beams would vibrate at the same frequency.[1]

This would explain why the forty-three granite beams above the chamber were rough-cut on one side. Before they were installed above the chamber, stonemasons specializing in sound removed areas from the granite slabs to achieve the desired frequency. In effect, the granite slabs were tuned.

Furthermore, acoustical tests confirm that the granite beams do resonate at a fundamental frequency. In fact, the chamber itself reinforces this frequency by producing dominant frequencies. Tests performed inside the upper chamber also reveal that the entire room is free standing from the surrounding limestone masonry—just like a high-fidelity equipment rack. The granite floor sits on corrugated limestone; the walls are supported from the outside and sunk five inches below the floor. The consequence is that the entire room is free to resonate at peak efficiency.[2]

According to Tom Danley, the sound engineer featured in *The Mystery of the Sphinx,* the Great Pyramid makes strange sounds because the granite chamber resonates from the rigidity of the stone. What he also discovered was that a number of low-frequency components existed even without a test signal present in the pyramid. (This means that the chamber was constructed for its resonance, and it naturally creates a frequency.) Most likely, he added, the low frequencies were a result of "Helmholtz resonances caused by the wind blowing across the entry tunnel." Another interesting find of Danley's was that "over a number of octaves, some of the resonant frequencies fell into the pattern that makes an F sharp chord."[3]

This brings up a question. Was the resonance in the Great Pyramid because of the granite chamber's dimensions—in other words, because of a mathematical relationship?

According to Danley, it was: "One of [those] things that was interesting was that the position of the sarcophagus and its resonances, in some cases, were coupled to the resonances of the room as well."

However, a compression wave emanating from the subterranean chamber would likely have a marginal effect on the granite in the upper chamber. What would be needed to localize the granite is a method to transform that compression wave into airborne sound. This would create enough vibration to activate the granite beams and create a standing wave of resonance in the granite room.

THE GRAND GALLERY

Key to making the upper (resonance) chamber vibrate in the manner suggested is a structure or device that focuses the vibrations from the compression wave rising from the subterranean chamber. According to Christopher Dunn, such is the purpose of the Grand Gallery. With its unique angles and surfaces, vibrations are reflected directly from this large hall-like room into the upper chamber. However, for this "resonance hall" to work, other equipment would be required—equipment that converted vibration into sound. According to Dunn, a device that would fit into the scheme of the Great Pyramid's design would be a device such as a Helmholtz-style resonator.[4]

A Helmholtz resonator responds to vibrations and maximizes the transfer of energy from the vibration's source, turning that vibration into airborne sound. This style of resonator is a hollow sphere with a round opening between one-tenth and one-fifth inch in diameter. It is normally made out of metal, but it can also be made of other materials. The frequency at which it resonates is determined by the sphere's size; if in harmony with its source, the resonator acts as an amplifier.

Although no equipment of any kind remains in the Grand Gallery, there are clues that structures of some kind had been installed. There are twenty-seven pairs of slots in the side ramps, which, as has been previously mentioned, have remained a mystery. They could have been fitted with wooden frames that held a resonator assembly. If so, each resonator assembly would have been equipped with several Helmholtz-type resonators installed in a series and tuned to different frequencies. Each resonator in the series would have responded at a higher frequency than the previous one, thereby raising the frequency of the vibrations coming from the subterranean chamber. To accomplish this, the pyramid engineers would have to have made the dimensions smaller for each succeeding resonator, reducing the distance between the gallery's two walls. Interestingly, in fact, the walls of the resonator hall step inward seven times in their height.

At their base, the resonators could have been anchored in the ramp slots by a wooden frame. Along the length of the wall's second corbel there is a groove cut into the stone. This may be where the resonators were held in place and positioned as they were installed into the slots. "Shot" pins placed in the groove would have held them in place. Vertical supports for the resonators were likely made of wood.

Although nothing resembling a resonator has ever been found in the Great Pyramid, according to Dunn, the Cairo Museum holds some of the most remarkable stone artifacts of ancient Egypt's civilization. Speculatively, given the shape and dimensions of some of these vessels, they may have been the Helmholtz-style resonators used in the Great Pyramid. One such item, a bowl, has a horn attached to it. Another bowl lacks the handles that are normally part of a domestic vase, but instead has trunnion-like appendages on each of its sides. These trunnions would be needed to hold the "bowl" securely in a frame.[5]

With vibrations from the compression wave moving up the structure of the pyramid, these resonators would also vibrate and emit sound to be

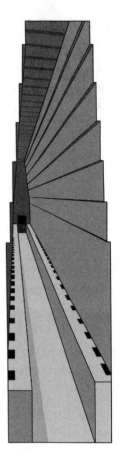

Fig. 9.2 (right). The Grand Gallery looking at the entrance to the antechamber (from the north)

Fig. 9.3 (below). The upper chamber's antechamber

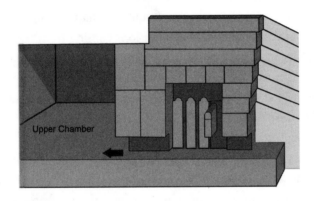

channeled into the granite resonance chamber. There, the vibrations of the granite ceiling beams would oscillate and spread to the forty-three granite beams above the chamber's ceiling. All the granite would then resonate in harmonic sympathy. As a result, a maximization of resonance would be achieved, and the entire granite chamber in the upper part of the pyramid would become a trumpet of sound.

FILTERING FREQUENCIES

Before sound reached the resonance chamber, however, there would have been some fine tuning. Between the resonance chamber and the resonator hall there is a small room known as the antechamber. Originally, this chamber was believed to hold in place a series of stone slabs that were slid into place after the body of the deceased was entombed in the upper chamber. According to tomb theory, the half-round grooves in the granite wainscoting supported wooden beams that served as windlasses to lower the blocks into place. According to Dunn, the idea that the blocks were slid into place may not have been far off the mark.

The architect of the Great Pyramid needed to focus sound of a specific frequency into the resonance chamber, which required an acoustic filter between the resonator hall and the resonance chamber. If baffles were placed inside this antechamber, sound waves coming from the resonator hall would be filtered as they passed through. Thus, according to Dunn, only a single frequency, or harmonic of that frequency, would enter the resonance chamber. The effect would be that interference sound waves would be unable to enter the resonance chamber and reduce the system's output.

For Dunn, such an analysis of the antechamber explains the half-round grooves visible on the west wall of the antechamber and the flat surface on the east wall. A likely purpose for these grooves is that baffles were secured in them. By rotating the cams, the off-centered shaft would raise or lower the baffles until the throughput of sound was maximized. Once they were tuned, the shaft suspending the baffles would have been locked into place in a pillar block located on the flat surface of the wainscoting on the opposite wall.[6]

There are other unusual features of the upper chamber. One is the granite box, partially broken on one corner, the sole contents of the chamber. If a lid to the box ever existed, it has been removed from the room without a trace. Not even portions of a lid, chunks or fragments, have ever been found in any of the passages or chambers. There also exist two shafts, one each in the north and south walls, approximately five feet above the chamber floor.

GETTING THE SHAFTS

The shafts in the middle and upper chambers are keys to understanding the functionality of the Great Pyramid. Today, we typically think of shafts as air ducts or access tunnels. We do so because these are commonplace in our society. Not so with the Great Pyramid.

Yet it was with intent that the builders of the pyramid designed shafts in the middle and upper chambers. Air shafts are meaningless in the middle chamber, since they terminate before reaching the exterior of the pyramid. Air shafts are also meaningless in the upper chamber, since there is no way of pushing air through except by the force of natural wind.

So what purpose do these shafts serve?

So far, it has been determined through experimentation and deductive logic that the subterranean chamber created a compression wave through the act of pumping water, and that the uppermost chamber resonated as the vibration from the wave was turned into sound in the Grand Gallery. With this in mind, a logical conclusion for the shafts of the upper chamber is that they were the final function of resonance, to produce and push sound into the atmosphere—in other words, to release a pressure wave into the atmosphere in a manner similar to a pipe organ.

Why?

Current research in physics has discovered that a pressure wave (sound) introduced into the atmosphere creates ionization. In other words, sound waves at certain frequencies moving through the atmosphere create an electrical field.

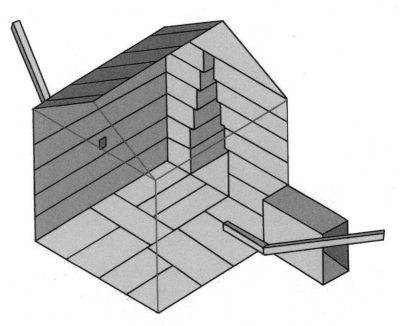

Fig. 9.4. The Great Pyramid's middle (Queen's) chamber

As for the shafts leading to nowhere in the middle chamber, it is logical to assume they terminate within the core of the pyramid on purpose, and for good reason. With vibrations continuously moving up through the pyramid, over time the structure would eventually begin to break apart because the sound wave would continue to build. Adding a dampener in the middle of the pyramid would assist in absorbing the constant vibration. The resonance of the middle chamber helped isolate the frequency required by the upper chamber. Thus, the shafts in the middle chamber lead where they are supposed to—to within the core of the pyramid.

The original condition of the middle chamber substantiates this theory. When it was first explored, the walls of the middle chamber were coated with lime plaster. In the *Great Pyramid of Giza,* published in 1877, James Boswick writes:

Two channels there [in the middle chamber] looked like the air-holes of the other Chamber, but were sealed up. When broken through, the space was horizontal for 7 feet, and then turned north and south at the angle 32°. *They might have been for acoustic purposes.* [author's emphasis][7]

It is interesting to note that one of the first people to enter the middle chamber noted that it might have had an acoustic function. If so, then the lime plaster acted as a damper for the signal emanating from the subterranean chamber. But why would any organization or civilization endeavor to build such an extraordinarily large structure to produce sound?

PYRAMID EXPERIMENTS

Long before "pyramid energy" became a popular topic, Verne Cameron performed some simple experiments at the Great Pyramid and discovered that there might be a positive downward flow of energy from the pyramid's summit and an upward flow from its base. Likewise, the British inventor Sir William Siemens observed that, from atop the pyramid, whenever he raised his hand with his fingers spread wide, he heard a ringing noise. Out of curiosity, he made a Leyden jar from a bottle and held it over his head. Sparks flew, and when he lowered the bottle one of his guides received a shock.[8]

A commercial from the 1970s boasted that a plastic banana hanger in the shape of a pyramid helped bananas stay fresh longer. My parents never bought one, and at the time I thought that the notion that three plastic bars in the shape of a pyramid could keep bananas fresh was a little ridiculous. Nonetheless, since the 1970s some people have claimed that energy does emanate from pyramid-shaped objects, and that this mysterious energy prevents foods from spoiling and ferrous metals from rusting. Needless to say, such claims have been the target of skeptics and debunkers, and through controlled experimentation have easily been dismissed, most recently in 2005 by Jamie Hyneman and Adam Savage of the Discovery Channel's *Mythbusters*.[9]

I too was skeptical of pyramid energy—that is, until I met Nick Edwards at a Denver trade show. Edwards, who calls himself "the pyramid man," has been researching pyramids and their effect on various objects for the past thirty years. He brought his self-made Tesla coil and pyramid to the trade show to use in a demonstration. According to Edwards, the pyramid shape collects and focuses ambient energy, energy that exists as a result of Earth's gravitational and magnetic fields.

It's easy to debunk this theory and its associated experiments, since the size of the object within the pyramid matters. The larger the object, the larger the pyramid needs to be to have an effect. For example, a single grape would be kept fresh longer under one of Nick's titanium pyramids, but a grapefruit would not. I tried this experiment myself and discovered that the grape under the pyramid did in fact stay fresh longer. The grape not under the pyramid reached a nonedible state four days before the grape under the pyramid. Of course, there needs to be more testing of this phenomenon. Nonetheless, it suggests the possibility that debunking attempts are just that—the purposeful disproving of a phenomenon.

Herein is one reason, it seems, that the pyramids of ancient Egypt needed to be so large. To collect any significant amount of energy, they had to be big, since the energy that surrounds us is very low in intensity. Perhaps it is also why the ancient Egyptians referred to the pyramids as Per-Neter, which translates as "house of nature." It may be the case that the ancient Egyptians understood this principle of nature and used it for the benefit of their society.

With the support of the Russian National Academy of Science, a number of Russian scientists have taken pyramid energy seriously. According to researcher John DeSalvo, strange atmospheric effects from a fiberglass pyramid built by Dr. K. Volodymyr Krasnoholovets were detected by Russian air force radar. The complete pyramid is composed of thirty sections; however, after the addition of the eleventh section, an energy field emanating from the pyramid was detectable by radar.[10]

According to Krasnoholovets, the source of the energy field is interons, a substructure of matter waves. Around every object that exists there are individual particles that overlap and form a common matter field. This field, generated by the friction of moving elementary particles through space, is what Krasnoholovets calls an interon field, and he believes that "the Great Pyramid was built intentionally in order to amplify basic energy fields of the Earth on a very subatomic, quantum level."[11]

THE GRANITE ENIGMA

The sparkling granite columns of Abu Sir and the magnificent curved granite ashlars on the Giza Plateau, the giant granite pillars fluted and incised with hieroglyphs of Giza's unknown temple—all are remnants. And yet they testify to a grand civilization that had developed the technology and the industry to build with granite on a massive scale. The people who created this civilization of granite were masters of its manipulation and have never been outdone in their stoneworking accomplishments—most notably, the rectangular box made of granite or other hard stone.

The most perplexing aspect of the expertly crafted granite boxes is not just the cutting expertise required to produce them. More than a few have been discovered, and although some were sealed shut, when opened they were found to be empty.

In 1925, upon excavating one of the Great Pyramid's satellite pyramids, George Reisner discovered a vertical shaft that was blocked by masonry along its entire length—ninety-nine feet.[12] This shaft contained the only undisturbed Old Kingdom burial ever found on the Giza Plateau, that of Queen Hetepheres, the wife of Seneferu and mother of

Khufu. After months of work to clear the shaft and chamber, a party of distinguished visitors and government officials attended the opening ceremony. Unfortunately, when all the visitors and officials had been lowered into the chamber and the alabaster lid pried open, there was no mummy to be found. In fact, the alabaster box was completely empty.[13]

What they did find, writes Egyptologist Ioreweth Edwards, was a "carrying chair, also made of wood partly cased with gold sheeting. It bore an inscription, written in hieroglyphs of gold set in ebony panels and repeated four times. It read: 'The mother of the King of Upper and Lower Egypt, followers of Horus, she who is in charge of the affairs of the harem [?] whose every word is done for her, daughter of the god [begotten] of his body, Hetepheres.'"[14]

For Edwards, there were no words that could do justice to the beauty, artistic excellence, and technical perfection of Hetepheres' equipment. "Tomb" furniture from later periods appears crude in comparison. According to Edwards, this Old Kingdom furniture's design was simple but exquisite. Only its woodwork has decayed with the passage of time.[15]

What puzzled Reisner, according to Egyptologist Barbara Mertz, was why elaborate care and secrecy had been expended on the burial for an empty sarcophagus. Was it really a burial?

Reisner insisted that the box had been used for a burial. The discoloration in the bottom of the box proved as much. The difficulty with this theory, however, according to Mertz, is that other sarcophagi have been found in place, unopened and empty. The Unfinished Pyramid at Zawaiyet el Aryan, which was supposed to be a step pyramid of considerable size, also contained a brilliantly finished alabaster sarcophagus, complete with its so-called funeral straps. When opened, it was also empty.[16] Interestingly, the work on the pyramid's superstructure was never started.[17]

It seems to me that the stone box was somehow an integral part of the pyramid design.

In 1953, aerial photographs discovered a rectangular shape on the sands close to the Step Pyramid at Sakkara. After being excavated by an Egyptian archaeologist, another step pyramid that was never completed was discovered. The structure from the aerial photograph turned out to be an enclosure wall. Based on the two courses that had been completed, the pyramid would have been as big as the Step Pyramid. In the upper part of the structure were 120 storerooms. They contained vases, jar stoppers, and gold bracelets. But the unfinished pyramid also contained an unusual granite box. This one had a sliding panel at one end, instead of a lid that fit on top of the box. And it was sealed with plaster. In May 1954 the box was opened, and like other sealed granite boxes, it was empty.[18]

Whatever had been placed inside them, if anything ever had been, was removed, but when and by whom? Why spend the time and trouble to carve a granite box, and then seal it while it is still empty?

There might a very good reason to place a granite box beneath the ground or inside the base of a pyramid, but to understand why, the latest in agricultural research first needs to be presented.

FERTILIZING WITH STONE

For the past fourteen years, inventor and physicist John Burke has been studying the use of electron bombardment to enhance seeds and has been extraordinarily successful in improving seed germination and stress tolerance. After eight years of laboratory testing and six years of field testing, his results have been very promising for the agriculture industry: quicker plant maturity and higher plant yields *without the use of chemicals or moisture.*

A number of universities and seed companies have collaborated with his company, Pro Seed Technologies, to test his process, which is called MIR/Stress Guard (Molecular Impulse Response). These universities and companies include Florida University, Iowa State University, Mississippi State University, Mississippi State Seed Company, North Dakota State University, Illinois Foundation Seed, Purdue University, Illinois Crop Improvement, Hoegemeyer Hybrids, and Ohio Foundation Seed. Early tests in 1998, at the University of Florida, achieved "marketable yields [that] were significantly increased," between 10 and 25 percent.[19]

How does electron bombardment enhance crop yields?

Seeds are showered with extremely low-energy (i.e., slow-moving) electrons, which are absorbed by the seed. As a result, the seed's cell mitochondria produce more free radicals, which in turn trigger the cell's natural defenses to produce more antioxidants. Once these antioxidants are produced, they destroy the free radicals and leave the seed with fewer free radicals to battle. Thus, the seed is stronger and better prepared to handle stress such as flooding, drought, and temperature extremes during its planting season.

Environmental stress damages the plant cell structure by increasing free-radical production. So the low-energy electron bombardment acts as an inoculation, making the seed's immune system stronger.[20]

Burke's patented MIR/Stress Guard System technology "improves the seed's antioxidant capacity (Source: Purdue University), and therefore its shelf-life (Iowa State University) and its ability to withstand a wide variety of environmental stresses. It also enhances growth in numerous ways and can be used in conjunction with traditional chemical seed coatings and on genetically-modified seed."[21]

In this process, seeds are passed in quantity between two electrodes calibrated to produce an electrical impulse specifically targeted for that type of seed, such as corn, wheat, or soybeans. The seed responds by releasing free radicals and then increasing its production of antioxidants to compensate and restore cell balance. In the end, the free-radical level is lower than it was before the MIR process.[22]

What does the bombardment of seed with low-energy electrons have to do with ancient Egypt's pyramids? Burke, who is also interested in ancient agriculture, has a possible answer.

Solving the Megalith Mystery

Ancient stone monuments, such as Britain's Stonehenge, have remained a mystery for thousands of years. Some megalithic sites are believed to have been calendars to mark the seasons. Other sites, such as Avebury in southern England, whose stones are arranged in a grid, seem to defy explanation. Burke suspected that there might be something much more significant than a calendar to these stones.

In researching his theory, Burke and his colleague, photographer Kaj Halberg, visited more than eighty different sites in North America, Europe, and Egypt. Armed with a fluxgate magnetometer (to measure Earth's geomagnetic field), an electrostatic voltmeter (to measure electric charge in the air or on objects), and ground electrodes (to measure naturally occurring current in the ground), they tested each site to see if a naturally occurring excess of electrons was present, as opposed to a normal amount in the atmosphere. There was. Furthermore, Burke and Halberg discovered that the source of this electromagnetic anomaly was a result of local land formations called conductivity discontinuities, and they began to look at how these land formations affect Earth's geomagnetic field.

One common geomagnetic anomaly you are likely familiar with is the aurora borealis, the "northern lights." Earth generates a magnetic field that exists all around us, which protects us from harmful solar radiation (high-energy particles). When Earth is struck by powerful solar winds, its geomagnetic field is pushed inward or depressed as it deflects these high-energy particles. As a result, air at the outer edge of the atmosphere becomes so excited in reaction to the solar radiation that it glows.

Another effect of Earth's geomagnetic field is its reaction to Earth's rotation. During the night, when solar radiation is at a minimum, the lines of the geomagnetic field lengthen. At dawn, the solar radiation returns, and as a result the geomagnetic field shrinks, making it stronger. At certain places on the Earth's surface, where unique land features exist, this surge of energy that occurs when the geomagnetic field returns to its daytime configuration is amplified.[23]

The underlying physical law behind this natural event is an electromagnetic principle called induction, which means that wherever there is a moving electric current, a magnetic field is generated, and a changing magnetic field generates an electric current in anything that conducts it. It is the same principle as a power station. The energy generated from burning coal turns a copper wire around a magnet, generating an electric current, which is then sent out on lines to be consumed by the machines of our electric-powered lives.

At dawn, what happens on Earth's surface is that the change in the magnetic field's strength generates weak direct electrical currents (DC) in the ground. Different types of materials have different levels of conductivity. As such, there are certain geographical places that conduct electricity more than others: ground that holds lots of water or ground with a high metal content conducts better than drier and less metallic ground.[24]

Where highly conductive land intersects with land that is relatively nonconductive (referred to as a conductivity discontinuity), Earth's magnetic field behaves differently. When the electrical current traveling through the ground runs into these conductivity-discontinuity features, Earth's magnetic field lines can be significantly strengthened or weakened. If the ground current's reaction to the geological discontinuity is to strengthen Earth's magnetic field, then, in turn, more electric current is generated. What's so special about this is that the ground current will attract electrified air molecules of the opposite charge: a positive ground current will attract negatively charged air molecules, and vice versa.[25]

According to Burke and Halberg, ancient cultures understood this principle and selected conductivity discontinuities as a place to build stone structures to take advantage of the electrical currents running through the ground. Stonehenge, for example, was built in the shape of a C, with a three-foot ditch at the perimeter of the C to trap and concentrate the current in the middle of the henge. In the Americas, native cultures built earthen mounds with flat tops on conductivity discontinuities to attract atmospheric field lines without attracting a lightning bolt.

While a thunderstorm is occurring, the atmosphere builds up with negatively charged air molecules (a process called ionization) until a threshold is met where it seeks the nearest positively charged object. And when the negatively charged air connects with that positively charged object, a lightning bolt occurs.

However, aside from a thunderstorm, Earth's surface typically has a negative charge and the atmosphere a positive charge. Where Earth's surface protrudes into the air, as with a mound, the positively charged field lines will concentrate. Likewise, the negatively charged field lines in the ground protrusion will concentrate in the smaller area of the mound's top. As a result, the area at the top of the mound becomes ionized, but not to the point where it discharges a lightning bolt. So seeds placed at the top of the mound would, at certain times, be exposed to slow-moving electrons, which, according to Burke's research, are then cajoled into creating antioxidants in order to soak up free radicals created by the ionized air. Thus, the naturally occurring energy serves as a natural flu shot for the seeds, which, when planted, grow faster and larger.[26]

So here is a possible reason why the pyramids were built. There could be no better motive for a civilization to expend so many resources to build pyramids in so many places in a line north and south along the Nile River.

Fertilizing the Nile Valley

According to Burke's research, everything about the Giza Plateau and the other large pyramids suggests that these structures were designed to focus electrical currents that were naturally occurring in the ground from the pyramid's base to its peak. Giza's three large pyramids, as well as the smaller satellite pyramids, were created from rock taken from the west bank of the Nile, a limestone rich in a manganese called dolomite. Because of the manganese, the dolomite effectively conducts electricity. Over its dolomite core, the Great Pyramid was cased with limestone containing low levels of manganese called Tura limestone, which acts as an insulator of electricity. Although very little of the Great Pyramid's casing stones remain, what does exist testifies to the fact that they were used for insulation.

The outer casing stones of the Great Pyramid were cut and polished with such precision ($^1/_{100}$ inch) that even today, as stated earlier, not even a razor will fit between two adjacent stones. Such precision takes time, so there must have been good reason to be so precise. Using the Tura limestone to create a blanket of insulation would require precision, for none of the charge created inside the pyramid could be allowed to leak out into the atmosphere.[27] With an insulator, the negative charge throughout the pyramid's base would be focused to its peak, which, according to legend, took the form of a gold capstone. (Gold is the most conductive of materials.)

Not only is the Giza Plateau at the intersection of two major limestone layers in the ground (the Mokkatam and the Maadi), but originally the plateau was not a naturally flat surface; it had to be leveled to support the Great Pyramid and the other two pyramids. Within the bedrock of the plateau, the limestone strata tilts down toward the river, which forms the edge of the Nile Valley aquifer. More importantly, water moving through rock creates electrical current,[28] and all three pyramids were built in a line where two aquifer layers rise to the surface, maximizing the concentration of current from the ground going into the pyramid. Furthermore, since the Giza pyramids were aligned along a tonguelike formation (peninsula) of the Mokkatam limestone, and the formation itself was narrowed by the quarrying of stone for the pyramid, the base of the Great Pyramid covered most of this tonguelike formation.

The result was that the placement of the pyramids on the plateau was deliberate and created an undisturbed causeway enclosed by a henge. For Burke, the placement of the pyramids is significant, since the existing ground current in the entire peninsula was concentrated in a small piece of ground right below the pyramids.[29]

In North Africa, with spring come sandstorms brought by strong desert winds. Known as Khamsin, these easterly gales out of the Sahara bring with them an excess of positively charged ions. (Friction between sand particles adds to the electrostatic charge of the wind.) These conditions set up an optimal situation for an ion generator, ideal for electric brush discharge (a faintly visible, relatively slow, crackling discharge of electricity without sparking) at the pyramid's peak. This is the same type of situation that exists in a thunderstorm, except that the threshold that creates the lightning bolt is not crossed. And, like a thunderstorm, brush discharge ionizes the atmosphere. In Egypt, during the Khamsin, ionized air molecules would be generated from the reaction between the negatively charged ions from the Great Pyramid and the excess positive ions in the atmosphere.

Unfortunately, ions emitted from a single peak would flow in all directions. Since Giza is situated to the west of the Nile Valley, only a small section of farmland would be affected. However, by placing smaller pyramids, which also have a negative charge, next to the large pyramids, the ionization flow could be directed to the desired area. Smaller pyramids placed to the south and southeast of the larger pyramids would direct the flow of ions to the south and east. This is precisely how the pyramids and their satellite pyramids were situated. If all pyramids are viewed as a system, from Meidum in the south to Giza in the north, it can be seen how a blanket of ionization would have flowed over the Nile Valley, perhaps twenty miles wide and forty miles long.

STONE TOWERS AS ENERGY CONDUCTORS

Entomologist Philip Callahan was stationed in Ireland during the Second World War and became fascinated with Ireland's round towers. Built by the Celts between the seventh and tenth centuries, these stone towers are an enigma. Without attached structures, such as a castle, they make a poor defensive structure. No one knows why they were built.

Today, there are twenty-five or more towers still standing in Ireland, and the remains of another forty-three pepper the countryside. Their oddest feature is that the doorway for these towers is always between nine and sixteen feet above the ground, and typically the tower is filled with dirt at the base. A clue to their purpose is that, for whatever reason, wherever these stone towers were built, the nearby farmers were always successful. For the cattlemen who drove their livestock to lands near the towers, the grass was always greener and beef more flavorful.[30] (See plate 39 of the color insert.)

The origin of the Celts is debated among historians, but it seems to be a good bet that they came from lands east of the Carpathian Mountains and were an Indo-European people. Whatever the case, Callahan discovered that they used impressive and sophisticated knowledge to improve their harvests. Ireland's stone towers weren't towers in the traditional sense, but antennae designed to collect and focus low-energy electromagnetic waves.

As everyone knows, the surface of our planet is bathed in energy from the sun, which is commonly referred to as light. However, there is a wide spectrum of energy that we cannot see that also bombards the planet. Infrared and ultraviolet energy are two examples. At the high end of this spectrum is the deadly gamma radiation that a nuclear explosion emits. At the low end are radio waves. Between the two is everything else, from microwaves to visible light. Although we cannot see these waves, they are constantly present.

Lightning, which is a continuous atmospheric phenomenon, creates waves of electromagnetic radiation at very low frequencies (VLFs) and extremely low frequencies (ELFs). If you have ever listened to an AM radio station during a thunderstorm, you may have noticed that something interferes with the broadcast. We call this static. This static is really extremely low frequencies created by the lightning. In fact, the outer atmosphere of our planet serves as a giant resonant cavity where standing energy waves of ELF and VLF created by lightning continually occur.[31]

The interaction between ELF magnetic fields and plants has been the subject of scientific studies for some time, and with promising results. To cite one example, Professors Hsin-Hsiung Huang and Show-Ran Wang of Taiwan's University of Science and Technology discovered that a 60-Hz sinusoidal magnetic field enhanced early growth of mung beans.[32]

In the Midwest it is common knowledge that thunderstorms are good for the vast fields of corn and beans as well as the home garden. They bring that extra "something" that water from the house spigot simply doesn't have.

For Callahan, the question was, could the towers be some form of dielectric radio antenna for focusing lightning-radio waves? Through experimentation at his home and in Ireland, he discovered that they were indeed designed in such a way as to collect and focus ELF electromagnetic waves into the surrounding fields.

Callahan measured the Glendalough tower at ground level and found no signal. But as he raised his oscilloscope up the tower, he got a weak signal and then a strong one. At the tower's door, which faces south-southeast and is 3.2 meters above ground level, the signal increased in strength to 20 mV right at the bottom of the doorway. Callahan plotted the ELF energy around the Glendalough tower and discovered that "in every measurement, the atmospheric ELF at 8 Hz, 2,000 Hz, and target wave region (from 300 Hz down to 0 at the middle and back up to 300), wherever the detector touched the tower, increased in amplitude from three to eight times."[33]

How does this happen?

The tower itself was built from mica-schist and granite, and, according to legend, the mortar was mixed using ox blood.[34] The link between these materials, according to Callahan, is that they are paramagnetic. In other words, the mortar was magnetic, but in a minute way.

"Paramagnetism is the alignment of a force field in one direction by a substance in a magnetic field, and diamagnetism [the opposite of paramagnetism] is the magnetization in the opposite direction to that of the applied magnetic field," Callahan notes. Diamagnetic substances are repelled by a strong magnetic field. Paramagnetic substances are attracted to it. In truth, according to Callahan, "all substances are diamagnetic, but it is a weak form of magnetism and may be masked by other, stronger forces, for instance a magnetic field. . . . Diamagnetism results from changes induced in the torque by bits of electrons that oppose the applied magnetic flux. There is thus a weak negative susceptibility to the magnet."[35]

Although different types of rock are paramagnetic in various degrees, rock and soil in general are paramagnetic. Water and plants are diamagnetic.

When shaped properly, structures made from paramagnetic materials naturally become open resonators and serve as waveguides for ELFs. Insects use this natural principle in their antennae, as Callahan discovered. The spine of the insect's antennae (sensilla) resonate to infrared frequencies emitted by living organisms. On the corn earworm moth, there are at least seven different shapes of antennae.[36] Insect antennae contain myriad shapes for resonance: corrugated spines, towers, and pyramids.

Callahan also demonstrates through experimentation that shape is important, particularly with relatively weak paramagnetic substances. Limestone, which is weak—unlike granite, basalt, and schist—will demonstrate its paramagnetic properties only when formed into a round tower.[37]

Determined to quantify the paramagnetism in rock or clay particles, Callahan ground up a clay pot and then weighed the amount of granules attracted to a magnet versus grains not attracted. The paramagnetic property of the limestone was so weak that only after a small chunk was shaped into a round tower did its cone-shaped end point toward the testing magnet. For Callahan, it was "this latter shape phenomenon that indicates that the paramagnetic force goes out in waves and can thus be studied using waveguide (radio) design (Maxwell's equations) mathematics." Another irrefutable proof that shape is important in paramagnetism, according to Callahan, is that ground-up rock or clay, after regrinding, will change its ratio of magnetic susceptibility to nonsusceptibility.[38]

If the Irish towers were low-frequency radio systems, then they had to be dielectric waveguide antennae for photon energy. Such a theory also explains why the bases of the towers were filled with dirt. A false ground nine or ten feet above the actual ground had to be created because of the small or nonexistent signal at actual ground level!

To further test his theory, Callahan built model towers to the exact dimensions of the tower on Devenish Island in County Fermanagh,

Ireland, and with a high-frequency oscillator (a Klystron) generated 3-cm wavelengths of radio energy. According to Callahan, since the Devenish tower is aligned to the night sky and is 25 meters high, it should resonate to meter-long wavelengths. When he placed his 10-cm-high, 3-cm-diameter sandpaper tower in the radio beam, the power meter went up from 6 to 9 decibels of energy, proving beyond any doubt that round towers were in fact waveguides for ELFs.[39]

There is a modern example of Nature's paramagnetic/diamagnetic duality. In the ancient tradition of the Zen garden, the placement of rocks is crucial to the growth of plants in the garden. A tall granite stone is placed in the center of several smaller granite stones. In another variation, a flat stone of quartz is placed next to a tall granite stone. Quartz is neutral or weakly diamagnetic, granite highly paramagnetic. According to the Zen gardener, by positioning these types of rocks in relationship to the sun and manipulating their relationship to each other, the gardener can control plant growth. Thus, the yin and yang principle of the Zen gardener is the subtle energy principle of paramagnetism and diamagnetism.[40]

A NETWORK OF PYRAMIDS

According to Callahan, the antennae of a wasp, the insect's sensory organs, display the pyramid shape and the corrugated shape, two of the best configurations for focusing and concentrating the paramagnetic force. Interestingly enough, according to Callahan, the vespid wasp hieroglyph is more common than the sacred scarab beetle hieroglyph and other carvings. Perhaps the ancient Egyptians understood Nature's principles far better than modern civilization would like to believe.

What does the Great Pyramid's pumping pressure waves (sound) into the atmosphere have to do with Ireland's round towers and dielectric waveguides for ELFs?

If you guessed that the Great Pyramid was a generator for the production of an electric field (ionization of the atmosphere) and that all the other pyramids downrange on the west bank of the Nile were part of an ELF-based fertilizer system, you guessed right.

Russian scientists have been experimenting with the use of sound to generate an electric field since 1993. Their work was published in 2005 in *Radiophysics and Quantum Electronics* in an article entitled "Electro-Acoustic Sounding of the Atmosphere." In scientific terms, these physicists were able to generate "a variable electric field using powerful acoustic waves on turbulent atmospheric regions containing local electric-charge irregularities."[41] In other words, using sound they created an electric field in an area of the atmosphere where a thunderstorm was developing.

At this point Callahan's research, in my opinion, merges beautifully with that of Burke. The brush discharge emanating from the Great Pyramid and the pressure wave emanating from the upper chamber created a bubble-shaped electrical field.

According to Burke's theory, the configuration of pyramids at Giza would naturally direct or "push" the electric field south to all the other pyramids. If so, logically the southern pyramids were also constructed to create and enhance subtle electrical fields. Furthermore, it might be the case that the pyramids downrange of the Great Pyramid also emanated negatively charged ions that would assist the flow further south.

If this were the case, each successive pyramid farther south would need to have an electric potential more positive (less negatively charged) than its neighbor to the north. To accomplish this, each successive pyramid to the south would need to be slightly shorter and smaller than its northern neighbor. Although not all pyramids have retained their original height, the general tendency is that each pyramid to the south is shorter. The Great Pyramid at Giza is 481 feet tall. At Dahshur, to the south, the Red Pyramid and the Bent Pyramid are 341 and 344 feet tall, respectively. Even further south, the final pyramid in the network, at Meidum, has been calculated to have been 306 feet tall after its completion.

Like-kind charges, such as negative and negative, repel each other, and opposite charges attract. In the case of negatively charged ions flowing to the south, as they approached each secondary pyramid, that pyramid's negative charge would repel the ions around the pyramid to the south and east, while at the same time assisting in attracting the flow of ions because of their lesser negative charge.

This might provide a clue to why the pyramid at Abu Rawash was abandoned early in its construction. A more suitable site was identified at Giza, where the natural land formations maximized the potential for electrical charge.

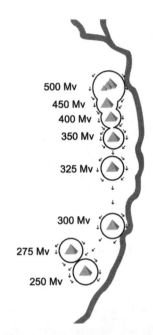

Fig. 9.5 (right). Ionization flow within the pyramid network (Voltages are not actual and are only given numerical values to depict the theory.)

Fig. 9.6 (below). ELFs and VLFs are reflected and scattered by the Great Pyramid's electric field toward the ground and sky.

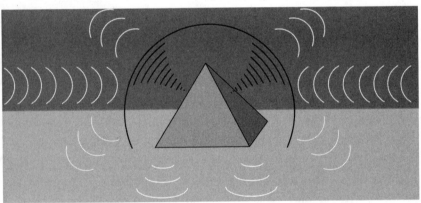

As did the builders of Ireland's stone towers, the pyramid builders were creating an open-resonance antenna to collect and diffuse ELFs and VLFs to boost crop growth. Here's how I think the system worked.

Extremely low and very low frequencies occur naturally throughout the atmosphere as a result of thunderstorms, dust storms, tornados, and volcanic activity; these frequencies propagate globally without excessive attenuation. Generally, these ELFs and VLFs move horizontally across the Earth's surface. In the skies above the Nile Valley, an electric field in the shape of a bubble was generated by the Great Pyramid's pressure wave,

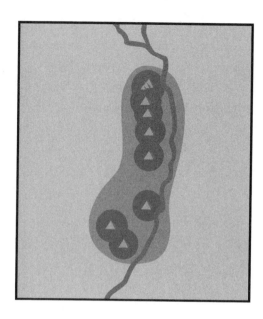

Fig. 9.7. Region fertilized by ELF and VLF

which served as a reflector to scatter ELF and VLF energy. Because of their design, all the other pyramids to the south of Giza resonated with the vibrations emanating from the Great Pyramid and shared in its electrical field. As a result, ELFs and VLFs were reflected to the fields around the pyramids.

Although the concept behind this system involved an understanding of atmospheric and electromagnetic theory, the design and implementation of the system are relatively simple. Once the pyramids were built and the pulse pump in the Great Pyramid started, little maintenance would be needed. Of course, the theory proposed here needs further research. Still, it offers rational and scientific answers to some of the most difficult questions posed by the design of Egypt's pyramids.

The pyramids were large because they needed to be. The area serviced by the reflected ELFs and VLFs is proportional to the size of the pyramid. With only a few exceptions, each pyramid contained a chamber near or at ground level or just below ground level and located in the middle of the pyramid. In this chamber a box carved from granite or other hard stone was placed. It is interesting to note here that in all the pyramids at Sakkara the chamber was located just below ground level. At Dahshur they were located just above ground level. With a resonance system such as this, it would be ideal to custom design a resonance cavity in each pyramid so that the pressure wave emanating from the Great Pyramid and moving downrange could be made coherent again, since the pressure waves (vibrations) weaken the farther they travel. In essence, they might have been putting a granite box in each respective chamber to "tune" the pyramid to the frequency emanating from the Great Pyramid.

10

A MESSAGE AT
DENDERAH

Gutzon Borglum devoted the last half of his life to sending the future of civilization a message, and the only way to ensure that those in the future received this message was to create a monument that would last for hundreds of thousands of years. Permanence was essential to his vision. So, with funding approved and appropriated by Congress, he carved the images of George Washington, Thomas Jefferson, Abraham Lincoln, and Theodore Roosevelt into one of the Black Hills' granite peaks, Mount Rushmore.

Borglum carved this monument because he believed that "ten thousand years from now our civilization will have passed without leaving a trace," and "a new race of people will inhabit the earth. They will come to Mount Rushmore and read the record we have made":[1]

> Hence, let us place there, carved high, as close to heaven as we can, the words of our leaders, their faces to show posterity what manner of men they were. Then breathe a prayer that these records will endure until the wind and the rain alone shall wear them away.[2]

Work began on Mount Rushmore in 1927, and over the course of fourteen years four hundred men armed with dynamite and jackhammers carved away the mountain, leaving the faces of four famous presidents. In October of 1941 Borglum's work had been completed.

Although not well known, Borglum also wanted to create a Hall of Records. According to the Mount Rushmore National Museum, "He often referred to ancient monuments such as the great heads of Easter Island and the Pyramids being left by earlier civilization without an adequate explanation of their meaning or intent."[3] So, above the head of Abraham Lincoln, in a canyon, he began drilling in July 1938. According to his plan, a tall tunnel would lead to a spacious room where the Bill of Rights, the Declaration of Independence, and the United States Constitution would be stored for all eternity. Congress, however, did not embrace this facet of Borglum's vision, and in July 1939 work on the Hall of Records ceased. It wasn't until the 1990s that a shaft was drilled in front of Borglum's entrance to the Hall of Records and the fullness of his vision realized.

In 1998, officials of the National Park System and the Borglum family watched in celebration as sixteen porcelain enamel panels with the United States Constitution, the Declaration of Independence, a history

Fig. 10.1. Granite carvings of Mount Rushmore

Fig. 10.2 (above). The
unfinished Hall of Records
(courtesy of the National
Park Service)

Fig. 10.3 (right). A worker
carving Mount Rushmore's
granite with an air-powered
jackhammer

Fig. 10.4. A worker suspended

Fig. 10.5. The viewing area with its granite pillars and patio

of Mount Rushmore, and a history of the four presidents, along with Borglum's biography and the history of the United States, were cased in a teakwood box and lowered into the titanium-lined shaft.

Much has changed at Mount Rushmore since the last time I was there. Granite buildings with granite tile patios, a three-tiered colonnade, and an amphitheater have been erected. The work accomplished by the National Park System is beautiful.

I could not help thinking that if Borglum's thoughts concerning the future someday came true—if a catastrophe occurred and civilization passed away without a trace—what would Mount Rushmore, the granite building, patios, and colonnades look like then?

Everything would have decayed, of course, and returned to the earth except for the granite. With this vision in mind, I could not help thinking of the Valley Temple and the Great Sphinx. The similarities between these man-made constructs in America and in Egypt are, at the very least, amusing, but ultimately ironic.

If a catastrophe does occur sometime in the future and a new civilization develops, how will the people of the new civilization view Mount Rushmore? If the English language is forgotten, perhaps the colonnades with their shops will be viewed as a temple, and the heads of Washington,

Fig. 10.6. Looking down the Memorial's colonnade

Fig. 10.7. Looking down the Valley Temple's colonnade

Jefferson, Lincoln, and Roosevelt as our "gods" whom we worshipped.

This raises the question: What's the difference between memorializing and worshipping?

A HISTORY OF CATASTROPHE

History is more than a written record of past events. It is also our cumulative memory as a civilization. Regardless if this cumulative memory is disseminated orally or through documents, how we know what occurred in previous years, centuries, or millennia relies on civilization being a continuous human endeavor. Yet there are gaps in our history where information is minimal or nonexistent. To fill in these gaps, those involved in the study of history create models based on the best available evidence, from such disciplines as archaeology and anthropology.

In constructing a model for our civilization's history, a beginning is determined and marked by the oldest written record or the oldest known public structure. Such a mark signifies civilization's origin. Today, based on the best available evidence, history marks the beginning of civilization as being approximately 3000 BCE, with the rise of hierarchical societies and the construction of public structures in the Indus, Mesopotamian, and Nile Valleys, as well as Caral in Peru.*

Before the nineteenth century, however, history's model was based on the Bible. The age of Earth was calculated to be four thousand years, according to the lineages of the Genesis patriarchs. Shortly thereafter, civilization began. In effect, the universe, Earth, mankind, and civilization were an act of divine creation.

During the nineteenth century, the discovery of bones from extinct animal species changed everything. Not only was Earth believed to be much older than previously thought, but mankind was no longer a divine creation. Instead, Man was the end product of a chance occurrence, given the correct mix of chemicals and the random mutations of form. Fueled by the burgeoning fields of geology and archaeology, histo-

---

*Caral is a large settlement in the Supe Valley, near Supe, Barranca province, Peru, some two hundred kilometers north of Lima. Inhabited between approximately 2600 and 2000 BCE, Caral is one of the most ancient cities of the Americas and possibly of the entire world. It is a well-studied site of the Norte Chico civilization.

rians now had a new model by which to interpret past events. Evolution became the darling of the scientific world. Everything was considered in terms of evolution: the evolution of animals, the evolution of man, the evolution of the cosmos, the evolution of cultures, even the evolution of religion. Almost every aspect of society is viewed in terms of evolution. And just like everything else, civilization is also believed to have evolved in a linear fashion.

Catastrophism, once the foundation of geology, was replaced in the middle of the nineteenth century by uniformitarianism: the assumption that environmental conditions of the past are the same as those of the present. Any changes occurred over a very long period. However, during the past twenty years, geologists have fully embraced catastrophism as being a major player in Earth's history. Catastrophism is now viewed as an important evolutionary ingredient responsible for five mass extinctions during the past five hundred million years: the Ordovician, Devonian, Permian, Triassic, and Cretaceous extinctions.

Past catastrophic events are not evident because our environment is self-maintaining. The atmosphere we live in and breathe is caustic. Over time everything decays and returns to the raw materials from which it was forged. Meteor craters from celestial impacts are smoothed out by rain and flowing water, then filled in with soil from seasonal winds. Very large craters disappear into fertile valleys of grasses and trees.

The evidence for Earth's violent past is obvious, according to our closest celestial neighbor. The moon displays numerous impacts, some extremely large, others quite small. Being much larger than the moon, Earth would have attracted many more stellar objects.

The most recent mass extinction occurred sometime between fifteen thousand and eleven thousand years ago, but there is no evidence of a devastating celestial impact. Wooly mammoths, mastodons, saber-toothed tigers, and other megafauna ceased to exist, and what happened to cause their extinction has baffled geologists. Some geologists theorize there was no catastrophe and that human overhunting practices were responsible.

Whatever the case, the extinction that ended the Ice Age decimated the animal species that inhabited Earth at that time, particularly mammalian species. Human cultures existed at that time, so they too lived through whatever circumstances brought an end to the age of the megafauna. Yet, according to the official historical record, humanity has no record or memory of this catastrophe. But if a global catastrophe reduced the human population to a few million individuals, or less, and if any civilization became sophisticated after a few thousand years, how *would* we know of the existence of any prior civilizations or life?

A small number of survivors would not have been able to maintain any civil infrastructure and would be forced to abandon their lifestyle in favor of survival, which means hunting and fishing and the employment of a rudimentary style of agriculture. Everything that had ever existed, unless built out of stone, would have disappeared.

As we know only too well, catastrophes do occur. The December 2004 tsunami that spread destruction on the shores of the Indian Ocean was a brutal reminder of Nature's awesome power. Countries from Asia to Africa were pounded by its devastation. With more than a quarter of a million people dead, it punctuated our current fascination and fear of cataclysms with a clear understanding of our own frailty and mortality.

Unfortunately, there are many interpretations of an event like the 2004 tsunami, some of which accompany self-assessment and a natural guilt about why such a terrible disaster would occur, particularly if a loved one suffered as a result. Blame for the catastrophe might be internalized, and those individuals dealing with it in this fashion might wonder what they did to invite the wrath of God Almighty. Even lesser tragedies invite a feeling of separation from Nature (or God) and are accompanied by grief and lament directed at the divine.

Anger and pain will dole out blame in many directions, but when anger turns into exhaustion, the pointing finger turns inward, and the mind rises above the pain, looking for an answer that will provide a feeling of control over the uncontrollable. Ultimately, that control is nothing more than an illusion; there is no control except over one's own self. Eventually, inner peace is achieved through reflection, and then comes the realization that if pain is God's punishment, selfish pleasure must be its cause.

We accept pain, for, in a sense, it makes us feel alive, even while we search for someone or something to pin it on. Such is the human experience, but the same principle works on civilization, at times, and does so pervasively.

History is filled with ancient legends of calamity and catastrophe, all of which come to us in the form of myth. This condition of history is global, and some of the oldest myths concerning catastrophe come from the ancient traditions of the Nile Valley.

THE FACE OF HATHOR

Hathor is very ancient, one of the oldest gods in the Egyptian religious tradition,[4] and similar in principle to the Great Mother goddess of prehistoric Europe. She represents the creatrix of life. Not only did she bring forth and maintain all biological life, but she also nurtured the souls of the deceased in the *duat* (the underworld). According to tradition, she came into being as the Eye of Ra[5] and functioned as the mother, consort, and daughter of the creator sun god. She is also the mother of the celestial falcon, the Lady of the Stars. Ultimately, Hathor was the mother of all gods[6] and the goddess of the sky. In the beginning, Hathor united with the Creator to create all that exists. She was the hand of Atum as he created as well and the divine "seed" from which the universe arose.

In Egyptian myth, Atum, the absolute and omnipotent God, gave birth to himself and created all that exists (the universe) by masturbating.[7] In a less symbolic version, Atum created the cosmos by projecting from his heart and brought forth the eight primary principles known as the Great Ennead of Heliopolis. These were the nine great Osirian gods: Atum, Shu, Tefnut, Geb, Nut, Osiris, Isis, Seth, and Nephthys. In the Pyramid Texts, Osiris, Isis, Seth, and Nepthys represent the cyclical nature of life and are in essence a part of Atum.

In principle, the ancient Egyptians expressed a reasoned theory of the universe's existence. They taught that before there was life, the universe existed in a state of chaos, which was described as a "dark watery domain of unlimited depth and extent."[8] They referred to this as Nun. From Nun came the eight gods known as the Ogdoad of Hermopolis, which consisted of four pairs of two, each pair being a male and a female. The Nu/Naunet pair represented the primordial or initial waters, Amun/Amunet the air (invisibility) or the void, Kuk/Kauket were darkness, and Huh/Hauhet were infinite space (eternity). The male gods were depicted with the head of a frog, and the goddesses with that of a serpent.

In the original version of the myth, the Ogdoad arose out of the waters and thrust up the primeval mound, also known as the Benben stone, which was honored at Heliopolis, where it was said that the sun was born. The power of the sun was the first light and came with the first appearance of the Creator. The sun put an end to the silent waters of darkness.[9] Amun-Ra and the goddesses Neith and Hathor then established *maat,* meaning "the divine order—the cosmos."

In the end, the Egyptians referred to the creator as the One Who Made Himself into Millions and viewed life and the cosmos as emanating from a single original force,[10] just as cosmologists today speculate in the Big Bang theory that all that exists was at one time a single indescribable point.

In ancient Egypt, the concept of a god or goddess does not refer to one particular entity, but to a condition or aspect of Nature that teaches us to understand the natural order of events. There is action and con-

Fig. 10.8. Hathor depicted as bovine woman

sequence, cause and effect, and no matter how hard you try to avoid it, what goes around comes around. In this manner Hathor symbolized life's duality.

Hathor literally means "House of Horus," and as such, she was the mother of Horus, symbolizing the mother of mankind. During the earliest dynasties Hathor represented the mother principle (a goddess) in a cosmic sense as well as the physical. In ancient Egyptian philosophy, Man is a representation of the cosmos and thus is the principle of the mother, creative in a cosmic sense as well as procreative in an earthly sense. Man as an archetype is a created being, and as a unique individual, a procreated being.

In a cosmic sense Hathor was responsible for the state of the world and the universe, and in an earthly sense she was responsible for music, dance, love, and sex, as well as childbirth. Although Hathor gave life, she could also take it away. As such, she was the goddess of destruction as well. However, Hathor's destructive side was not limited to the consequences of indulgence. It extended to destructive natural events in a more dramatic expression of her powers.

An elegant temple was built in Hathor's honor at Denderah, north of Luxor. Today it is one of the most enigmatic sites in all Egypt. In ancient times Hathor's Temple was known as the Castle of the Sistrum and Per Hathor, the House of Hathor, or the Domain of Hathor. Throughout Egypt's dynasties it is said to have been a place of pilgrimage and worship, but after the ruin of the pharaonic way, Denderah was abandoned, and then the wind and sand became its sole occupant. For nearly two thousand years Hathor's temple remained half buried in sand.

Like other temples of the Nile, Hathor's Temple has a long history and has been modified a number of times. Its current form dates to the Ptolemaic and Roman eras during the first century BCE. The Romans constructed a birth house (where babies were born) next to the temple entrance. Later, Coptic Christians erected a church there. During the New Kingdom (1550–1070 BCE), Thutmose III, Amenhotep III, and Ramses II and III are believed to have added to the temple complex. There is also an older birth house and an Eleventh Dynasty chapel dedicated to King Nebhepetre Mentuhotep II. But there is also reason to suspect its original foundation dates back to dynastic Egypt's earliest history. In *A Thousand Miles Up the Nile,* the nineteenth-century writer Amelia Edwards notes:

> The names of Augustus, Caligula, Tiberius, Domitian, Claudius, and Nero are found in the royal ovals; the oldest being those of Ptolemy XI, the founder of the present edifice, which was, however, rebuilt upon the site of a succession of older buildings, of which the most ancient dated back as far as the reign of Khufu, the builder of the Great Pyramid. This fact, and the still more interesting fact that the oldest structure of all was believed to belong to the inconceivably remote period of the Horshesu, or "followers of Horus" (i.e., the petty chiefs, or princes, who ruled in Egypt before the foundation of the first monarchy), is recorded in the following remarkable inscription discovered by Mariette in one of the crypts constructed in the thickness of the walls of the present temple.
>
> The first text relates to certain festivals to be celebrated in honour of Hathor, and states that all the ordained ceremonies had been performed by King Thothmes III (XVIIIth dynasty) "in memory of his mother, Hathor of Denderah. And they found the great fundamental rules of Denderah in ancient writing, written on goat-skin in the time of the Followers of Horus. This was found in the inside of a brick wall during the reign of King Pepi (VIth dynasty)." In the same crypt, another and a more brief inscription runs thus:—"Great fundamental rule of Denderah. Restorations done by Thothmes III, according to what was found in ancient writing of the time of King Khufu." Hereupon Mariette remarks "The temple of Denderah is not, then, one of the most modern in Egypt, except in so far as it was constructed by one of the later Lagidæ. Its origin is literally lost in the night of time."[11] [See plate 40 of the color insert.]

Yet all these additions pale in comparison to the breathtaking magnificence of the temple itself. It is difficult to describe with words because the temple was specifically designed to be more of an experience than a structure. Edwards accurately captures its splendor:

The immense girth of the columns, the huge screens which connect them, the ponderous cornice jutting overhead, confuse the imagination, and in the absence of given measurements appear, perhaps, even more enormous than they are. Looking up to the architrave, we see a kind of Egyptian Panathenaic procession of carven priests and warriors, some with standards and some with musical instruments. The winged globe, depicted upon a gigantic scale in the curve of the cornice, seems to hover above the central doorway. Hieroglyphs, emblems, strange forms of Kings and Gods, cover every foot of wall space, frieze and pillar. Nor does this wealth of surface-sculpture tend in any way to diminish the general effect of size. It would seem, on the contrary, as if complex decoration were in this instance the natural complement to simplicity of form. Every group, every inscription, appears to be necessary and in its place; an essential part of the building it helps to adorn.[12]

When gazing on the magnificent columns of Hathor's Hypostyle Hall, it seems that a regret of cosmic proportion occurred. Fortunately, this magnificent hall is one of the most well-preserved and impressive architectural masterpieces in all Egypt. Each column (there are twenty-one in all) has a capital with Hathor's bovine/human face carved on four perfectly orthogonal sides. On most of the pillars, however, Hathor's face has been carefully and systematically chiseled away. With no eyes, nose, or mouth, Hathor is now faceless.

Early Christians who abhorred idols are said to have been the vandals of Hathor's Temple. However, in ancient Egypt when a ruler fell from favor, the succeeding regime often systematically defaced his graven images and removed his name from the records. For example, in 1353 BCE, when Amenhotep III died, masons methodically chiseled away any mention of Amun, the god of the great pharaoh. Likewise, after Akhenaten's death in 1334 BCE, masons again entered Amenhotep III's mortuary temple, recarved Amun's name, and erased all mention of Akhenaten. It might be the case that in the collective ancient Egyptian mind, Hathor was decommissioned as a principle of Nature. Without the ability to see or breathe, Hathor's spirit could not exist.

Why the ancient Egyptians decommissioned Hathor is a story

contained in her myths, and like all other stories from great antiquity, it tells a tale of destruction. Hathor serves as an aspect of the sun, the eye of Ra.

HATHOR'S WRATH

The story of Hathor as the eye of Ra echoes the tragedy of catastrophe that, from time to time, befalls our planet. It is in this context of Nature and the cosmos that the destruction of Hathor's face can best be understood.

According to myth, humanity plotted against Ra, so he summoned the gods in the primeval waters for their advice. After council, Nun and the other gods recommended that he send his Eye—the Eye of Ra (*Utchat*)—against the rebels, for no one was more able to smite them than Hathor. So Hathor, the Eye of Ra, was sent and overpowered mankind, slaughtering them and then wading in their blood. There were survivors, so the next day she was to finish the task. But for whatever reason Ra changed his mind and ordered his high priest on Earth to make beer, mix it with red ochre, and pour it into the fields to a depth of the palm. When Hathor arrived the next morning to resume the killing, she saw her beautiful reflection in the flooded fields. Instead of continuing the slaughter, she decided to drink the mix of beer and ochre. Now drunk, she returned to Ra and spared what was left of mankind.

According to the Book of the Heavenly Cow, Earth would never again be the same. Ra, now sick and tired, rode away on the back of Nut, who transformed into a cow during a time when Earth was enveloped in darkness.[13] The survivors asked Ra to stay and shoot at his enemies, but he refused and, upon his departure, put Osiris in charge of mankind. With this change, a new era began, with the lesser gods ruling the world. According to tradition, death came into being, and from that point onward mankind had to maintain the divine order of the cosmos.

In another later myth, Tefnut, as the Eye of Ra, went to Nubia to live as a bloodthirsty lion after being separated from her father, Ra. Thoth was sent in an attempt to persuade her to return, but to no avail. She died and became Hathor, the goddess of the sky.

In another version Tefnut transformed into a cat—the goddess

Bast—who then turned into a lion when angry; a great disturbance occurred in the order of the universe when the Eye of Ra was removed from Ra. And only when the Eye of Ra was returned to Ra was cosmic order restored. In yet another version, according to the Jumilhac Papyrus, Isis transformed herself into Hathor and destroyed with fire all the followers of Seth. Mankind, at that time, was divided by the gods into the Followers of Horus and the Followers of Seth, where the latter represented evildoers.[14]

Although there are several versions of this myth telling of the destruction of mankind, what is clear is that a catastrophe occurred that decimated whatever civilization then existed, and it had something to do with events in the sky. Both the Eye of Ra and Hathor, who was Ra's daughter, are associated with the celestial realm. In the ancient Egyptian language the word for eye (*irt*) sounded similar to another word in their language that meant "doing" or "acting." So it may be the case that the word *eye* would be what we today refer to as an "act of God"—in other words, a natural catastrophe.

It was Egyptian tradition to identify the eyes with different aspects of the Creator, almost exclusively celestial bodies: the sun, the moon, the morning star (Venus), and Sopdet (Sirius). But Hathor, the eye goddess, was not associated with any known celestial body, so she appears to be special. Among her attributes were water and fire. According to Geraldine Pinch, "Her fiery glance destroyed the enemies of the divine order while her tears created life."[15]

Little credence has been given to these stories to help describe history because they occurred in so-called mythical times. But is there really such a thing as mythical times? Perhaps a more pertinent question is, why are these times considered mythical?

The most probable answer is that they are considered mythical because the events in the stories associated with these times occurred before the age of writing—before our civilization existed—and thus are difficult to interpret. Their metaphorical language makes it extremely hard to determine exactly what happened and when it happened.

In 1969, history of science professors Giorgio De Santillana and Hertha Von Dechend published a book entitled *Hamlet's Mill* in an attempt to break the metaphorical code of mythology. The findings of their research dictate that those who are serious about understanding the past should look at myth more as a scientific language than as religious rhetoric. Their argument that ancient mythology was effectively an understanding of natural principles (science) is justified by their exhaustive work into the meaning of mythology. Myth is a specific type of ancient language, they contend, that we are only now beginning to understand.[16]

Let's look at the temple at Denderah, for instance. It was dedicated to Hathor and her myths. On the temple's ceiling is a grand mural. Nut, as the sky, is seen in typical form bending over Earth. But what is so unusual about this engraving is that the world is upside down. And Hathor, with a contemptuous look on her face, rains down from the sun through what appear to be cones of energy.

Nut, upside down, can be nothing other than the world being proverbially turned upside down. And Hathor, in the stream of rays coming from the sun, must be the cause of those rays. In relating this temple scene to Hathor's myth, the pertinent question is, what is the eye of Ra?

Our first clue is that the principal characters in the stories, Hathor and the Eye of Ra, are really a single character. Hathor as the daughter of Ra is the Eye of Ra. We also know that Hathor, although associated with a number of human traits, was predominantly a celestial or sky goddess and responsible for giving life to mankind. Our second clue is that, whatever event the myth is referring to, it was cataclysmic and global, decimating mankind.

So in order for the myths of Hathor and the Eye of Ra to symbolize an actual event, there needs to be a celestial and cataclysmic event that decimated mankind. Although a meteor or comet impact are likely candidates for such a cataclysm, there are two problems with this idea. First, subsequent to the Chicxulub (Yucatan) impact 65 million years ago, there is no evidence of a meteor or comet impact on Earth's surface that would be large enough to have global consequences. Second, a comet or meteor large enough to be witnessed as a celestial event while still in its approach to Earth would likely be sufficiently large to destroy all life on Earth. (The meteor that led to the extinction of the dinosaurs was only six miles wide.)

Despite these two problems, a global catastrophe did occur at the end of the Ice Age, beginning about fourteen thousand years ago.[17] Whatever happened, we know from the fossil record that its effects lasted for several thousand years and resulted in the mass extinction of numerous species, particularly large animals such as the mammoth and mastodon. The majority of them died out between fourteen thousand and eleven thousand years ago. Yet what this catastrophe was and what impact it had on human populations remains a mystery.

GENESIS AND DISASTER

When in prehistory did this unknown granite civilization, this Civilization X, exist? The only source we have to go on is the word of the ancient Egyptians themselves. According to their records, from 38,000 BCE to 14,800 BCE was a blurry period of their history when "the gods" ruled. After 14,800 BCE the Shemsu-Hor (Followers of Horus) ruled until Narmer established dynastic Egypt in 3100 BCE.

Exactly what, or who, "the gods" were is unknown. At the time the Turin Papyrus was written (ca. 1200 BCE), a period of 13,600 years had elapsed since the time that the gods had reigned. However, other ancient sources may shed light on these gods, particularly the Bible and other ancient texts.

The first five books of the Bible are attributed to Moses, who was born in Egypt and raised in the house of the pharaoh. As Egyptian royalty, he grew up a prince and attended the finest schools, where he learned math, philosophy, and history according to the Egyptian educational system of the time. Although the Bible has long been a source for theological exegesis, the books of Moses were much more.

At a time of political turmoil in Egypt, Moses led a movement of independence for a group of people known as the Hyksos, people with Semitic origins from Asia. After centuries of living in the Nile delta, the Hyksos had become too politically powerful for the Egyptian government. The Hyksos lived in a strategically significant part of the eastern delta where any invasive force would likely march if it came from the northeast.

As tensions mounted between the Hyksos and the native Egyptians, Moses (most likely along with other Hyksos leaders) decided it was best to leave and create a new independent state apart from Egyptian rule. But to do so would require much effort, an army, and the documents necessary to create a government. Such was the purpose of the books of Moses. They were theological and philosophical as well as a provider of laws. However, they were also historical and explained the course of mankind according to the history of the time, particularly the book of Genesis, where there is a possible historical reference to a remote time in history where not gods, but sons of God existed as men of importance. In the introduction to the story of Noah's Flood:

> When men began to increase in number on the earth and daughters were born to them, the sons of God saw that the daughters of men were beautiful, and they married any of them they chose. . . .
>
> The Nephilim were on the earth in those days—and also afterward—when the sons of God went to the daughters of men and had children by them. They were the heroes of old, men of renown. [Gen.: 6.4]

Biblically, no more is written about these sons of God, but in the Book of Enoch (one of the apocryphal books) they were responsible for bringing civilization to mankind. Also referred to as Watchers, their teachings cover a long list of attributes: knowledge of the clouds; signs of the earth, sun, and moon (calendar systems); observation and knowledge of the stars; astrology; the science of the constellations; the use of spices, sorcery, and enchantments; and the use of paint, cosmetics, and jewelry. They also instructed in the supernatural, smiting spirits and demons, and the medical, smiting an embryo in the womb (abortion). But the most defining qualities of civilization the Watchers are credited with disseminating are those for which we are now so famous, the art of war and the methods of writing.

The essence of this ancient text has long been hidden behind a host of theories that explain the Watchers as demons, or evil spirits, that somehow mated with women to sire a breed of giants called the Nephilim. Unfortunately, over the past three thousand years, the evolving meaning of demons and angels has clouded the significance of this passage. The terms *demon* and *angel* were originally used to characterize a person, such as "She is an angel" because she is kindhearted, or "He is a demon" because he is meanspirited and filled with anger. We still use those words today in their original meaning.

The significance of these sons of God, these "heroes of old and men of renown," is that they lived prior to a great catastrophe that the Bible refers to as Noah's Flood, and that they carried on the skills and teachings of civilization. A similar tale (from Genesis 11:1–9) is told about the Tower of Babel:

> Now the whole world had one language and a common speech. As men moved eastward, [or from the east; or in the east] they found a plain in Shinar [Babylonia] and settled there.
>
> They said to each other, "Come, let's make bricks and bake them thoroughly." They used brick instead of stone, and tar for mortar. Then they said, "Come, let us build ourselves a city, with a tower that reaches to the heavens, so that we may make a name for ourselves and not be scattered over the face of the whole earth."
>
> But the Lord came down to see the city and the tower that the men were building. The Lord said, "If as one people speaking the same language they have begun to do this, then nothing they plan to do will be impossible for them. Come, let us go down and confuse their language so they will not understand each other."
>
> So the Lord scattered them from there over all the earth, and they stopped building the city. That is why it was called Babel [Babylon; Babel sounds like the Hebrew for "confused"]—because there the Lord confused the language of the whole world. From there the Lord scattered them over the face of the whole earth.

At face value, the Tower of Babel is just another fable where God exercises his "will" on the world because mankind has been up to no good, building a tower to reach the heavens, presumably in defiance of God. Whether the tower existed is not the point. The point is that a civilization was at one time unified by a single language and could accomplish anything. But after God's intervention, mankind was scattered across the world and its languages became diverse.

In 3000 BCE, long before the Tower of Babel story was recorded in Genesis, no single language existed. However, some linguists speculate that very early in prehistory a single language *did* exist. This is a highly debated topic in linguistics. Some linguists are certain that no such language existed, but Joseph Greenberg (1915–2001), a prominent linguist and African anthropologist, believed that it did and made it his life's work to understand the historical relationships between the world's languages.

According to Greenberg, there were twelve super-families of language that may have been derived from a single ancestral human language. This is a concept that is supported by geneticists who have traced human DNA to a single small human population in Africa two hundred thousand years ago.

We may never definitively know whether a single ancestral language existed at some remote time in the past. Nonetheless, geneticists think it is a possibility, and history as it was viewed by ancient cultures of the Middle East viewed it as fact. However, the real question is, did the story of the Tower of Babel relay actual events, or was it a morality tale about the evils of mankind? Since this story and other stories in Genesis were widespread during ancient times, it is a fair assumption, in the tradition of De Santillana and Von Dechend, to conclude that it represents actual events. If so, what could the Tower of Babel story be referring to?

For me, it is clear that the single language and technical ability of mankind in the Tower of Babel story refer to ancient Egypt's Civilization X.

In the insurance business, there is a clause that protects the insured from what are referred to as "acts of God." These are nothing more than natural disasters, whether the disaster be a thunderstorm, hailstorm, tornado, or flood. Five thousand years ago people surely blamed God for natural disasters just as they do today. Thus, what the Tower of Babel story is likely referring to is a natural disaster of immense proportions. The civilization that existed was decimated, leaving only isolated pockets of survivors. Over many generations those survivors struggled back onto the road of civilization, but because of their isolation, unique languages developed in various regions. In both the story of Noah's Flood and that of the Tower of Babel, a civilization is interrupted by a catastrophe. Although the Genesis author does not state precisely what the catastrophe was in the Tower of Babel story, the story of Noah clearly describes a flood generated by torrential rains. However, a flood by water might be an allegory for a different type of flood.

The difficulty with a global flood is that five times the amount of water that currently exists on Earth today would be required to cover the surface of the planet at a level topping the highest of the world's mountain peaks. Furthermore, if such an event occurred, it would likely permanently change the composition of the atmosphere. The story of Noah's Flood has a predecessor in the Sumerian Epic of Gilgamesh. The latter story seems to be more about the heavens than about the life of a person surviving a great flood.

Although the Sumerians first recorded the story of Gilgamesh as early as the beginning of the second millennium BCE, its origin is much older. Its popularity in ancient times was unmatched by any other story. Hurrians, Hittites, Assyrians, and Babylonians rehearsed it in various ways throughout ancient times.

In the Epic of Gilgamesh, Enkidu the wild man is seduced by a harlot who lures him into the city. There he encounters Gilgamesh, one of the earliest kings of Uruk. They fight. Gilgamesh wins, but he decides Enkidu is worthy of friendship. So together they plan an expedition to the great forest to slay the terrible monster Humbaba (the appointed guardian of the great forest), where "his roaring is the Great Flood."

Humbaba was called a "god" in the texts because *hum* means "creator." Humbaba (Hum is the father) is the "guardian of the cedar of paradise." This corresponds to the Elamitic god Humba or Humban, who shares the title of "prevalent" and "strong" with the planets Mercury and Jupiter and with Procyon (alpha Canis Minoris). He also occurs in a star list, carrying the determinative *mul*, which appears in the names of stars such as mulHumba. More appropriately, Humbaba is actually a type of "god of the intestines." His head, except for the eyes, is often depicted as being made from intestines in a single winding line.

No!

De Santillana and Von Dechend, the authors of *Hamlet's Mill*, believe that Humbaba is referring to the planet Mercury, Venus, or possibly Jupiter. But the latter would never make a convincing lord of entrails, or any other outer planet, for that matter. Their orbits do not allow for such notions—and Venus is much too regular for this role. Mercury, however, makes an appropriate god of the intestines, since its orbit is the most erratic of the major planets.

In the Epic story, when the heroes reach the cedar forest, they decapitate Humbaba with the help of the powerful Shamash (the sun), who sends a great storm to blind the monster. Upon returning to Uruk, Gilgamesh washes his hair and dresses in festive attire. As he puts on his crown, Ishtar, the goddess of love, enthralled by his good looks, asks him to marry her. Gilgamesh declines, reminding her of the fate of her previous mates, particularly Tammuz (Adonis).

No!

Who is Ishtar? Only two celestial personalities are possible candidates for the role of Ishtar: the planet Venus and Sirius. Both have the reputation of a harlot.

Scorned, Ishtar goes up to heaven in a rage and persuades Anu to send down the Bull of Heaven to avenge her. The Bull, awesome to behold, descends and kills a hundred warriors with his first snort. The two heroes tackle him. Enkidu grabs the bull by the tail and Gilgamesh, running between the bull's horns, makes the kill. Ishtar then appears on the walls of Uruk and curses the two heroes who have shamed her. In disgust, Enkidu tears off the right thigh of Heaven's Bull and flings it in her face amid brutal taunts. Celebration follows.

The story continues, but it is clear at this point that its characters, much like Greek mythology, *are symbolic of the movements of heavenly bodies.* Later, Tablet IX* tells the story of Enki's (God's) direct intervention in human affairs in order for Ziusudra to build an ark and survive the Great Flood. However, Ziusudra's construction of an ark has nothing to do with a literal flood. This ark corresponds to the constellation of Argo. This, of course, has obvious and far-reaching implications.

According to De Santillana and Von Dechend, in ancient times "floods refer to an old astronomical image, based on an abstract geometry."[18] It is not an easy picture to see, considering the objective difficulty of the science of astronomy. However, simply put, the plane of the celestial equator divides the constellations into two halves. The northern half of the constellations, those between the spring and autumn equinox, represents dry land. The southern half, those between the autumn and spring equinoxes, including the winter solstice, represents the waters below. The four points on the zodiac (the two equinoxes and the two solstices) define the conceptual plane of the flat earth.

Therefore, a constellation that ceases to mark the autumn equinox,

---

*The Epic of Gilgamesh is an ancient story originally carved into twelve clay tablets.

thereby falling below the equator, sinks into the depths of the water. *It is in this abstract way that a celestial flood occurs.* This makes it easier to understand the Gilgamesh flood, as well as to grasp the ideas from similar myths, such as the Greek story of Deucalion, where devastating waves were ordered back by Triton's blowing of the conch.

Like the story of the Eye of Ra, the Epic of Gilgamesh must have represented some grand celestial occurrence, and a dividing of history into "before" and "after." It is a fair assumption that these ancient and famous stories—the Eye of Ra, the Epic of Gilgamesh, Noah's Flood, the Tower of Babel, and all the other flood myths from around the world—all refer to the same event. If the Turin Papyrus is reasonably accurate, then a catastrophe brought on by some celestial event occurred sometime around 14,800 BCE when the reign of the Egyptian "gods" ceased and that of the Shemsu-Hor began. Ironically, this approximate date between the gods and the Shemsu-Hor also corresponds with the end of the Ice Age and a catastrophe that resulted in mass extinction.

11

AN INVISIBLE CATACLYSM

As we know, the Great Pyramid was built on a massive scale from limestone, with its upper chamber formed from seventy-ton granite slabs. Given this, it is impossible for me to accept that simple people with simple tools were responsible for its construction. Two and a half million blocks of limestone were used, weighing somewhere near 6 million tons, costing an adjusted $18 billion. This was more stone than would be used in all of Egypt's construction projects for the next 1,500 years. There is little choice but to accept the evidence that only a sophisticated system of quarrying, transportation, logistics, designing, planning, and constructing could have accomplished such a project.

Neither was the Great Pyramid project an isolated event. Pyramids were built in a line down the west bank of the Nile River. Three were built at Giza, and the pyramids of Abu Rawash, Sakkara, Dahshur, Abu Sir, Abu Gorab, and Meidum were built as well. Huge temples adorned with colossal statues were built in the Delta, at Tanis, at Memphis, and in an extraordinary way, in the south, at Thebes. All were stamped with the name of Ramses and a geometrically idealized statue of Man. This statue did not necessarily deify an individual but it expressed an understanding of Nature in which mankind was the perfected expression of consciousness and self-perception.

Such a civilization could never have been primitive or simple. The industry required to create this grand granite civilization must also have had the academic system needed for the development of knowledge and the civil engineering skill to implement that knowledge. And any sophisticated industry requires large numbers of people who specialize in certain tasks to manufacture goods and provide services. This achieves a scale of economy whereby that particular society can produce increasingly more sophisticated products as well as projects on a larger scale. This is a principle of economics that was as valid a thousand or ten thousand years ago as it is today.

Simple tools limited to copper implements and stone hammers do remove stone, but these tools have never been sufficiently tested in a manner that would convince me that they were the only implements of a civilization as great as that of ancient Egypt. The stone at Abu Rawash, the basalt blocks displaying machine-tool markings, and the perfect pink granite boxes testify to that. They are irrefutable evidence that whoever built these structures had achieved a very advanced degree of skill and knowledge.

Until now, this grand prehistoric civilization, Civilization X, has been denied its legacy. With no other evidence except the structures themselves, the paradox that these structures create has been swept away by a willingness to confuse fact with theory and evidence with the interpretation of the evidence. Opponents to a theory that a sophisticated prehistoric civilization existed claim that since there is no trace of this civilization before 3000 BCE, it simply did not exist.

There are a considerable number of traces left by this civilization, however, from thousands of magnificently carved stone vessels at Sakkara, to the machine-feed lines at Giza and Abu Rawash, to the ancient legends and stories of a civilization that once was. But what happened to this granite civilization remains a puzzle. Any civilization in the past, primitive or otherwise, would have been at the mercy of Nature, celestial and terrestrial, and it is unlikely that whatever caused the mass extinction of mammals at the end of the Ice Age did not also affect human cultures.

TERMINAL PLEISTOCENE EXTINCTION

Terminal Pleistocene extinction is the scientific term for the cataclysm that occurred some ten thousand years ago. We more commonly refer to it simply as the end of the Ice Age; it is synonymous with the disappearance of the wooly mammoth, mastodon, saber-toothed tiger, and many other species. In all, 45 percent of all mammalian species became extinct at this moment in Earth's history.[1]

Professor Frank Hibben, one of the pioneers of American archaeology, who traveled from Arizona to Alaska in search of the first Americans, states bluntly, "The Pleistocene period ended in death."[2] And it wasn't ordinary. It was "catastrophic and all-inclusive."[3] He found evidence for this almost everywhere: Florida, New Jersey, Texas, California, and as far south as Mexico and South America. He compares the evidence of violence found here to scenes of liberated death camps in Nazi Germany: "Such piles of bodies of animals or men simply do not occur by any ordinary natural means."[4]

Siberia and Europe were equally affected. The European rhinoceros and cave bear, as well as the herds of bison and mammoth in Siberia,

Fig. 11.1. Mammoth/mastodon "kill sites" in North America
(from the mammoth site at Hot Springs, South Dakota)

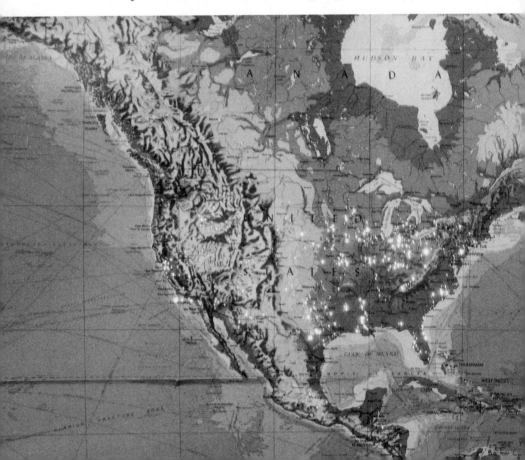

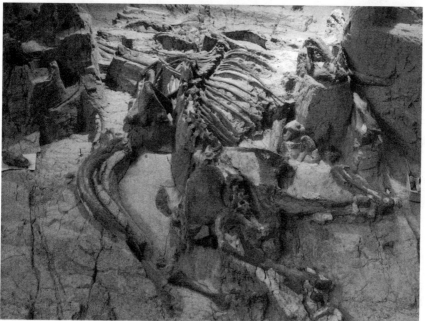

Fig. 11.2 (top). Mammoth "dig" at Hot Springs, South Dakota
Fig. 11.3 (bottom). Full skeleton of a mammoth at
Hot Springs, South Dakota

disappeared forever. The extinction seems to have affected most of the Northern Hemisphere. With regard to the Southern Hemisphere, only some parts of it, as well as Australia, escaped destruction.[5]

North America seems to have been the most affected by this catastrophe. Across the breadth of the United States there are hundreds of mammoth "death sites." They are concentrated mostly in the Midwest, but also exist in the Rocky Mountains, on the Great Plains, and on the West Coast.

In Alaska, the evidence of cataclysmic death is clear. Frozen deposits of soil, rock, and plant and animal remains (known as muck), are common geological features. In many places, writes Hibben, this muck is "packed with animal bones and debris in trainload lot [including] bones of mammoths, mastodons, several kinds of bison, horses, wolves, bears and lions."[6] They met their end in the icy waters of a monumental flash flood.

Hibben also found something unexpected. Within the frozen muck were parts of animals and trees mixed with chunks of ice interlaced with layers of peat moss. According to Hibben, "It looks as though in the midst of some cataclysmic catastrophe of ten thousand years ago the whole Alaskan world of living animals and plants was suddenly frozen in mid-motion like a grim charade. . . . Twisted and torn trees are piled in splintered masses. . . . At least four considerable layers of volcanic ash may be traced in these deposits, although they are extremely warped and distorted."[7]

Although more than three thousand miles away, a similar situation exists in southern California's La Brea tar pits. According to George McCready Price, a large portion of the bones there were discovered "broken, mashed, contorted and mixed in a most heterogeneous mass."[8] More than five hundred species of animals were fossilized in the sticky black tar some eleven thousand years ago. In 1906, after the first season of excavations, more than seven hundred saber-toothed tiger skulls were found. The tiger skulls averaged an amazing twenty per cubic yard.[9] In the tar pits there were actually more bones than tar.

On the other side of the Arctic Circle, mammoths were being killed in the same manner. In 1977, John Massey Stewart estimated that more than half a million tons of mammoth tusks were still buried along Siberia's arctic coastline.[10] In recent times, several dozen frozen mammoth carcasses, such as the Jarkov mammoth, have been found with their flesh still intact.[11] Other mammoths have been found with undigested grass, bluebells, wild beans, and buttercups still in their stomachs.

Whatever catastrophe occurred also affected human cultures. The brilliant painters of the Magdalenian (Cro-Magnon) culture that populated western Europe and were responsible for the beautiful works of cave art found at Pech Merle, Chauvet, and Cussac, among other places, seemingly disappeared around the same time as the mammoths and mastodons. Their successors, known as the Azilian culture, appear later as scattered communities peppering the land. Whatever happened at the end of the Ice Age, human cultures were certainly affected.

BIRTH OF A NEW AGE

How mankind fared during this period of mass extinction has been as much a mystery as why the world's climate changed so abruptly. What seems apparent, though, is that as soon as the climate stabilized, people began gathering wild cereals and established permanent agricultural settlements. This was particularly the case in the Levant and eastern and central Anatolia (Turkey), where some villages housed up to ten thousand occupants. In Turkey there were approximately thirty major villages.[12]

During the twelfth to the tenth millennia BCE the Natufians, named from the Wadi en-Natuf just north of Jerusalem, were the first to build permanent villages and farms.[13] They were of slender build with a dolichocephalic (oblong) cranium. For clothes they wore animal skins and lived in caves or on hilltops close to freshwater springs. As artisans they left an unprecedented quantity of bone implements and stone artifacts. They also made ornaments from a variety of materials, exotic as well as common.[14] Interestingly, they were also the founders of Jericho, the first known city, established sometime around 10,000 BCE.

Jericho is well known from the biblical tale of military conquest; its ruins lie in an oasis of the Jordan Valley, north of the Dead Sea. Excavations reveal almost continuous occupation from its establishment in 10,000 BCE to 1580 BCE. Between 8300 and 7300 BCE, Jericho's occupants built circular brick houses surrounded by a perimeter wall and a stone tower west of the city, complete with an internal stairway. Rectangular houses with plaster floors and walls were added later. By the sixth millennium BCE Jericho's inhabitants had domesticated sheep and were cultivating a variety of plants.

Sometime during the middle of the seventh millennium BCE another city sprang up east of the Carsamba River on Turkey's Anatolia Plain; it was called Çatalhüyük. Nearly twice the size of Jericho, at one time Çatalhüyük housed a population close to ten thousand people in an astonishing network of dwellings similar to a Taos Pueblo village in the southwest United States or a Dogon village in Mali, West Africa.[15] Built from mud brick and wood, one house stood alongside a neighboring house in condominium fashion.

Each self-sufficient house had an entrance provided by a hole in the roof. Dwellings contained a living room, kitchen, storage room, and a fourth area believed to have been a shrine. Kitchens used nearly one-third of the available floor space and were equipped with small, hearth-style ovens set into the walls. Plaited baskets for grains, tools, and other supplies were also found in the storage rooms near the kitchen. Inside the house, ceilings were made of clay pressed into reeds, and windows were set at the top of walls near the roof. Floors were created from a lime-based plaster and covered with woven reed mats. Plaster walls were painted with designs in white, red, yellow, and black. Benches and small niches were built along the walls for sitting and sleeping.

Like the inhabitants of Jericho, the people of Çatalhüyük engaged in the domestication of plants such as barley and wheat and animals such as swine, sheep, and cattle. An amazing number of personal items— things you would find in any modern household—were also found at Çatalhüyük. Glasslike rock from a nearby volcano was used to craft mirrors. Wood was used to make boxes, bowls, platters, cups, and spatulas. Animal bones were crafted into needles, plastering tools, cups, spoons, spatulas, fishhooks, hammers, and handles for blades. Baskets, woven in spiral fashion, were made of straw, as were mats for floor coverings. Clay was used for making pots. Numerous clay balls, both large and small, were also unearthed; most likely they were a heat-transfer device used in cooking.

There is little doubt that domestic life as we recognize it was fully developed. Accessories and articles of personal adornment suggest a high degree of sophistication. Some items appear to be toggles, belt buckles,

rings, stone and clay beads, bone pendants, beads for anklets, and bracelets. An exceptional flint dagger with a decorative bone handle was found
as well. There is also evidence of textile manufacturing with wool or flax,
as well as a trading network with other villages in the region. Anatolian
trade goods have been found throughout the Middle East. Thus,
Çatalhüyük must have been a hub for the commercial trading of obsidian, textiles, skins, food, and even technology. Stamp seals were found of
various designs, possibly used to decorate fabric or walls, but they may
also have been used to stamp exported products indicating that they were
made in Çatalhüyük.

One of the relatively unknown aspects of Çatalhüyük and Jericho is
the mortar they mixed for construction. According to materials scientist
Joseph Davidovits, the mortar was high quality:

> The oldest known remains of high-quality cement are found in the
> ruins of Jericho in the Jordan valley. They date from 9,000 years
> ago. We know that white lime vessels, based on the synthesis of zeo-
> lites, were produced in Tel-Ramad, Syria, 8,000 years ago. Mortar
> from this era has also survived from Catal Hujuk, Turkey. The exis-
> tence of these ancient products suggests that the earliest stonemak-
> ing technology migrated into Egypt.[16]

During the middle of the fifth millennium BCE, however, Çatalhüyük
was abandoned for reasons unknown, and the farming culture of Anatolia
left no mark on any other cultures of that time. Whether the inhabitants of Çatalhüyük migrated south into Africa is unknown. It would be
another two thousand years before Sumer and Egypt established civilizations in their respective regions.

Why these towns in the Near East quickly developed after the end
of the Ice Age is a fascinating question. A consensus of the historical
disciplines assumes that the change in climate at the end of the Ice Age
spurred the invention of agriculture and animal domestication, and from
the archaeological record this appears to be the case. Why did it happen
first in Anatolia and the Levant as opposed to other places?

One explanation is that this area suffered the least in the changing global climate, so those who survived were better equipped with

manpower and knowledge to forge a new life. Another explanation is that the regions of Anatolia and the Levant were the heart of whatever civilization existed prior to the end of the Ice Age, and that the towns springing up in these regions were attempting to restore some rudimentary means of civil order. Wouldn't it be a logical act of the survivors to immediately band together in townlike fashion?

WHAT CAUSED THE MASS EXTINCTION?

The five previous extinctions in Earth's history are well researched, but the mass extinction that occurred at the end of the Ice Age is not so well understood. The mass extinction of large mammalian species is fact, but the cataclysm is a phantom. Theoretical events that brought about the end of the Ice Age and mass extinction range from the sensational, such as an upheaval in Earth's crust, to the mundane, like a gradual climate change resulting from a change in Earth's orbit.

But something was missing in all these theories, and it would take space technology to put a finger on it.

In 1967, the United States military deployed a number of satellites to monitor the Soviet Union and its adherence to the 1963 Nuclear Test Ban Treaty, but the evidence they gathered was not what was expected. The satellites discovered cosmic rays, gamma-ray bursts—the most lethal source of radiation known to humanity. According to the data, the source for these gamma-ray bursts appeared to be nearly everywhere outside our galaxy. At first, colliding neutron stars were suspected; later supernovae, which emitted more energy in their last few seconds of life than in their entire previous existence, also became a suspect. Whatever the source, a concentrated amount of these cosmic rays would to be lethal for us and our planet.

More than thirty years later, on August 27, 1998, NASA's Ulysses spacecraft, armed with high-energy radiation detectors, registered a gamma-ray burst from a star named SGR1900+14, located in our own galaxy in the constellation Aquila, twenty thousand light-years away. At the time, it was the most powerful wave of gamma radiation observed from this type of star, from near zero to several thousand electrons per second. The burst was extraordinary. It was estimated that in a few seconds the Aquila explosion released as much energy as our sun would release in 300 years.

Astronomers named this type of superlarge starburst a magnetar. So dense is a magnetar that immediately before it explodes, its magnetic field becomes nearly a thousand trillion times stronger than Earth's magnetic field. These superstars are so intense that they emit a steady stream of x-rays peppered by brief but powerful bursts of gamma rays, and an intense occasional flare.[17]

Cosmic rays (high-energy gamma rays) are not visible, and in general are deflected by Earth's magnetic field. But according to NASA, a sufficiently intense gamma-ray burst originating in our galaxy within six thousand light-years of Earth would be cataclysmic, a likely catalyst for mass extinction.[18] Gamma rays interacting with the atmosphere would burn away the ozone layer, the outer layer of Earth's protection. Although the atmosphere below the ozone layer would soak up most of the gamma rays, the nitrogen and oxygen molecules in the air would break up into a poisonous brew of nitrogen oxides, particularly nitrogen dioxide.[19]

Deadly ultraviolet radiation would reach the surface and lead to a widespread outbreak of disease and cancer. Some scientists, such as Arnon Dar, Ari Laor, and Nir Shaviv of the Israel Institute of Technology, theorize that these lethal fluxes of atmospheric particles, called muons, would destroy the ozone layer and make the environment radioactive. They would also cause birth defects from mutated DNA in the children of those who survived the cataclysm.[20]

According to Dar, after a supernova's initial burst, some of the ejected material would fall back into its core, generating a hyperdense neutron star. An accretion disk (a swirling disk of matter) would then develop around the exploded star. Whatever material fell back into the star would be hurled into space in the opposite direction of the star's rotation. As the ejected matter overtook the material from the initial explosion, a gamma-ray burst would be generated. Dar refers to this scenario as the "cannon ball" model and claims there is a growing body of direct and indirect evidence to support its occurrence.[21] According to University of Kansas astrophysicist Adrian Melott, there is paleontological evidence that a gamma-ray burst in our galaxy occurred at the end of the Ordovician period 443 million years ago, bringing to Earth a mass extinction of animal life. The Ordovician extinction is one of five major extinctions that have occurred in the past 500 million years.

Could it have happened since the Ordovician extinction? A University of Hawaii particle astrophysicist thinks so. According to Professor John G. Learned, gamma-ray bursts occur on average every one hundred to three hundred million years. Astronomers have also discovered that gamma-ray emissions can originate at the center of galaxies. In 2000, astronomers from Cambridge University and the Joint Astronomy Centre in Hawaii created the most detailed map to date of our galaxy's center. Vast, dense clouds of gas and giant streams of energy serve as a womb for the birth of stars. There is also a wide network of wispy filaments and other strange structures formed by the intense stellar winds and magnetic fields. And at the very center of the core there lies a monster known as Sagittarius A*, the remnants of an explosion one hundred times more powerful than a supernova. Astronomers have dubbed this ultrasuper explosion a "hypernova." Although no one knows for sure what Sagittarius A* is, it is believed by some astronomers to be a supermassive black hole.[22]

Although it is yet to be proven that a single galaxy has a black hole at its center, the possible number of galaxies that might contain a black hole is on the rise. Some galactic cores emit vast energies and are much brighter than others. These high-energy galaxies are said to have an "active galactic core" and thus are labeled as active galaxies.

Active galaxies are believed to have a supermassive black hole at their core that hurls tremendous jets of energy into space, and through the production of a black hole, gamma-ray bursts are created. When a large star explodes, its core collapses and a black hole forms; the explosion sends a blast wave through the body of the star. When the blast wave collides with material within the star's body, gamma rays are created and burst out from the star's surface in front of the blast wave. The blast wave and its cache of stellar material then rockets through space at near the speed of light. As it travels it collides with gas and dust and emits even more photons, which results in an "afterglow" that has a distinct blue color.

Our galaxy is inactive, but if it ever became active through the creation of a newly formed hypernova, its telltale sign would be ominous. Cosmic rays emitted from the core as a superwave would be visible as a large blue star in the night sky.[23] A thousand times brighter than the brightest star in the sky, it would be unmistakable and a warning of impending doom.

THE CARBON-14 ANOMALY

If a galactic core burst had sent gamma radiation speeding through our galaxy at some time in the past, it would have affected the biology of our planet and left its fingerprint as part of the archaeological record. This fingerprint would appear through the release of neutrons, which would dramatically increase the amount of carbon-14 in the atmosphere. In turn, excess carbon-14 would show up in biological remains like wood and bone, as well as other organic material from that period.

Carbon-14 is created when the reaction of cosmic rays with the ionosphere precipitates neutrons through the atmosphere. These neutrons react with nitrogen-14, creating carbon-14, which immediately upon creation begins to decay.

Organic material absorbs carbon-14 at a constant rate, and knowing what the level of carbon-14 in an organic entity was before it died, scientists can measure the amount remaining and calculate the entity's age. Apart from normal variations, carbon-14 stays at a constant level in Earth's atmosphere. However, modern nuclear activities have increased the level of carbon-14 in the atmosphere, and subsequently in everything organic.

When Willard F. Libby first discovered radiocarbon dating in 1947, archaeologists and Egyptologists ignored it. They questioned its reliability, as its results did not coincide with the known historical dates of the artifacts being tested.[24] Today, carbon-14 dating is an accepted practice. However, the radiocarbon time scale contains uncertainties, including errors as great as a thousand years. The further back into history carbon-14 researchers went, the larger the discrepancies became. The original assumption on which carbon-14 dating was based is that its level in the atmosphere is the same at all times. Archaeologists and the carbon-dating scientists were, therefore, in contradiction with each other. The archaeologists would not budge. So scientists were forced to reevaluate their findings and search for an accurate method of calibrating carbon-14 to validate its usefulness.

The answer came in the form of tree-ring dating. The tree that eventually provided the means to accomplish this accurate carbon-14 dating was the bristlecone pine of the southwestern United States. As the oldest living tree on Earth, the bristlecone pine enabled scientists to develop the chronology to calibrate carbon dating and adjust the clock. As it turned out, the archaeologists were correct in their dates, and the original carbon-14 results were in error. In some cases, for distant dates, the error was as much as eight hundred years. But this finding had more than one interpretation. Archaeologists may be correct in their historical timeline, or there may have been an unexplained infusion of carbon-14 into the atmosphere at some prehistoric time.

Archaeologist David Wilson summed up the argument this way:

> If present day measurements of the radiocarbon remaining in objects which died in, say, 2500 BCE give a date of 2000 BCE, then there is "too much" carbon-14 left that is not decayed, perhaps it is that there was "too much" carbon-14 in the object originally in 2500 BCE. This is now generally accepted as being the case, but that still leaves the question open as to *why* there was more carbon-14 in the atmosphere and biosphere.[25]

One way to explain the excess carbon-14 is to hypothesize that an immense nuclear explosion occurred sometime prior to 10,000 BCE, releasing vast amounts of neutrons into the atmosphere. This would most assuredly result in an elevation of carbon-14. But, to the best of our knowledge, no civilization with nuclear capabilities existed at any time in the past. The only other way to explain the evidence is by intense cosmic rays from a solar, coronal mass ejection, which in turn might have been triggered by a galactic core burst. Such is the theory proposed by physicist Dr. Paul LaViolette.

According to LaViolette, such a shower of thermal neutrons would have "changed nitrogen in [animal] remains into carbon-14."[26] Any exposed organic matter at the time of the solar conflagration would have been made artificially young, from a chemist's perspective.

Archaeological anomalies appear to support this cosmic-ray scenario. According to nuclear physicist Richard Firestone and archaeologist

William Topping, animal remains found in the northeastern region of North America from the Pleistocene are younger, sometimes by as much as 10,000 years, than what is found in western areas of the country. Some dates are seriously incorrect, such those from the Gainey site in Michigan. Carbon-14 dating places the material at 2,880 years old, where thermoluminescence (TL) dating shows that the item is 12,400 years old. This evidence prompted Firestone and Topping to write an article entitled "Terrestrial Evidence of a Nuclear Catastrophe in Paleoindian Times."[27]

According to the article, North America was bombarded with cosmic particles, with the heaviest concentrations being in the region of the Great Lakes, thereby creating "a catastrophic nuclear irradiation that produced secondary thermal neutrons from cosmic ray interactions." The energy released on this occasion was so great that the atmosphere over the state of Michigan reached 1,832°F (1,000°C) and melted vast amounts of glacier ice. As for animal and plant life, the radiation would have been lethal.[28]

Firestone and Topping have continued their research and theorize that a 6.5-mile-wide comet, possibly resulting from a supernova, exploded over the Midwest 13,000 years ago. Furthermore, they added, "This event was preceded by an intense blast of iron-rich grains that impacted the planet roughly 34,000 years ago."[29] More recently, their theory has been published in the academically prestigious *Nature* magazine.[30]

Two other archaeologists have reported similar dating results. In 1999, Robson Bonnichsen and Richard Will reported in *Ice Age Peoples* that tests of thirteen prehistoric sites in the northeast United States all arrived at carbon-14 dates regarded as being too young for the remains discovered there. According to *Mammoth Trumpet* writer James Chandler, "Many anomalies reported in the upper United States and in Canada cannot be explained by ancient aberrations in the atmosphere or other radiocarbon reservoirs, or by contamination of data samples (a common source of error in radiocarbon dating)."[31]

The editors of *Mammoth Trumpet* were so intrigued by the story that they reprinted Firestone and Topping's article in its entirety. Firestone and Topping's conclusion was that "the only phenomenon capable of creating such imbalances . . . is massive neutron bombardment, probably from a supernova."[32]

Data obtained from polar ice cores also reveal evidence of this cosmic event. During 1981 and 1982, using neutron activation analysis, LaViolette found high levels of iridium and nickel in samples from Greenland ice that were between 35,000 and 73,000 years old. Five years later, glaciologists discovered beryllium-10 isotope peaks in Ice Age polar ice, more evidence that cosmic-ray bombardment was very high on occasion during prehistoric times.

GALACTIC CORE BURST

The core of our galaxy became active around 16,150 years ago and emitted a deadly burst of cosmic radiation, according to LaViolette.[33] Its effects spanned a period lasting several thousand years and triggered vast increases in solar flare activity. Some of these intense coronal mass ejections would have been large enough to temporarily engulf Earth and the moon.[34] For Earth, the consequences were cataclysmic: a sudden increase in temperature, rapid ice-sheet melting, global flooding, and the mass extinction of animal life.

In *Earth Under Fire,* LaViolette paints a detailed, ominous picture of the events for this invisible catastrophe. Whether from a black hole or megastar, the core of our galaxy periodically becomes active and enters an explosive phase, generating a burst of cosmic radiation. According to LaViolette, our galactic core emits a burst of gamma rays about once every thirteen thousand to twenty-six thousand years.[35] This cosmic superwave of energy travels out from the galactic core at close to the speed of light, and on its 23,000-light-year journey toward Earth, it beams a blue light.

When the cosmic rays reach the outer shell of the solar system (the magnetic-field shield from solar wind generated by the sun), a luminous filament of weblike structures emanates from the blue star. According to LaViolette, a shockwave would then form, producing a gravity wave traveling ahead of the cosmic superwave. Electrons of the superwave would become trapped and vaporize the ice of the Oort Cloud.* The shockwave would then push dust and gas from the Oort Cloud into the inner

---

*The Oort Cloud is a spherical cloud of comets and debris in which our solar system exists.

regions of the solar system and alter the levels of solar radiation reaching the planets.

The immediate effect on Earth would be the arrival of an electromagnetic pulse (EMP). Shortly afterward, a large gravity wave would move through Earth, pulling the planet at its seams (tectonic plates), resulting in a rash of earthquakes. Darkness would follow as cosmic dust and debris from the outer shell of the solar system reached the inner planets. In the dust, the sun would react violently and behave like a T-Tauri star, emitting excess x-rays and ultraviolet and infrared radiation.[36] Solar flares would also result and would increase the sun's brightness.

Over time, the cumulative effects on Earth's climate would be devastating. Dust filling the solar system would reflect radiation back to Earth, and in effect create a "hothouse." The gaseous clouds surrounding the galactic core would become luminous from the cosmic radiation and form an oval shroud around the blue star. For those on Earth, this would appear to be a blue eye in the sky—the eye of Ra, a sign of cosmic punishment. Those who survived the radiation burst would suffer through devastating environmental changes. People living in coastal areas would suffer from destructive floods. But more importantly, with the intense heat, weather patterns would become unpredictable, and the air would become toxic as nitrogen and oxygen broke down into brown smog. Famine would be the number-one killer. Only people who were fortunate enough to be near clean water and a ready supply of food would be able to survive.

Other independent evidence appears to support LaViolette's theory. In 1977, after studying moon rocks, NASA astronomers published an article entitled "Solar Flare Activity: Evidence for Large-scale Changes in the Past." Their conclusion was that prior to ten thousand years ago, solar flare activity must have varied by as many as fifty times more than what it has been in the last ten thousand years. Although the NASA astronomers qualified their theory somewhat, they were confident that "the conclusion nevertheless remains the present 'best' explanation for the observed data trends."[37]

Herbert Zook, a NASA physicist for the Johnson Space Center, appeared in the documentary *Earth Under Fire* in support of LaViolette's theory. He concluded "that there is rather good evidence that the sun was more active, possibly much more active, 10,000 to 20,000 years ago."[38]

THE GEMINGA SUPERNOVA

Nine years after the publication of *Earth Under Fire,* scientists Richard Firestone, Allen West, and Simon Warwick-Smith published findings in general agreement with LaViolette's theory, with one important distinction: the source of radiation was the Geminga supernova, as opposed to a galactic core burst. Backed by years of study, the detailed geological and archaeological evidence described in *The Cycle of Cosmic Catastrophes* tells of a sequence of events beginning in 41,000 BCE and culminating in 13,000 BCE; according to the authors, these were responsible for Earth's last great extinctions.

Today, at five hundred light-years away, the Geminga pulsar is the closest pulsar to Earth. However, forty-one thousand years ago it was much closer, a mere 150 light years away. Furthermore, at that time the pulsar was an ordinary star. Unfortunately for us, it was at the end of its life. Geminga became a supernova and sent out a burst of radiation that set off a series of events that affected our planet for the next thirty thousand years.[39]

This burst of radiation directly impacted the eastern portions of the southern hemisphere, eliciting widespread extinctions in Australia and Southeast Asia. For ten seconds, plant and animal life exposed at the surface was irradiated by dangerous levels of gamma rays. In those areas, the human race was decimated. For those alive at the time, the flash from the Geminga supernova was bright enough to be a second sun during the day or another moon at night. For six months Earth had two suns. Over a period of many years, the supernova's luminescence gradually faded until it was no longer visible.

Whoever survived the initial burst of radiation was subject to plummeting temperatures and unstable weather. The dead and dying vegetation served as kindling for devastating fires ignited by frequent lightning strikes. Aside from the excess ozone created by the flood of radiation, nitrates in the atmosphere made a poisonous brew.[40] (See plate 41 of the color insert.)

The shock wave from Geminga's explosion finally reached Earth thirty-four thousand years ago, bringing with it more radiation and bombarding Earth with small ions and particles as well as comets and asteroids. It was so powerful it nearly reversed Earth's magnetic field. Then, a second shock wave struck Earth sixteen thousand years ago and brought with it another round of radiation, comets, and asteroids. The most devastating effects of the Geminga supernova, however, arrived thirteen thousand years ago.

From the Oort Cloud, the outer shell of our solar system, the blast wave from Geminga pushed a vast amount of dust, debris, and ice into the core of the solar system. Some of the debris hit the sun, touching off a series of large solar flares. A large comet, traveling at thousands of miles per hour, entered Earth's atmosphere just above Lake Michigan and impacted the ice sheet.[41]

The impact of the comet ejected a vast amount of rock and ice across the Northern Hemisphere, creating a starburst of craters from the Carolinas to Texas and the West Coast. The impact of ejected rock triggered earthquakes and volcanic eruptions as well as intense firestorms on a monstrous scale. In northern climes, heat from the impacts vaporized hundreds of thousands of cubic miles of ice and collapsed various regions of the glacial ice sheet. The rapidly melting ice quickly inundated coastlines, while trapped water surged below the ice, creating unique land formations called drumlins. The rain of exploding rock also triggered massive underwater slides, which produced enormous tsunamis that bombarded the Atlantic coast and released trapped methane gas from the ocean's floor.[42]

The cascading effect of the comet impact devastated the climate, and for more than one thousand years, Earth returned to Ice Age–like conditions. Scientists refer to this period as the Younger Dryas. Rain and snow fell for weeks. Wildfires pumped untold amounts of carbon dioxide into the atmosphere. The cold water that was dumped into the North Atlantic stopped the climate-warming ocean currents. And the vaporized water and rock created thick clouds that covered Earth for many years.

It was the "nuclear winter" that the generation of the 1980s was so afraid of. The darkness and cold temperatures, along with fire, destroyed nearly all of the plant life in the northern hemisphere. With little to eat, the surviving animals faced starvation during the next few months. As a result, animal and human life was also destroyed. The most unfortunate species were those with large bodies; they became extinct. The biological void created allowed disaster species to flourish. In the standing water left behind, algae grew exponentially and left a black mat of decay over the ground.[43]

Europe and North Africa were similarly affected. Drawing on the meteorite database in London's National History Museum, Firestone, West, and Warwick-Smith mapped the locations of 3,411 European, African, and Middle Eastern meteorite impacts.[44]

The carbon-14 anomaly had been solved. Something caused a considerable increase in radiocarbon in the atmosphere forty-one thousand years ago. With its gamma rays, cosmic rays, and neutrinos, nothing could be more potent than a nearby supernova.

REMEMBERING HISTORY AS MYTH

Whether due to a galactic core burst or a nearby supernova, the catastrophic events described above answer a number of historical questions and enigmas, particularly having to do with various myths of mankind's decimation, such as the Eye of Ra, the Epic of Gilgamesh, Noah's Flood, and Deucalion's Flood. These events also offer a plausible answer to the ancient tradition of separating the ages into post- and antediluvian. As well, they provide a possible explanation for the mass extinctions and sudden global warming at the end of the Ice Age, as well as a potential rationale for the enigmatic and anachronistic structures of Egypt's granite civilization.

A previously unidentified civilization that I refer to as Civilization X existed before the end of the Ice Age. It had the technical know-how to build on an extraordinary scale with limestone and granite, and to build with the precision of modern manufacturing. Not only did the people of this civilization build with skill, they also built with purpose the network of energized pyramids that fertilized their fields. The existence of such a civilization explains the evidence of the magnificently carved granite statues of Thebes, Memphis, and Tanis and the monumental pyramids that line the west bank of the Nile in Lower Egypt. It also explains the stone at Abu Rawash, which Christopher Dunn believes is the waste material of a casing stone created by a circular power saw.

The most fascinating aspect in this detective story of Earth history and our history is that the survivors of this civilization would never forget the celestial changes that brought about disaster, because the glow of the galactic core, the blue star, would have been visible for some time.

And when the cosmic superwave made its way past the outer rim of the galactic core, dense gas clouds created a luminous oval around the blue star. In the night sky, it really would look like an eye, the Eye of Ra. And as we have noted earlier, in the daytime it would appear as a second sun in size and brightness.[45] This sight of this blue eye would have been incredible. The entire eye would have been thirty-two times the size of the sun, and the eye's pupil would have been four times the size of the sun.[46]

In this striking passage from an ancient Egyptian incantation, we can clearly connect the metaphorical to the literal, the Eye of Ra to the blue glow of radiation:

> Great will be your power and mighty your majesty over the bodies of your enemies. They will fall howling on their faces, all mankind will cringe beneath you and your might, they will respect you when they behold you in that vigorous form which the Master of the Primeval Gods gave you. . . .
>
> Look . . . O Primeval Ancestors! upon this spirit who comes today, taking the form of a beam of light, coming from the Isle of Fire. . . .
>
> "I have to raise my hand to shade myself, for fear of the fire of her mouth," says one of the elder gods.
>
> "Behold it [the Eye] will be stronger than all the gods,
> It has mastered the dwellers at the ends of the Earth,
> it is sovereign over every god."
>
> . . . No one will come who can withstand me, except Atum, for it was he who originally moved and put me before him so that I could wield power and throw out my heat.[47]

Considering the impact that such an event would have had on civilization, along with an illumination of the galactic core, no wonder it inspired ancient myths about mankind being punished by the cosmic Eye of Ra. No wonder the survivors systematically removed Hathor's face from her temple residence, as Amelia Edwards describes:

It is not without something like a shock that one first sees the unsightly havoc wrought upon the Hathor-headed columns of the facade at Denderah. The massive folds of the head-gear are there; the ears, erect and pointed like those of a heifer, are there but of the benignant face of the goddess not a feature remains. [Even on the ceiling] every accessible human face, however small, has been laboriously mutilated.[48]

On the ceiling of the temple at Denderah there is a beautifully carved zodiac presenting the Egyptian constellations in a polar projection format. The symbols for the constellations are symmetrically oriented around the celestial polar axis, and the zodiac symbols around the ecliptic pole. What is interesting about this zodiac carving is that the summer solstice is oriented to true north, and the spring and autumnal equinoxes are oriented due east and west.

According to LaViolette, the carving's depiction of polar displacement (a result of precession) and its appropriate orientation relative to true north suggest that whoever designed the relief understood astronomical principles and was using the precession of the equinoxes to indicate the key date of 13,687 BCE, give or take twenty years.[49]

Consequently, the Denderah zodiac is much more than an artistic display of the zodiac and its constellations. It is a map pointing to a specific date more than fifteen thousand years ago. Interestingly, a special hieroglyph designates this key date by being positioned on the celestial equator close to the summer solstice transect. The marker is, of course, Hathor, the cow of Isis, adorned with a star.

LaViolette also points out the uniqueness of the ancient zodiac signs. Sagittarius and Scorpio are the only signs in the zodiac depicted with arrows. For Sagittarius, it is the arrow of the archer, and for Scorpio, the arrow of the scorpion is its tail. Sagittarius and Scorpio are also adjacent to each other as if intentionally pointing at the galactic center. Today they miss the galactic center by 2.5 degrees of longitude. However, 15,870 years ago, they pointed directly toward the center of the galaxy.[50] Ironically, this division between post- and pre-catastrophe is strikingly close to the time when the Shemsu-Hor (the Followers of Horus) began their reign in Egypt in 14,800 BCE.

Could it be that Egypt's mythical period when the gods reigned is in reference to a dim memory of a great civilization, and that the Shemsu-Hor are the survivors of the cataclysm that ended the Ice Age? Perhaps this is the essence of the tale that the priests of Sais told Solon, and the same one that Plato spun into a story of morality and Nature's wrath.

12

A CASE FOR
CIVILIZATION X

There shall come in the latter end of the days scoffers,
according to their own desires going on, and saying,
"Where is the promise of his presence? For since the fathers
did fall asleep, all things so remain from the beginning
of the creation"; *for this is unobserved by them willingly,*
that the heavens were of old, and the earth out of water
and through water standing together by the word of God,
through which the then world, by water having been
deluged, was destroyed. [author's emphasis]

2 PETER 3:3–6, YOUNG'S LITERAL TRANSLATION

History has only two perspectives: that of those who lived it and that of
those who did not. Those who lived it know the events to be fact. Those
who did not are reliant on those who did for an accurate portrayal of past
events. Such is the flow of information from generation to generation,
and with each successive generation the details of the story might change,
given the subjective nature of storytelling.

History is a story and will always be a story. It cannot be tested in
a laboratory and will never be scientific fact. History requires facts, but
even more, it requires eyewitness testimony to explain what happened.

Those who deny our earliest history—mankind's earliest history—and substitute a fabrication according to their own interpretation of the evidence perform a great disservice not only to society but to the children they love and cherish. History is much more than a set of events, dates, and places. History is our identity as well as our destiny. Those who forget it fall prey to repeating it. Without memory (history), there is no self-awareness or self-perception. There is no learning, language, or knowledge. Life is reduced to the simple biological desire of the moment.

We do a great disservice to society and to our children when we claim that the myths and mythology of our ancient ancestors are primitive and superstitious, a fabrication to explain "why things are." In the post-apocalyptic world of 10,000 BCE there would be little room for pen and paper, or books and libraries. The truth of what happened—the history at that time—would have to be disseminated as a story. Thus, stories and legends about the Great World Fire and the Great Flood were remembered in almost every ancient culture. Over time, however, memories faded, and the storytelling eventually stopped. What was once an oral history became the fantasies and fables of a primitive people.

HISTORY'S EGYPTIAN FRINGE

Written records before 2000 BCE are rare, and there are no written historical records prior to 3000 BCE to help explain any human events that may have occurred at the time of the terminal Pleistocene extinction. There is history, though, that has been remembered and later written down—the ancient Egyptian's kings' list, for example. This list is a written record of all of Egypt's past rulers according to *their* history, a history that reaches forty thousand years into the past.

For Egypt's post-apocalyptic generations, only a dim memory existed of their ancestors' grand civilization. Thousands of years later, all the great achievements of this grand civilization were attributed to "the gods." The survivors of this ancient civilization would have carried forward that civilization's culture as best they could. The Shemsu-Hor, the Followers of Horus, with the knowledge and skill that had been passed down to them, would have been viewed as a ruling class, a dynastic race, whether they were in fact a ruling class or not.

Diodoros of Sicily reports history in a similar manner. According to several chroniclers, gods and heroes originally ruled Egypt for 18,000 years. Afterward, mortal kings governed for 15,000 years, bringing the length of Egyptian history to 33,000 years. Manetho attributes 15,150 years to prehistoric divine dynasties and 9,777 years to the kings reigning before Menes, for a total of 24,927 years.

According to E. A. Wallis Budge in *A History of Egypt,* George the Syncellus claimed that the Egyptians possessed a tablet they referred to as an ancient chronicle. It mentioned thirty royal dynasties after the reign of the gods, which comprised a period of twenty-five Sothic cycles, which is 36,525 years, one Sothic cycle being 1,461 years.[1] Herodotus also mentions a long history for ancient Egypt in that, on four separate occasions, "the sun moved from his wonted course, twice rising where he now sets, and twice setting where he now rises."[2] Herodotus says that according to the Egyptians priests, from the current King Hephaistos to the first king of Egypt there had been 341 generations of human beings. And since 300 generations are equal to 10,000 years (given that 100 years is three human generations), 11,340 years have passed from the first king to Hephaistos. During that time, the Egyptians said, "there had arisen no god in human form; nor even before that time or afterwards among the remaining kings who arise in Egypt."[3]

Herodotus was taken by the priests to a great temple and shown colossal wooden statues representing 345 men who served as chief priests during the 341 generations of kings. Each statue was a son succeeding his father. The priest, going from image to image, told Herodotus their names until he had reached the one who had died last.[4]

The Egyptian priests also claimed:

> In this time they said that the sun had moved four times from his accustomed place of rising, and where he now sets he had thence twice had his rising, and in the place from whence he now rises he had twice had his setting; and in the meantime nothing in Egypt had been changed from its usual state, neither that which comes from the earth nor that which comes to them from the river nor that which concerns diseases or deaths.[5]

Thus, according to the ancient Egyptians' records, the spring equinox had twice been located in the constellation of Aries, and it also passed twice in the opposing constellation of Libra. In other words, one-and-a-half precessional cycles occurred during all of ancient Egypt's historic and prehistoric periods, approximately thirty-nine thousand years.[6]

Manetho articulated the same historical information that the Palermo Stone* and Turin Papyrus† recorded. According to Herodotus (before the reign of kings that the priest spoke of), "Before these men they [the priests] said that gods were the rulers in Egypt."[7] Although Egyptologists today would surely object to a history of Egypt that dates far into prehistory, earlier finds by archaeologists appear to corroborate such antiquity.

University of Southern California Professor Walter Wallbank, the 1951 winner of the Watumull Prize for *India in the New Era,* wrote in his world history textbook coauthored with Alastair Taylor:

Artifacts have been discovered in Egyptian tombs that go back as far as 15,000 BCE. These remains show that the early Egyptians passed through the main divisions of the Old and New Stone Ages and had even begun to use copper for tools before the time of the Old Kingdom. Progress was apparently rapid, and soon people lived in crude houses, had weapons of flint and copper, and engaged in agriculture. Examinations of grain and husks found in the stomachs of corpses in ancient tombs has shown that as early as 10,000 BCE the ancient Egyptians had developed superior strains of barley seed which could be easily cultivated and which produced heavy yields. The earliest Egyptians, whose race has not yet been conclusively ascertained, wore linen garments and were especially remarkable for their artistic skill, particularly in pottery. Their polished red-and-black ware was never surpassed by their descendents, even in the periods of highest Egyptian accomplishments.[8]

---

*The Palermo Stone is a large fragment of a stela known as the Royal Annals of the Old Kingdom of ancient Egypt and contains records of the kings of Egypt from the first to the fifth dynasty.

†The Turin Papyrus is an ancient Egyptian map from approximately 1160 BCE. It is generally considered to be the oldest surviving map of topographical interest from the ancient world.

The textbook in which this section of text appears, *Civilization: Past and Present,* is still published today, although probably, in its current edition, it does not include claims that grain and husks found in Egyptian corpses date to Paleolithic times. Yet such a claim is consistent with the ancient Egyptians' documented history.

To explain Egyptian history and reconcile it with evidence of a megalithic granite civilization, a logical conclusion is that the Egyptian Followers of Horus reoccupied the buildings that their ancestors erected and attempted to continue a post-apocalyptic civilization. Although they gradually lost their skills, early on, with the catastrophe fresh in their minds, wouldn't such a powerful and advanced civilization leave a permanent record for its posterity? The carver of Mount Rushmore left a permanent record, without the threat of impending cataclysm. Not only did he carve the gargantuan granite faces of Washington, Jefferson, Lincoln, and Roosevelt, he also created a Hall of Records behind the mountain. According to geologists, Mount Rushmore will outlast all other structures and should be visibly intact for the next two hundred thousand years.

Could there be an Egyptian Hall of Records?

In one of his "readings," psychic Edgar Cayce claimed there was, underneath one of the front paws of the Sphinx. Although the area under the Sphinx has never been excavated, according to Robert Schoch's 1991 seismic survey, there is a rectangular chamber underneath the front paws. Whether we will ever know depends on the Egyptian Supreme Council of Antiquities. Nevertheless, there may have been more than one Hall of Records.

The Gulf of Egypt

The ancient Egyptian kings' list and anecdotal evidence from ancient historians is not easily dismissable. During prehistoric times the landscape of northern Egypt was very different than it is today. According to Herodotus, the Egyptians told him that at one time the land north of Memphis formed a gulf of the Mediterranean Sea, lying between the two ranges of hills. From his own observations at the time, he was convinced this was true, for the land of Egypt "projects into the sea beyond the coast on either side; I have seen shells on the hills and noticed how salt exudes from the soil to such an extent that it affects even the pyramids."[9]

In 1737, Danish explorer and naval captain Frederick Louis Norden was sent to Egypt by the king of Denmark and traveled down the Nile into Nubia. After his death in 1742 his notes from Egypt were published in French, *Voyage d'Egypte et de Nubie* (Copenhagen, 1755), and soon afterward in English. According to Norden, at the time he visited Giza there were still a great number of shells on the plateau as well as petrified oysters. He also commented that seashells were attached to the pyramid, implying that the pyramids originally or at one time were sitting in the sea.[10]

The formation of the Nile River began around 120,000 years ago. At that time northern Africa received substantial rainfall and was endowed with rivers and lakes. The White Nile was the Nile's primary source of water. Rivers and streams in the Ugandan highlands flowed west and drained into the Atlantic Ocean. The current source of the Nile, Lake Victoria, did not exist before 10,000 BCE. Recent uplift because of tectonic forces gave the lake its altitude and enabled its flow into the Nile River.[11]

Giza's Fourth Pyramid

Norden also wrote that there was a fourth pyramid on the Giza Plateau, one built of black stone. According to Norden, this black pyramid was one hundred feet farther to the west than the third pyramid. It was closed and without any casing stones. It resembled the others, but it lacked a temple. Up to its middle, this pyramid was composed of stone that was blacker than common granite, and at its summit was a single large stone, a cube, which, according to Norden, appears to have been a pedestal. From the middle to the summit the builders used a yellowish stone. Unlike the other three pyramids, this black pyramid was built more to the west so as to be in line with the Great Pyramid and the middle pyramid. Norden writes:

> These four great pyramids are surrounded by a number of others that are smaller. To the west of the first pyramid, we find a great number of others, but all likewise ruined. Opposite the second pyramid, there are five or six of them, which have all been opened, and in one, I have observed a square well, thirty feet deep.[12]

According to Budge in *A History of Egypt,* Strabo also testifies to the existence of a pyramid built with black stone:

> At the distance of forty stadia from Memphis is a brow of a hill, on which are many pyramids, the tombs of the kings. Three of them are quite large. Two of them are reckoned among the "Seven Wonders of the World." They are a stadium in height, and of a quadrangular shape. Their height somewhat exceeds the length of each of the sides. One pyramid is a little larger than the other. At a moderate height in one of the sides is a stone, which may be taken out; when that is removed, there is an oblique passage [leading] to the tomb. These two pyramids are near each other, and on the same level. Farther on, at a greater height of the mountain [hill], is the third pyramid, which is much less than the two others, but constructed at much greater expense; from the foundation nearly as far as the middle, *it is built of black stone.*[13]

There are additional accounts of Giza's Black Pyramid. According to Tony Bushby in *The Secret in the Bible,* the Maori of New Zealand have a book explaining the pyramids and the black pyramid. In 1926, a series of interviews with a Maori elder permanently recorded the story, which was entitled *Sacred Legend;* it was later published in a book called *Maori Symbolism.*

In *Sacred Legend,* the pyramids are said to have been built of concrete blocks made from an aggregate of sand, solid mud, rushes, and reeds.[14] Ironically, such a statement has its modern-day supporter in Joseph Davidovits,* whose 1986 theory put forth in *The Pyramids: An Enigma Solved* claims to have solved the means by which the pyramids were constructed: with poured concrete blocks.

According to the Arab historian and geographer Muhammed Taki Al Makrizi in his book *Hitat,* in the fourteenth century Arabic and Coptic manuscripts were discovered in a Cairo library, which were possibly the tenth-century writings of the Arab historian Masoudi. Whatever the

---

*Joseph Davidovits is a materials scientist and the discoverer in 1979 of geopolymer chemistry.

case, Al Makrizi's *Hitat* tells the story of an unusual discovery in a Giza pyramid. According to this text, the builder of the "Western Pyramid"— meaning the Black Pyramid—made thirty treasury chambers within the structure and filled them with instruments, picture columns, and precious stone. Also, the ancient text claims, the rooms contained equipment of fine ironlike weapons that do not rust, glass that can be folded without breaking, strange charms and lanterns, various kinds of simple and mixed medicines, and deadly poisons. Corpses of the soothsayers were placed in sarcophagi carved from black granite. Beside each soothsayer lay a book relating all his magical arts, his life's story, and the works he had accomplished.[15]

Masoudi also claims to have seen mechanical statues in the subterranean tunnels of Giza: "I have seen that one does not describe for fear of making people doubt one's intelligence . . . but still I have seen them."[16]

What happened to this Black Pyramid?

According to Bushby, Masonic literature states that in 1759 the pyramid was dismantled by a Scottish faction of the Masons, who were motivated by the possibility of hidden treasure.[17] The black stones were sold to fund the operation. Bushby claims that the square floor of the Black Pyramid can be seen approximately three hundred feet west of the third pyramid, and his book contains an aerial photo of it. If true, the pyramid would have been almost 160 feet tall, with its cube capstone about six feet tall.[18]

The Great Pyramid

Other legends claim that the Great Pyramid was originally painted and inscribed with symbols of some peculiar sort of wisdom. An ancient scroll in the Bodleian Library written by the astronomer/astrologer Abou Balkhi states:

> Two of those [pyramids] exceeded all the rest in height, being 400 cubits high, and as many broad, and as many long. They were built of large blocks of stone, and so well joined together that the joints were scarcely perceptible. Upon the exterior of one structure [The Great Pyramid] was inscribed every charm and wonder of physics.[19]

In 1988, Davidovits analyzed the red coloration from the Great Pyramid's interior stones and corroborated Balkhi's statement. Using a microscope, he inspected two cracks in some of the red coating. One crack was deep and exposed the white limestone underneath. The other crack was very old; it was filled with a substance of red color. This second crack had obviously been painted over. Davidovits commented, "The coating and coloration are truly remarkable alchemical product, showing no blistering or other appreciable deterioration after about 4,500 years."[20]

Masoudi also seems to corroborate the unusual décor of the Great Pyramid. He writes that the celestial spheres were inscribed on the Eastern Pyramid (Great Pyramid), as well as the positions of the stars and their circles. Also included in these inscriptions was the history of past times and of that which is yet to come, and "the fixed stars and what comes about in their progression from one epoch to another . . . and images made of their forefathers' creations."[21]

There are other legends claiming that the upper section of the Great Pyramid was once painted. Early in the nineteenth century, chunks of rusty-colored casing stones were found at the pyramid's base. Analysis at the Sorbonne University in Paris determined that the casing stones had, at one time, been painted with a color made with an iron oxide base, most likely either red or yellow.[22]

Like the Great Pyramid, the Turah limestone quarries, where the rock for the casing stones was cut, show only a hint of their former greatness. Early in the nineteenth century the Turah quarries were once again opened for operation, and within one hundred years modern quarrymen had erased the precision cutting and the systematic removal of stone of its former owners. One man recorded what he had experienced:

> The extraction of stone was carried on with a skill and regularity which denoted ages of experience. The tunnels were so made as to exhaust the finest and whitest seams without waste and the chambers were of an enormous extent; the walls were dressed, the pillars and roofs neatly finished, the passages and doorways made of a regular width, so that the whole presented more the appearance of a subterranean temple than of a place for the extraction of building materials.[23]

The City and the Subway

In Egypt, nearly every site of ancient ruins is accompanied by fields of granite and limestone rubble, and for the past two thousand years these sites have been plundered for their wealth of stone. Almost everyone, I am sure, would like to know to what extent ancient Egyptian civilization had built their cities. We view them more than two thousand years since their demise.

During the thirteenth century an Arab doctor from Baghdad moved to Cairo to teach philosophy and medicine. While in Egypt, the doctor, Abd'el-Latif, recorded in his journal a description of Cairo and its environment. He also visited Giza and surveyed the Sphinx and the Great Pyramid. According to Abd'el-Latif, a considerable amount of ancient stone structures covered the area, so much so that "it requires a half day's march in any direction to cross the visible ruins." Based on the average speed a person can walk in half a day, the area of Giza's ruins was approximately a diameter of twenty-five miles.[24] Eighteenth-century writer Richard Pococke recorded the plundering in his *Travels in Egypt:* "They are every day destroying these fine morsels of Egyptian antiquity, and I saw some of the pillars being hewn into mill-stones."

Herodotus also testifies as an eyewitness to such a magnificent place. He recounts:

> They decided to leave a common memorial of their reigns, and for this purpose constructed a labyrinth a little above Lake Moeris, near the place called the City of Crocodiles. I have seen this building, and it is beyond my power to describe; it must have cost more in labour and money than all the wall and public works of the Greeks put together—though no one would deny that the temples at Ephesus and Samos are remarkable buildings.[25]

He also commented that the pyramids surpassed description, but that the Labyrinth surpassed the pyramids. It had twelve roofed courts, six facing north and six south. A single wall surrounded the entire building, and on the inside there were three thousand chambers, half underground and the other half above ground. Although he didn't descend into the underground, he said of the chambers above ground that they surpassed all human production:

The upper rooms, on the contrary, I did actually see, and it is hard to believe that they are the work of men; the baffling and intricate passages from room to room and from court to court were an endless wonder to me, as we passed a courtyard into rooms, from rooms into galleries, from galleries into more rooms, and thence into yet more courtyards. The roof of every chamber, courtyard, and gallery is, like the walls, of stone. The walls are covered with carved figures, and each court is exquisitely built of white marble and surrounded by a colonnade. Near the corner where the labyrinth ends there is a pyramid, two hundred and forty feet in height, with great carved figures of animals on it and an underground passage by which it can be entered.[26]

The underground chambers, Herodotus was told, contained the sepulchers of the kings who built the Labyrinth, and those of the sacred crocodiles. He was not allowed to see these underground chambers.

In 1935, what were possibly parts of this labyrinth were discovered at Giza by archaeologist Dr. Selim Hassan; they were announced with great fanfare in *The Daily Telegraph*. On Monday, March 4, 1935, the headline stated: "Subway found below the pyramids—New Discoveries in Egypt—Colonnaded Hall in Rock." According to the article, a subway connecting Khephren's Pyramid to Cheops's Pyramid had been discovered in recent excavations. The subway had been cut through living rock. More remarkable still, a shaft 11 yards long was found that led from the subway to the heart of the rock; it ended in a chamber 18 feet by 33 feet. On one side of the chamber there was a second shaft that led down into the rock another 48 feet. This ended in a hall somewhat larger than the upper chamber, which contained seven smaller chambers. In two of them basalt sarcophagi were found. From one of these side chambers a third tunnel ran down another 42 feet into the rock and ended in a colonnaded hall where three more basalt sarcophagi were found. The chamber furthest down, about 195 feet below the causeway, was partly under water and has not been explored.[27]

According to Hassan, the chambers are from the Saitic period, or about 600 BCE. Between the Saitic and Ptolemaic periods, 600 BCE to 200 BCE, the pyramid area was used as a burial ground, and materials from Fourth Dynasty tombs were used for later burials. (Later burials have almost always been discovered above the earlier ones.[28])

London's *Sunday Express* published an article headlined "City of the World's First Queen—The Mystery of the Pyramids—May Be Solved by New Excavations" concerning the same discovery. In the article, by Edward Armytage, a city had been discovered whose existence had not even been suspected and that promised to throw new light on a highly organized civilization that existed four thousand years ago. Armytage also wrote that the discovery might provide the key to the mystery of how the pyramids were built.

For years Egyptian archaeologists have virtually ignored an incomplete pyramid on Giza, regarding it as nothing but a mound of debris. Then Hassan declared that it was undoubtedly the tomb of a ruler. The article also stated that close by the remains of a wonderful city had been unearthed: "The city has a perfect drainage system and other amenities which were not introduced into Europe until 200 years ago!"[29]

According to Bushby, "Archaeologists were bewildered at the city—most beautifully planned—temples, pastel painted peasant dwellings, workshop, stables, other buildings including a palace. This is underneath the plateau and extends eastward."[30] Bushby also asserts that officials falsely claimed that there was no temple adjoining the Sphinx, and that the area around the Sphinx and pyramids had been explored deeply and thoroughly. "On matters outside official policy," Bushby contends, "there appears to be a hidden level of censorship in operation, one designed to protect both Eastern and Western religions."[31]

DENDERAH'S CRYPTS

In chapter 10 we learned that the existing Temple of Hathor at Denderah was rebuilt on the site of a succession of older buildings, the most ancient of which dates back to the Old Kingdom reign of Khufu. According to an inscription discovered by Auguste Mariette (1821–1881) in one of Denderah's crypts, the oldest structure is believed to be the work of the Followers of Horus, who, as we know, were an Egyptian people that predated dynastic Egypt.

At Denderah, perhaps the builders of the original Hathor Temple, the

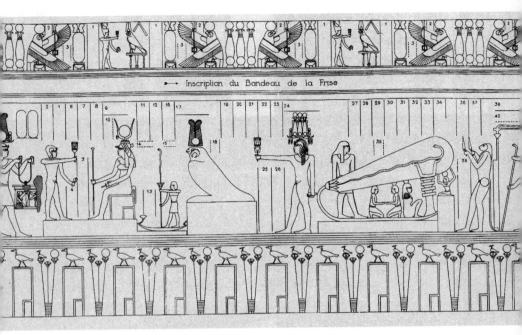

Fig. 12.1. Illustration of the north wall of the southern crypt at Denderah (from Le Temple de Dendara *by Emile Chassinat)*

Followers of Horus, saw fit to bury treasure—not in the form of precious jewelry or golden furniture, but information. Before any structures were ever erected at Denderah, the temple grounds were excavated and subterranean vaults installed. Today, these vaults are known as crypts. Three crypts were created, one for the east, west, and southern exposures of the main temple. Only the southern crypt is open to the public. The other two crypts are restricted, and public access is denied.

Accessing the southern crypt is not easy. There is no designed formal entranceway. There is only a square hole in the floor, as if a floor block was never installed, or was removed by some explorer long ago. Access to the southern crypt is through a three-foot-square opening. Inside, the crypt is equally narrow and appears more like a hall than a room. All of its walls are carved in relief and adorned with murals. Unlike the mural of Hathor carved into the temple ceiling, the crypt murals contain mysterious life-sized figures of men and women.

One of the more notable murals is the now-famous "Denderah light

Fig. 12.2. Illustration of the south wall of the southern crypt at Denderah (from Le Temple de Dendara *by Emile Chassinat)*

bulbs." The strange carving exhibits two men facing each other, each holding a large object shaped like a giant light bulb, but more elongated. At the back of the bulbs a cord is attached that runs along the floor into a box. Inside each bulb is a serpent with its tail at the base of the bulb where there appears to be a socket. The serpent's head reaches near the bulb's tip as its body stretches the length of the bulb. The end of one bulb is propped up on a *djed* pillar. There is also a human figure that looks like a baboon, which is holding two knives in his hands and standing in front of a bulb.

The closest modern visual representation to these "Denderah bulbs" would be a Crookes tube.* However, some Egyptologists believe these bulbous objects are of a mystical and religious nature and that the "bulb" is really a lotus flower spawning the primordial serpent from within.

---

*Invented by the British physicist William Crookes, a Crookes tube is an experimental electrical tube in which cathode rays (electrons) were discovered.

The official explanation for these crypts is that they were storage vaults for statues of Hathor and other ritual furnishings for celebrations. Carvings in the main temple's staircase depict scenes of rituals that were held for statues at various times of the year.

Denderah's Temple of Hathor, like most temples, was used over a very long period. Since everything is relatively old, the separation between different periods of construction may be hard to tell. But there is little doubt that the temple was used as a place of worship during later times, and the crypts *may* have been used to store statues. Yet the crypts must have originally been intended for something much more important. A cellar only four feet across adorned with carved murals defies logic, except if the purpose of the cellar is to conceal and protect. But what would the ancient Egyptians be attempting to conceal and protect?

The official view is that the crypts were designed to hold secrets of the prophets and the goddess herself. And the fact that they were beautifully carved and painted indicates that the crypts must have been used for sacred rites of Hathor. However, if the story told in the crypts is the same religious and philosophical concept that is told by the architecture and art in the temple of Amun-Mut-Khonsu, why were the crypts completely concealed?

The secret had to have been something else. Was it technical information and the story of a grand civilization in a time when "the gods" reigned? Are the Denderah crypts a time capsule in the same way Gutzon Borglum designed Mount Rushmore's Hall of Records? Why would two of them be closed to the public?

MAKING THE CASE FOR CIVILIZATION X

I read books describing how the Great Pyramid was built for entertainment as much as I do for knowledge, not so much because any one author has solved the mystery of its construction or its purpose, but because a mental paradox is always created in my mind. Whatever theory is put forth on the technique the pyramid builders used, it always rests on assumptions, which means that to believe it, a step of faith is required.

Whatever the case may be, the Great Pyramid was built with precision. In his new book *The Great Pyramid,* veteran Egyptologist John Romer states:

> The first thing I had discovered was that, unlike the royal tombs of Thebes, the combination of the Great Pyramid's colossal size and extraordinary precision—for the accuracy of its architecture can be measured on occasion within fractions of an inch—easily defeats the efforts of a modern draftsman.[32]

And:

> As well as being the most accurately surveyed building in the modern world, the Great Pyramid is also one of the most accurate the human race has ever made; some of the elements of its architecture are yet precise to within a fraction of an inch.[33]

Such an observation by Romer is reminiscent of Arab Hekekyan Bey's statement, "Had they been merely an agricultural people they could not have disposed of superfluous wealth and labor in prosecuting with such constancy undertakings which were un-remunerative."[34] Whatever the age, one thing is clear, he insists: "The people were then highly civilized."[35]

Yet in the same breath, Romer attributes a "single construction plan" that was used in the construction process to a "pre-literary age" in which the particular specifics of "the Great Pyramid's construction were integral to its design . . . and that subtle harmonies held within its architecture are the product of the methods of its manufacture; of its craftsmen and their specific use of their materials."[36] How could the pyramid builders not be literate and achieve such splendor?

It's the same old story: in their brilliance and genius, the pyramid builders designed and constructed with precision the most monumental and majestic structure known to mankind, but used only the simplest of handheld tools: copper chisels and wooden mallets. The chisel marks on the Great Pyramid's limestone course blocks and in the southern quarry are proof enough, or so it is thought. Yet is it really possible that a man carved out the descending passageway 350 feet, lying upside down, banging away at the stone and bedrock with a copper chisel, and was precise to within a quarter of an inch? It would have taken a super race to accomplish such a feat.

At one time automobiles were built with hand tools, and to some extent they still are, although computer-driven robots have come of age in the manufacturing process. What is missing in this explanation of automobile manufacturing is that other industries that use machining processes were employed to help manufacture the car. If a Model T Ford was somehow preserved in the ground and then excavated ten thousand years in the future, along with a crescent wrench, a screwdriver, and a ball-peen hammer, would a logical conclusion be that the Model T was built with only those tools that were found with it? Because we know that manufacturing an automobile requires more than a few hand tools, we would say, "No, of course not."

So shouldn't we apply the same treatment of logic to the great pyramids and all the other wonderful artifacts of this granite civilization, this Civilization X? We should, and the stone at Abu Rawash with its clearly defined feed lines cries out to every machinist, every carpenter, and every person who has used power tools to advertise the fact that simple hand tools were not the only tools used in the process of pyramid building.

The theory that best fits the evidence is this one: in 4000 to 3000 BCE, settlers and migrating cattlemen found a derelict and sparsely populated civilization in the Nile Valley. The granite temples and pyramids of Abu Rawash, Giza, Sakkara, Abu Sir, Abu Gorab, Dahshur, and Meidum already existed. Because these structures were self-contained and had no obvious entrances, the new caretakers of the pyramids assumed they were tombs. What else could they be? Naturally, the people migrating to the Nile Valley reoccupied these ancient sites and added new structures to the old. Out of mud brick and small stones, villages were built, such as the houses erected along the causeway that links the middle pyramid to the Sphinx, or the small irregular houses built near Giza's third pyramid.

These feebly built structures were reduced to rubble and covered with sand long ago. When discovered in 1932 by Hassan, their walls were chest high and still displayed some red, white, and black paint. Today there is little remaining of them except a dark spot on the ground.

According to Egyptologists, the eastern town of Giza was a very crowded place. Domestic granaries, storage bins, and grinding stones have been found there, as well as traces of alleyways between houses. More than five thousand mud "sealings" were also found, some of them bearing the names of Khafre and Menkaure, two rulers of the Fourth Dynasty.[37]

Where there is a village, there will also be a cemetery, which is what Egyptologists have always claimed Giza was designed to be. Adjacent to the Great Pyramid are two mastaba fields, typical burial mounds of early dynastic Egyptians. However, at Giza's southern end is a cemetery where commoners were put to rest. Its lower portion contains six hundred simple graves and thirty larger tombs.[38] According to examination, half of those interred here were female; children accounted for 23 percent of the total.[39] One tomb was built with a square courtyard, its walls made from broken limestone. It also, however, contained pieces of granite, basalt, and diorite, the same type of stone used to build Giza's pyramids and temples.

If these Old Kingdom villages belonged to the pyramid builders, assuming that Giza was intended to be a necropolis, surely these families would have moved elsewhere after the pyramid projects were finished. Why would the rulers of the Old Kingdom allow families to stay on sacred ground unless they too lived among them? Yet no royal mansions attributable to the Old Kingdom have been found.

In no way can these Giza villages be considered evidence of those who built the pyramids. Nor can the existence of a cemetery be proof that it contains the remnants of those who built the pyramids. Such thinking escapes the objectivity of science. The only thing that this evidence definitely tells us is that people lived on the Giza Plateau during the early part of the second millennium BCE.

A much better explanation of the evidence is that at some time in the remote past, a technically advanced civilization existed. It had the skills and power to quarry, move, and dress multiton blocks of stone. It also had the technology to cut and shape granite into beautiful temples. And if a technically advanced civilization did exist in prehistory, it should also be the case that its existence, its legacy, was remembered and carried forward in legend, myth, and story.

Although ancient legends and myths are highly suspect today, they were an important part of ancient cultures. With a very small percentage of the population being literate, and the task of creating documents tedious and expensive, the most effective way of disseminating knowledge and history was through the art of storytelling. Stories are much easier to remember than a list of facts.

Fortunately for us, as civilization progressed, so did the need for documentation, for business reasons as well as aesthetic ones. A class of scribes developed and grew, as did institutions for learning. As such, our ancient ancestors wrote down these stories and legends that were so popular in ancient times. For the Hebrew people, what history exists can be found in the early chapters of Genesis, Noah's Flood, the Tower of Babel, and the story of Abraham. For the Egyptians, it is the kings' list of the Turin Papyrus and the Palermo Stone and a web of various myths and legends.

In our narrow-minded approach to the past, we have consistently attributed these myths and legends to the religious fascination of primitive-thinking people and discarded any other means of interpretation, mostly as a result of improperly translating the Egyptian word for "god." *Neter* is the Egyptian word that, for the Greeks and Hebrews, eventually came to mean god, although it originally referred to principles of nature, and there are many principles to describe, such as digestion, respiration, and procreation, to name a few. And in Egyptian thought, animals were chosen as a way of expressing a natural principle according to that animal's natural qualities.

For example, the jackal, which scavenges food, can eat almost anything, even rotten meat. As such, the jackal is an apt symbol for the principle of digestion, and when the head of a jackal is depicted on a human body, the artist is referring to the principle of digestion as it relates to humans. Thus, there is an explanation for placing the deceased's stomach in a jar whose lid is carved in the shape of a jackal's head. Likewise, the lid of the jar that holds the deceased's liver is in the shape of a man's head, since the liver appears to be a critical organ for the human personality. Liver ailments can significantly alter one's personality.

With this symbolic approach to understanding the legends and myths of ancient Egypt, a better understanding of their knowledge can be achieved, as well as a better understanding of what they might have viewed as their history and legacy. Like the Hebrews, the Egyptians had their own tradition of catastrophe. And like Noah's Flood and the Tower of Babel, mankind suffered decimation at the hands of "God," but for the Egyptians the culprit was known as Hathor, a cosmic principle that gave life to all.

Symbolism is not science but neither is history, nor is its investigation scientific. Constructing a history purely based on physical evidence leaves a wide gap for the historian to conjure whatever chronology he or she chooses to accept. Ignoring what ancient historians wrote, too, is a mistake.

The first Egyptologists were confused by the evidence they uncovered. In order of what was expected, there was evidence of a relatively primitive people who lived in and around the Nile Valley between 5000 BCE and 3000 BCE. They lived simply, using flint tools and making clay pottery. But there was also evidence of a highly sophisticated people who crafted magnificent jars and vases out of stone and built wondrous structures that have withstood the test of time.

Throughout the Nile Valley this civilization erected obelisks, statues, temples, and pyramids of limestone and granite like no other civilization has since. The first Egyptologists assumed that those responsible for this magnificence were the dynastic Egyptians of 3000 BCE. But explaining how primitive predynastic people blossomed into the majesty of dynastic Egypt was a problem. Ignoring Herodotus and all the other ancient historians, Egyptologists solved the problem by creating fictitious invaders from another land.

Today, with John Cadman's modeling and demonstration that the subterranean region of the Great Pyramid was a hydraulic pulse pump, John Burke's scientific investigation into the use of stone structures as a means of crop fertilization, Christopher Dunn's analysis of the stone at Abu Rawash (that it was the result of a powered saw), and John West and Robert Schoch's redating of the Sphinx, there is little reason to believe our standardized and approved "history of civilization" textbooks. Skepticism, as you see, works both ways.

I suspect that the vast majority of stone structures were extant by 14,500 BCE, long before historical Egypt's First Dynasty, and that the survivors of the calamity that befell our planet at the end of the Ice Age, the Followers of Horus, struggled their way back from near-extinction and restarted their ancestors' once-great civilization. The technical know-how to build big had disappeared many thousands of years prior in favor of subsistence. Nonetheless, what the survivors could pass down was the knowledge, the philosophy, and the dim memory of a once-great civilization. To their descendents—primitive people that they were—the men and women of Civilization X would have appeared as gods.

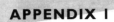

ARABIAN HISTORY

History is a story, a tradition—oral and written—but most of all, it's our story, and as old as time itself. As such, it is encoded in myth and legend.

John Greaves (1602–1652), an English mathematician and historian, collected a considerable number of Arabic, Persian, and Greek manuscripts. He also visited Egypt, where he conducted the most accurate survey, of his time, of the pyramids, which resulted in the publication of *Pyramidographia* (*A Description of the Pyramids in Egypt*).

While in Egypt, Greaves had the opportunity to collect the Arab traditions concerning the pyramids, those stories that were handed down to the Arabs from the native Egyptians *they* had conquered a thousand years earlier. Much of what they told him, he refused to believe. Yet he found the accounts of Ibn Abd Al Hokm more credible than all the others.

According to Arab historians of the time, the pyramids were built before the deluge. Firouzabadi, although not very clear on the subject, states that the pyramids were erected "by Edris, to preserve there the sciences, and prevent their destruction by the Deluge; or by Sinan ben-almo schaishal sehaishal, or by the first men, when informed by observation of the stars of the coming Deluge; or to preserve medicines, magic, and talismans."[1]

There are two versions of this tradition. In the first tradition, the story begins with the king of Egypt, Saurid Ibn Salhouk, three hundred years before the flood. The king, while asleep, saw that the whole Earth was turned over, along with its inhabitants. People were lying face down and the stars were falling, striking one another with a terrible noise. After he saw the first stars falling to Earth, what resembled white birds snatched people up and carried them between two great mountains. Then the shining stars became dark.[2]

Upon awakening, the king assembled the 130 chief priests from the provinces of Egypt and told them of his dream. The priests discussed the matter, made their prognostication, and foretold of a deluge, which would destroy the country. However, it would be a number of years before this happened. So the king ordered the building of pyramids. A vault would be made where the Nile River flows, and would run into the countries of the West.

Once the pyramids were built, he filled them with talismans, riches, treasures, and strange things and engraved in them all the profound sciences, the sciences of astrology, arithmetic, geometry, and physics, as well as the words of wise men and the names of the *alakakirs* (magical, precious stones)—their uses and abuses.

In building the pyramids, vast columns and wonderful stones were cut and massive stones brought from the Ethiopians, which were used as the foundations of the three pyramids; the stones were fastened together with lead and iron. After the final pyramid was finished, it was covered with colored Satten (marble), and it was announced that there would be a solemn festival for all the inhabitants of the kingdom.

In the West Pyramid, the king placed thirty treasuries and filled it with a store of riches, utensils, signatures made of precious stones, instruments of iron, vessels of earth, metal that doesn't rust, and glass that bends. In the pyramid he also placed strange spells, several kinds of *alakakirs,* single and double, and deadly poisons, among other things. In the East Pyramid, he placed knowledge of the celestial spheres and stars, and how they operate; perfumes; and the books that tell of these matters.

In the third pyramid, the colored pyramid, were placed the commentaries of the priests in chests of black marble. With every priest there was placed a book telling the wonders of his profession, his actions, his nature, and what was accomplished in his time, and what is and shall be from the beginning to the end of time.

In 1584, Murtadi* told another version of the story. Three hundred

---

*Murtadi was an Arab historian who lived in the tenth century.

years before the deluge, King Saurid, the son of Sahaloc, dreamed one night that he saw Earth overturned along with its inhabitants. People were cast down on their faces, and out of the heavens came falling stars. A year later he dreamed that he saw the fixed stars fall to Earth in the form of white birds, which carried people away and cast them between two great mountains. Then, the shining stars became dark and were eclipsed.[3]

Upon awakening, astonished, he entered into the Temple of the Sun, and beset himself to bathe his cheeks and to weep. The next morning he ordered all the princes of the priests, and magicians of all the provinces of Egypt, to come together for a meeting. They did so, 130 priests and soothsayers, and he told them of his dream. The priests found the dream of great consequence, and they interpreted it to mean that a very great accident would fall on the world.

The priest Acimon, the greatest of all and chief in the king's court, said to him that his dream was admirable, and that he had also had a frightening dream. The chief priest dreamed that he was with the king on the top of "the mountain of fire," which is in the midst of Emsos. There the saw the heaven sink down below its ordinary position. The stars covered and surrounded them like a great basin turned upside down. The stars then intermingled among men in diverse figures, and the people implored the king's assistance. They ran to the king in multitudes to seek refuge. So the king lifted up his hands and endeavored to thrust back the heaven to keep it from coming down so low. So did the chief priest.

While they were in that posture, a part of the heavens opened and a bright light came out of it. Afterward, the sun rose out of the same place. The chief priest said that the heaven would return to its ordinary position after 300 courses. Then the king commanded them to take the height of the stars, and to consider what accident they portended, whereupon they declared that there would be a deluge and after that, fire. Thus, the king commanded pyramids to be built, where they soon secured their most esteemed treasuries.[4] One of the more intriguing traditions comes from the Coptites. In their books, there is said to exist this inscription:

I Saurid, the king, built the Pyramids in such and such a time, and finished them in six years; he that comes after me, and says he is equal to me, let him destroy them in six hundred years; and yet it is known that it is easier to plucke down then to build; and when I had finished them, I covered them with Szttin, and let him cover them with slats.[5]

For Greaves, Egyptian history according to the Arabs contained so many of their own inventions that the truth had been extinguished, rendering it little more than a romance. Boswick called the ancient Arab traditions a yarn, but were they?

It seems to me that in the past twenty years, researchers such as John Anthony West, Robert Schoch, John Cadman, Christopher Dunn, and John Burke have justified, at the very least, the need for further scientific study of our prehistoric past.

All history suffers from a kind of embellishment that is capable of distorting the truth. This is as true today as it was eons ago. Despite the embellishment that George Washington chopped down a cherry tree in his youth, much to his father's dismay, it doesn't remove him as general of the Continental Army or president of the United States.

Other sources already covered in this book corroborate elements of ancient Egyptian history as it was told to the Arabs, indicating that there was a cosmic deluge in the tradition of Gilgamesh and the Eye of Ra. The deluge was cosmic in the sense that Earth suffered a celestial calamity in the manner described earlier in this chapter. If this is true, then the pyramids were constructed sometime around 14,500 BCE.

THE ATLANTIS QUESTION

Plato's legend of Atlantis describes the conflagration and cataclysm that occurred at the end of the Ice Age: earthquakes, tsunami waves, rising sea levels, and the destruction of an island nation. Plato claims to have heard the tale of Atlantis from his Uncle Solon, who heard it from the Egyptians while visiting Egypt. If true, then the Atlantis story is an Egyptian story.

In modern times, ever since Francis Bacon's 1627 publication *The New Atlantis,* much ado has been made of Plato's Atlantis. Even today, the hunt for Atlantis continues, but the evidence is always sketchy and vague. Atlantis may never be found for the simple reason that it may never have existed. It also seems likely that Plato's dialogues of Critias and Timaeus may have been works of fiction, moral stories to provide imagery and examples for an audience. Even so, like the myriad myths and legends telling the tale of catastrophe, Plato's story of Atlantis is a part of history. The fascinating question is, why?

Crantor, a student of Xenocrates, who was a student of Plato, is said to have visited Egypt to verify the Egyptian story of Atlantis. Although Crantor's commentaries on Plato are lost, Proclus (412–485 CE) declares in his commentaries on Plato that Crantor did visit Egypt and viewed the columns that contained the Egyptian story of Atlantis. Plato never mentions any columns in *Critias and Timaeus;* nonetheless, it might be the case that Solon heard the story from another Egyptian source. If the story was commonly known to the temple priests at that time, certainly there would be a number of ways to learn the story.

Aside from the Egyptian story, there are numerous other legends from various cultures about a time when mankind suffered through and was decimated by conflagration and cataclysm. Although not all of them recall an island continent sinking into the sea, some do. Could it be mere coincidence that the natives of Mexico's Yucatan peninsula have, in their oral tradition, a tale similar to Plato's Atlantis?[1]

Geneticists claim that anatomically modern man has existed for the last 150,000 years, and that human origins began in Africa. Yet history only accounts for a little over 3 percent of time, as we understand the scope of time. If it is true that modern man has existed for the last 150,000 years (and there is no reason to doubt the geneticists, since the archaeological record suggests the same), why isn't it possible for civilization to have been established earlier than 3000 BCE?

There is the opportunity as well as the motivation. Human cultures certainly had enough time in the last hundred thousand years to accumulate enough knowledge and skill to organize and reach some level of civil sophistication. Coming out of the Dark Ages, our own civilization accomplished much more in only a thousand years. It makes me wonder if there is any truth to the accounts of stainless-steel and clear-plastic objects, among other riches, allegedly placed in ancient Egypt's pyramids, and if there really was a fourth, black pyramid at Giza.

If the pyramids of Giza did not exist, and if Iorweth Edwards had not described Queen Hetepheres' equipment as objects to which words cannot do justice, I would have to say, "Absolutely not." But with Edwards' choice of words—"artistic excellence and technical perfection"—in describing Queen Hetepheres' equipment buried in tunneled bedrock deep below the Giza Plateau, I have to wonder what else lies buried beneath the sand. Call it Atlantis or not, there is more than enough evidence to suggest that civilization already existed at a time long before the end of the Ice Age. Plato's Atlantis may be a tale of morality, but history itself makes a strong case for Civilization X.

NOTES

CHAPTER 1. A CIVILIZATION IN GRANITE

1. Ian Shaw, *The Oxford History of Ancient Egypt* (New York: Oxford University Press, 2002), 97.
2. George A. Reisner, "The Harvard-Boston Egyptian Expedition," *Harvard Alumni Bulletin* 24, no. 7 (June 22, 1922): 943.
3. Christopher Dunn, "The Amazing Boxes of the Serapeum," at www.gizapower .com/Precision.htm (accessed September 29, 2009).
4. Christopher Dunn, *The Giza Power Plant* (Rochester, Vt.: Bear & Co., 1998), 83.

CHAPTER 2. A PREHISTORIC SPHINX

1. R. A. Schwaller de Lubicz, *Sacred Science: The King of Pharaonic Theocracy* (Rochester, Vt.: Inner Traditions, 1982), 96 (see footnote 29).
2. *Monumental Mysteries: Aging the Great Sphinx,* BBC/Discovery Channel documentary, 1997.
3. *Mystery of the Sphinx,* documentary, BC Video, 1993. (This documentary was based on the research of John Anthony West.)
4. Robert Schoch, "Redating the Great Sphinx of Giza," *KMT: A Modern Journal of Ancient Egypt* 3, no. 2 (Summer 1992): 52–59, 66–70.
5. Ibid.
6. Ibid.
7. Ibid.

8. Ibid.

9. *Mystery of the Sphinx.*

10. Colin Reader, "Khufu Knew the Sphinx: A Reconciliation of the Geological and Archaeological Evidence for the Age of the Sphinx and a Revised Sequence of Development for the Giza Necropolis" (October 1997, revised August 1999), at www.ianlawton.com/as1.htm (accessed September 29, 2009); "A Geomorphological Study of the Giza Necropolis, with Implications for the Development of the Site," *Archaeometry* 43, no. 1 (2001): 149–65.

11. Robert M. Schoch, "Geological Evidence Pertaining to the Age of the Great Sphinx," at www.robertschoch.com/geodatasphinx.html (accessed September 29, 2009).

12. P. Morel, F. von Blanckenburg, M. Schaller, et al., "Quantification of the Effects of Lithology, Landscape Dissection, and Glaciation on Rock Weathering and Large-Scale Erosion as Determined by Cosmogenic Nuclides in River Sediments," *Annual Report: The Institute for Particle Physics,* ETH Zürich, Swiss Federal Institute of Technology, 2001.

13. John Stone and Paulo Vasconcelos, "Studies of Geomorphic Rates and Processes with Cosmogenic Isotopes Examples from Australia," Cambridge Publications, Goldschmidt 2000 Conference: An International Conference for Geochemistry, Oxford, UK, organized by the European Association for Geochemistry and the Geochemical Society, 2000.

14. Table data from sources cited in notes 12–14, and from the following: National Parks Service, U.S. Department of the Interior, at www.nps.gov/miss/features/geology/geology.html (accessed in 2004, from *Before the Pharaohs*) and www.factmonster.com/ce6/sci/A0817621.html (accessed September 29, 2009), whose source is *The Columbia Electronic Encyclopedia,* 6th ed. (New York: Columbia University Press, 2005); National Parks Service, U.S. Department of the Interior Geology Fieldnotes: Grand Canyon National Park, at www.2nature.nps.gov/geology/parks/grca (accessed in 2004, from *Before the Pharaohs*); The Niagara Parks Commission Geology of the Falls, at www.niagaraparks.com/nfgg/geology.php (accessed September 29, 2009); and "Origins of Niagara: A Geologic History," at www.iaw.com/~falls/origins.html (accessed September 29, 2009).

15. A. Matmon, E. Zilberman, and Y. Enzel, "The Development of the Bet-Ha'Emeq Structure and the Tectonic Activity of Normal Faults in the Galilee," *Israel Journal of Earth Sciences* 49 (2000): 143–58.

16. Robert J. Wenke, "Egypt: Origins of Complex Societies," *Annual Reviews Anthropology* 18 (1989): 129–55.

17. Kevin Allred, "Some Carbonate Erosion Rates of Southeast Alaska," *Journal of Cave and Karst Studies* 66, no. 3 (December 2004): 89–97.

18. E. A. Wallis Budge, *A History of Egypt,* vol. 2 (London: Adamant Media, 2005), 49.

19. Ibid., 51.

CHAPTER 3. A MECHANICAL METHOD OF CUTTING STONE

1. Walter Bryan Emery, *Archaic Egypt* (Baltimore, Md.: Penguin, 1961), 214.

2. Ibid., 215.

3. Ibid.

4. Ibid.

5. Barbara Mertz, *Temples, Tombs, and Hieroglyphs* (New York: Coward-McCann, 1964), 54.

6. Ibid., 55.

7. Ibid.

8. Ibid., 59.

9. Ibid., 21–22.

10. Ibid., 22.

11. William Flinders Petrie, *The Pyramids and Temples of Gizeh* (London: Field & Tuer, 1883), 173.

12. Ibid., 174.

13. Ibid., 176.

14. Ibid., 174–75.

15. Ibid., 175.

16. Ibid., 176.

17. Ibid.

18. Ibid.

19. Ibid., 177.

20. Christopher Dunn, "Return to the Giza Power Plant," at www.gizapower.com/Articles/return.html (accessed September 29, 2009).

21. Ibid.

22. Petrie, *Gizeh,* 75–76.

CHAPTER 4. A NEW ROSETTA STONE

1. Miroslav Verner, *The Pyramids: The Mystery, Culture, and Science of Egypt's Greatest Monuments* (New York: Grove Press, 2001), 221.
2. Ibid., 152.
3. Christopher Dunn, "Mega Saws of the Pyramid Builders," *Atlantis Rising,* no. 70 (July/August 2008): 32–33, 64–65.
4. Ibid.
5. Ibid.
6. Ibid.
7. Ibid

CHAPTER 5. A PHILOSOPHY IN STONE

1. Joyce Tyldesley, *Ramses: Egypt's Greatest Pharaoh* (New York: Penguin, 2000), 100.
2. Terry Landau, *About Faces: The Evolution of the Human Face* (New York: Anchor, 1989), 69.
3. Samuel A. B. Mercer, *Earliest Intellectual Man's Idea of the Cosmos* (London: Luzac, 1957), 16.
4. Ernst Kjellberg and Gosta Saflund, *Greek and Roman Art: 3000 BC to AD 550,* trans. Peter Fraser (New York: Thomas Y. Cromwell, 1968), 69.
5. W. Stevenson Smith, *The Art and Architecture of Ancient Egypt* (New York: Penguin, 1965), 111.
6. Tyldesley, *Ramses,* 100.
7. Mercer, *Idea of the Cosmos,* 17.
8. Schwaller de Lubicz, *Sacred Science,* 98.
9. Ibid., 99.
10. Ibid., 238.
11. Ibid.

CHAPTER 6. A PYRAMID OF ASSUMPTIONS

1. Mertz, *Temples, Tombs, and Hieroglyphs,* 81.
2. Verner, *Pyramids,* 449.
3. *Mysteries of the Pyramids.*
4. Michael A. Hoffman, *Egypt before the Pharaohs* (New York: Dorsett, 1979), 270–71.

5. Ibid., 278.

6. Verner, *Pyramids,* 45.

7. *Where Did It Come From? Ancient Egypt: Iconic Structures,* Popular Arts Entertainment, The History Channel, September 21, 2006.

8. Verner, *Pyramids,* 70.

9. Ibid., 69

10. Ibid.

11. Ibid., 70.

12. Rudolf Gantenbrink, "Ascertaining and Evaluating Relevant Structural Points Using the Cheops Pyramid as an Example," at www.cheops.org/startpage/publications/publications.htm (accessed February 2006).

13. Cheikh Anta Diop, *The African Origin of Civilization: Myth or Reality?* (Chicago, Ill.: Lawrence Hill Books, 1989), 234.

14. Petrie, *Gizeh,* 200–201.

15. Ibid.

16. Ibid., 201.

17. Ibid.

18. Paul Lunde, "The Seven Wonders," *Saudi Aramco World* (May/June 1980): 14–27, at www.saudiaramcoworld.com/issue/198003/the.seven.wonders.htm (accessed September 29, 2009).

19. Herodotus, *The Histories* (New York: Penguin, 1972), 127.

20. Thomas W. Africa, "Herodotus and Diodorus on Egypt," *Journal of Near Eastern Studies* 22, no. 4 (October 1963): 254.

21. Aristotle, *The Basic Works of Aristotle* (New York: Modern Library, 2001), 1464.

22. Verner, *Pyramids,* 23.

23. Schwaller de Lubicz, *Sacred Science,* 217.

24. Verner, *Pyramids,* 69.

25. Ibid.

26. I. E. S. Edwards, *The Pyramids of Egypt* (New York: Penguin, 1986), 250.

27. Ibid., 241.

28. Ibid., 89.

29. Ibid., 91.

30. Bob Briar, "How to Build a Pyramid," *Archaeology* (May/June 2007): 24–25.

31. Richard Noone, *5/5/2000 Ice: The Ultimate Disaster* (New York: Harmony, 1986), 105.

32. Michel W. Barsoum, "The Great Pyramids of Giza: Evidence for Cast Blocks" (presentation), Department of Materials Science and Engineering, Drexel University, Philadelphia, Pa., December 2006, at www.materials.drexel.edu/pyramids/PyramidPresentation_Lores.pdf (accessed September 29, 2009).

33. Joseph Davidovits and Margie Morris, *The Pyramids: An Enigma Solved* (New York: Hippocrene, 1988), 26.

34. Ibid., 49.

35. Ibid., 52.

36. Ibid., 186.

CHAPTER 7. A BETTER INTERPRETATION OF THE EVIDENCE

1. Lunde, "Seven Wonders."

2. Martin Bernal, *Black Athena: The Afroasiatic Roots of Classical Civilization,* vol. 1, *The Fabrication of Ancient Greece 1785–1985* (New Brunswick, N.J.: Rutgers University Press, 1987), 272.

3. Ibid., 273.

4. Ibid.

5. Ibid., 276.

6. Ibid., 273.

7. Ibid.

8. Ibid., 275.

9. Ibid., 277

10. Ibid., 275 (see note 189).

11. Ibid., 279 (see note 191).

12. Ibid., 278.

13. William Flinders Petrie, *Ten Years Digging in Egypt,* at web.ukonline.co.uk/gavin.egypt/flinders1.htm (accessed September 29, 2009).

14. Ibid.

15. William Flinders Petrie, *Ten Years Digging in Egypt 1881–1891* (New York: Fleming H. Revell, 1893), 150.

16. Emery, *Archaic Egypt,* 38–39.

17. Edward F. Malkowski, *Before the Pharaohs: Egypt's Mysterious Prehistory* (Rochester, Vt.: Bear & Co., 2006), 279.

18. Emery, *Archaic Egypt,* 38–39.

19. Donald B. Redford, *Egypt, Canaan, and Israel in Ancient Times* (Princeton, N.J.: Princeton University Press, 1992), 24.

20. Ibid., 13.

21. Douglas E. Derry, "The Dynastic Race in Egypt," *Journal of Egyptian Archaeology* 42 (December 1956), 81.

22. Ibid.

23. Ibid.

24. Ibid., 82.

25. Ibid., 85.

26. Emery, *Archaic Egypt,* 39.

27. Ibid., 40.

28. Ibid., 31.

29. Mertz, *Tombs, Temples, and Hieroglyphs,* 36.

30. Emery, *Archaic Egypt,* 30.

31. Ibid., 31.

32. E. A. Wallis Budge, *A History of Egypt,* vol. 1 (London: Adamant Media, 2005), 23.

33. Ibid., 24.

34. Ibid., 25.

35. Ibid., 26.

36. Ibid., 27.

37. Ibid., 28.

38. Ibid., 29.

39. Ibid.

40. Ibid., 27.

41. Ibid., 53.

42. Ibid., 35.

43. John A Wilson, *The Burden of Egypt: An Interpretation of Ancient Egyptian Culture* (Chicago, Ill.: University of Chicago Press, 1951), 156.

44. Schwaller de Lubicz, *Sacred Science,* 96.

CHAPTER 8. A PULSE GENERATOR INSIDE
THE GREAT PYRAMID

1. John Romer, *The Great Pyramid: Ancient Egypt Revisited* (New York: Cambridge University Press, 2007), 317, 318.

2. Interview with Bob Briar, *Coast to Coast AM with George Noory,* December 1, 2008.

3. Gantenbrink, "Cheops Pyramid."

4. Verner, *Pyramids,* 91.

5. Ibid., 89.

6. Ibid., 199.

7. Ibid., 202.

8. www.britannica.com/EBchecked/topic/387468/Lake-Moeris (accessed September 29, 2009).

9. Spotlight Interview 2000, Dr. Zahi Hawass, at www.zahihawass.com/interview_2000.htm (accessed January 20, 2008).

10. Zahi Hawass, "The Osiris Shaft," at http://guardians.net/hawass/osiris1.htm (accessed September 29, 2009).

CHAPTER 9. A NETWORK OF PYRAMIDS

1. Dunn, *Giza Power Plant.*

2. Ibid., 141.

3. "ProSoundWeb Live Chat with Tom Danley," March 12, 2002, transcript, at *www.prosoundweb.com/chat_psw/transcripts/danley3.shtml* (accessed September 29, 2009).

4. Dunn, *Giza Power Plant,* 166–68.

5. Ibid., 171–72.

6. Ibid., 173–74.

7. James Boswick, The *Great Pyramid of Giza: History and Speculation* (New York: Dover, 2003), 34.

8. Tony Bushby, *The Secret in the Bible* (Queensland, Australia: Joshua Books, 2003), 250.

9. *Mythbusters,* The Discovery Channel, Episode 32, aired June 9, 2005.

10. John DeSalvo, *Decoding the Pyramids* (New York: Metro Books, 2008), 103.

11. Ibid.

12. Edwards, *Pyramids of Egypt,* 116.

13. Mertz, *Temples, Tombs, and Hieroglyphs,* 79.

14. Edwards, *Pyramids of Egypt,* 117.

15. Ibid.

16. Mertz, *Temples, Tombs, and Hieroglyphs,* 79.

17. Ibid., 72.

18. Ibid., 71.

19. J. M. White, "Sweet Corn Seed Enhancement Increases Early Plant Fresh and Dry Weights and Yield," *Proceedings of the Florida State Horticultural Society,* 1999, at www.proseedtech.com/FL_State.htm (accessed November 15, 2007).

20. John Burke, at www.proseedtech.com/faqs.htm (accessed November 15, 2007).

21. John Burke, at www.proseedtech.com/MIR_process.htm (accessed November 15, 2007).

22. John Burke, at www.proseedtech.com/MIR_process.htm (accessed November 15, 2007).

23. John Burke and Kaj Halberg, *Seed of Knowledge, Stone of Plenty: Understanding the Lost Technology of the Ancient Megalith Builders* (San Francisco: Council Oak Books, 2005), 10.

24. Ibid.

25. Ibid.

26. Ibid., 14.

27. Ibid., 159.

28. Ibid., 161.

29. Ibid., 163.

30. Philip S. Callahan, *Paramagnetism: Rediscovering Nature's Secret Force* (Austin, Texas: Acres USA, 1995).

31. Ibid., 55.

32. Show-Ran Wang and Hsin-Hsiung Huang, "The Effects of 60Hz Magnetic Fields on Plant Growth," *Nature and Science* 5, no. 1 (2007).

33. Callahan, *Paramagnetism,* 70.

34. Ibid.

35. Ibid., 46.

36. Philip S. Callahan, *Ancient Mysteries, Modern Visions* (Austin, Texas: Acres USA, 2001), 42.

37. Callahan, *Paramagnetism,* 70.

38. Callahan, *Ancient Mysteries,* 71.

39. Ibid., 23.

40. Ibid., 46–47.

41. V. O. Rapoport, N. A. Mityakov, V. A. Zinichev, et al., "Electro-Acoustic Sounding of the Atmosphere," *Radiophysics and Quantum Electronics* 48, no. 1 (January 2005): 2–33.

CHAPTER 10. A MESSAGE AT DENDERAH

1. Poster, Mount Rushmore National Memorial Museum.
2. Ibid.
3. Ibid.
4. Anthony S. Mercatante, *Who's Who in Egyptian Mythology,* ed. and rev. Robert Steven Bianchi (New York: Barnes & Noble, 1998), 53.
5. Geraldine Pinch, *Egyptian Mythology: A Guide to Gods, Goddesses, and Traditions of Ancient Egypt* (New York: Oxford University Press, 2002), 138.
6. Ibid., 137.
7. Ibid., 138.
8. Ibid., 58.
9. Ibid., 59.
10. Ibid., 61.
11. Amelia Edwards, *A Thousand Miles Up the Nile* (London: George Routledge, 1890), 121.
12. Ibid., 120.
13. E. A. Wallis Budge, *Legends of the Gods: The Egyptian Texts* (London: Kegan Paul, Trench and Trübner, 1912), 25.
14. Pinch, *Egyptian Mythology,* 75.
15. Ibid., 129.
16. George De Santillana and Hertha Von Dechend, *Hamlet's Mill: An Essay Investigating the Origins of Human Knowledge and Its Transmission Through Myth* (Boston: David R Godine, 1992).
17. Ian M. Lange, *Ice Age Mammals of North America* (Missoula, Mont.: Mountain Press Publishing, 2002), 181.
18. De Santillana and Von Dechend, *Hamlet's Mill,* 57.

CHAPTER 11. AN INVISIBLE CATACLYSM

1. Lange, *Ice Age Mammals,* 185.
2. Frank C. Hibben, *The Lost Americans* (New York: Thomas Y. Crowell, 1968), 157.
3. Ibid.
4. Ibid., 158.
5. Ibid., 159.
6. Frank Hibben, "Evidence of Early Man in Alaska," *American Antiquity* 9 (1943): 254.

7. Ibid., 254–59.

8. George McCready Price, *The New Geology: A Textbook for Colleges, Normal Schools, and Training Schools; and for the General Reader* (Mountain View, Calif.: Pacific Press Publishing Association, 1923), 579.

9. Immanuel Velikovsky, *Earth in Upheaval* (New York: Doubleday, 1955), 59.

10. John Massey Stewart, "Frozen Mammoths from Siberia Bring the Ice Ages to Vivid Life," *Smithsonian* 8 (1977): 60–69.

11. *Raising the Mammoth,* documentary, Discovery Channel, March 12, 2000; also on DVD by Discovery Home Studios, July 23, 2002.

12. Ian Hodder, *The Leopard's Tale* (New York: Thames & Hudson, 2006), 15.

13. Ibid., 20.

14. Anna Belfer-Cohen, "The Natufian in the Levant," *Annual Review of Anthropology* 20 (1991): 167–86.

15. Ibid., 25–26.

16. Davidovits, *Enigma Solved,* 113–14.

17. NASA Jet Propulsion Laboratory, "Ulysses Captures Gamma-Ray Flare from Shattered Star," October 1, 1998, at www.jpl.nasa.gov/releases/98/ magnetars .html (accessed September 11, 2006).

18. Lyn Jenner, "Explosions in Space May Have Initiated Ancient Extinction on Earth," at www.nasa.gov/vision/universe/starsgalaxies/gammaray_extinction .html (accessed September 29, 2009).

19. Jeff Hecht, "Gamma Rays May Have Devastated Life on Earth," at www .newscientist.com/article.ns?id=dn4198 (accessed September 29, 2009).

20. Arnon Dar, Ari Laor, and Nir J. Shaviv, "Life Extinctions by Cosmic Ray Jets," Department of Physics and Space Research Institute, Technion-Israel Institute of Technology, Haifa, Israel, *Physical Review Letters,* May 16, 1997.

21. Robert Roy Britt, "Cosmic Cannon: How an Exploding Star Could Fry Earth," at www.space.com/scienceastronomy/astronomy/gammaray%20_ bursts_010522-1.html (accessed September 9, 2006).

22. David Whitehouse, "Journey to the Galactic Core," BBC News Online, at news.bbc.co.uk/1/hi/sci/tech/1078352.stm (accessed September 29, 2009).

23. Paul LaViolette, *Earth Under Fire* (Rochester, Vt.: Bear & Co., 2005), 71.

24. David Wilson, *The New Archaeology* (New York: Knopf, 1975), 97.

25. Ibid., 112.

26. LaViolette, *Earth Under Fire,* 194.

27. Richard B. Firestone and William Topping, "Terrestrial Evidence of a Nuclear

Catastrophe in Paleoindian Times," *Mammoth Trumpet* 16, no. 2 (March 2001): 9–16.

28. Ibid., 9.

29. John Tiffany, "Was Ice Age America Victimized by a Massive Supernova?" *Barnes Review* (September/October 2006): 36.

30. Rex Dalton, "Blast in the Past," *Nature* (May 17, 2007): 256–57.

31. James M. Chandler, "Carbon, and Radiocarbon Dating: A Primer," *Mammoth Trumpet* 16, no. 2 (March 2001): 8.

32. Ibid., 9.

33. LaViolette, *Earth Under Fire*, 88.

34. Ibid., 165.

35. Ibid., 89.

36. Ibid., 161.

37. H. A. Zook, J. B. Hartung, and D. Storzer, "Solar Flare Activity: Evidence for Large-Scale Changes in the Past," *Icarus* 32 (1977): 106–26.

38. *Earth under Fire—Humanity's Survival of the Apocalypse*, DVD (Venice, Calif.: UFO TV, 2005).

39. Richard Firestone, Allen West, and Simon Warwick-Smith, *The Cycle of Cosmic Catastrophes* (Rochester, Vt.: Bear & Co., 2006), 174.

40. Ibid., 133.

41. Ibid., 147.

42. Ibid., 148.

43. Ibid.

44. Ibid., 293.

45. Tiffany, "Massive Supernova," 39.

46. LaViolette, *Earth Under Fire*, 73.

47. LaViolette, *Earth Under Fire*, 76. (New York: Thames & Hudson, 1859), 221–23. LaViolette quotes R. T. Rundle Clark, *Myth and Symbol in Ancient Egypt*.

48. Amelia B. Edwards, "A Thousand Miles Up the Nile," at http://web.ukonline.co.uk/gavin.egypt/amelia.htm (accessed September 29, 2009).

49. LaViolette, *Earth under Fire*, 80.

50. Ibid., 36.

CHAPTER 12. A CASE FOR CIVILIZATION X

1. Budge, *History of Egypt*, vol. 1, 163.

2. Schwaller de Lubicz, *Sacred Science*, 87.

3. Herodotus, *Histories,* 186.

4. Ibid.

5. Ibid.

6. Schwaller de Lubicz, *Sacred Science,* 87.

7. Herodotus, *Histories,* 187.

8. T. Walter Wallbank and Alastair M. Taylor, *Civilization: Past and Present,* vol. 1 (Chicago: Scott, Forsman, 1949), 56.

9. Herodotus, *Histories,* 133.

10. Bushby, *Secret in the Bible,* 123.

11. "Introduction to the Nile," at www.utdallas.edu/geosciences/remsens/Nile/geology.html (accessed September 29, 2009).

12. Bushby, *Secret in the Bible,* 125.

13. Budge, *History of Egypt,* vol. 2, 38.

14. Bushby, *Secret in the Bible,* 126.

15. Ibid., 127.

16. Ibid., 165.

17. Ibid., 128.

18. Ibid., 129.

19. Ibid., 135.

20. Davidovits, *Enigma Solved,* 93.

21. Bushby, *Secret in the Bible,* 135.

22. Ibid., 132.

23. Ibid.

24. Ibid., 137.

25. Herodotus, *Histories,* 188.

26. Ibid., 189.

27. Bushby, *Secret in the Bible,* 168.

28. Ibid.

29. Ibid., 171.

30. Ibid., 172.

31. Ibid.

32. Romer, *Great Pyramid,* 3.

33. Ibid., 4.

34. Boswick, *Great Pyramid of Giza,* 63.

35. Ibid.

36. Romer, *Great Pyramid,* 4.

37. Jim Kamil, "Who Built the Pyramids?" *Al-Ahram Weekly*, no. 847, May 31–June 6, 2007, at www.weekly.ahram.org.eg/2007/847/he1.htm (accessed January 21, 2008).

38. Zahi Hawass, "The Discovery of the Tombs of the Pyramid Builders at Giza," at www.guardians.net/hawass/buildtomb.htm (accessed September 29, 2009).

39. Joyce Tyldesley, "The Private Lives of the Pyramid-Builders," at www.bbc.co.uk/history/ancient/egyptians/ pyramid_builders_03.shtml (accessed January 21, 2008).

APPENDIX 1. ARABIAN HISTORY

1. Boswick, *Great Pyramid of Giza,* 114.

2. Ibid.

3. Ibid.

4. Boswick, *Great Pyramid of Giza,* 115–18.

5. Ibid., 72.

APPENDIX 2. THE ATLANTIS QUESTION

1. Firestone, *Cosmic Catastrophes,* 328.

BIBLIOGRAPHY

Africa, Thomas W. "Herodotus and Diodorus on Egypt." *Journal of Near Eastern Studies* 22, no. 4 (October 1963).

Allred, Kevin. "Some Carbonate Erosion Rates of Southeast Alaska." *Journal of Cave and Karst Studies* 66, no. 3 (December 2004).

Belfer-Cohen, Anna. "The Natufian in the Levant." *Annual Review of Anthropology* 20 (1991).

Bernal, Martin. *Black Athena: The Afroasiatic Roots of Classical Civilization.* Vol. 1, *The Fabrication of Ancient Greece 1785–1985.* New Brunswick, N.J.: Rutgers University Press, 1991.

Bonwick, James. *The Great Pyramid of Giza: History and Speculation.* New York: Dover, 2003.

Briar, Bob. "How to Build a Pyramid." *Archaeology* (May/June 2007).

Budge, E. A. Wallis. A *History of Egypt.* Vol. 1. London: Adamant Media, 2005.

———. *A History of Egypt.* Vol. 2. London: Adamant Media, 2005.

———. *Legends of the Gods: The Egyptian Texts.* London: Kegan Paul, Trench and Trübner, 1912.

Burke, John, and Kaj Halberg. *Seed of Knowledge, Stone of Plenty: Understanding the Lost Technology of the Ancient Megalith Builders.* San Francisco: Council Oak Books, 2005.

Bushby, Tony. *The Secret in the Bible.* Queensland, Australia: Joshua Books, 2003.

Callahan, Philip S. *Paramagnetism: Rediscovering Nature's Secret Force.* Austin, Texas: Acres USA, 1995.

Chandler, James M. "Carbon and Radiocarbon Dating: A Primer." *Mammoth Trumpet* 16, no. 2 (March 8, 2001).

Dalton, Rex. "Blast in the Past." *Nature* (May 17, 2007).

Dar, Arnon, Ari Laor, and Nir J. Shaviv. "Life Extinctions by Cosmic Ray Jets." *Physical Review Letters*, 80, no. 26 (May 16, 1997).

Davidovits, Joseph, and Margie Morris. *The Pyramids: An Enigma Solved*. New York: Hippocrene Books, 1988.

De Santillana, George, and Hertha Von Dechend. *Hamlet's Mill: An Essay Investigating the Origins of Human Knowledge and Its Transmission through Myth*. Boston: David R. Godine, 1992.

Derry, D. E. "The Dynastic Race in Egypt." *Journal of Egyptian Archaeology* 42 (December 1956).

Dunn, Christopher. *The Giza Power Plant*. Rochester, Vt.: Bear & Co., 1998.

———. "Mega Saws of the Pyramid Builders." *Atlantis Rising*, no. 70 (July/August 2008).

Edwards, I. E. S. *The Pyramids of Egypt*. New York: Penguin, 1986.

Emery, Walter Bryan. *Archaic Egypt*. Baltimore, Md.: Penguin, 1961.

Firestone, Richard B., and William Topping. "Terrestrial Evidence of a Nuclear Catastrophe in Paleoindian Times." *Mammoth Trumpet* 16, no. 2 (March 2001).

Firestone, Richard B., Allen West, and Simon Warwick-Smith. *The Cycle of Cosmic Catastrophes*. Rochester, Vt.: Bear & Co., 2006.

Hibben, Frank C. *The Lost Americans*. New York: Thomas Y. Crowell, 1968.

———. "Evidence of Early Man in Alaska." *American Antiquity* 8, no. 254 (1943).

Hodder, Ian. *The Leopard's Tale*. New York: Thames & Hudson, 2006.

Hoffman, Michael A. *Egypt before the Pharaohs*. New York: Dorsett, 1979.

Kamil, Jim. "Who Built the Pyramids?" *Al-Ahram Weekly* 31, no. 847 (May/June 2007).

Kjellberg, Ernst, and Gosta Saflund. *Greek and Roman Art: 3000 BC to AD 550*. New York: Thomas Y. Cromwell, 1968

Landau, Terry. *About Faces*. New York: Anchor, 1989.

Lange, Ian M. *Ice Age Mammals of North America*. Missoula, Mont.: Mountain Press Publishing, 2002.

LaViolette, Paul. *Earth Under Fire*. Rochester, Vt.: Bear & Co., 2005.

Massey, John Stewart. "Frozen Mammoths from Siberia Bring the Ice Ages to Vivid Life." *Smithsonian*, no. 8 (1977).

Matmon, A., E. Zilberman, and Y. Enzel. "The Development of the Bet-Ha'Emeq Structure and the Tectonic Activity of Normal Faults in the Galilee." *Israel Journal of Earth Sciences*, no. 49 (2000).

Mercer, Samuel A. B. *Earliest Intellectual Man's Idea of the Cosmos.* London: Luzac, 1957.

Mertz, Barbara. *Temples, Tombs, and Hieroglyphs: The Story of Egyptology.* New York: Coward-McCann, 1964.

Morel, P., F. von Blanckenburg, M. Schaller, et al. "Quantification of the Effects of Lithology, Landscape Dissection, and Glaciation on Rock Weathering and Large-Scale Erosion as Determined by Cosmogenic Nuclides in River Sediments." *Annual Report: The Institute for Particle Physics.* Zürich: Swiss Federal Institute of Technology, 2001.

Noone, Richard. *5/5/2000 Ice: The Ultimate Disaster.* New York: Harmony Books, 1986.

Petrie, William M. Flinders. *The Pyramids and Temples of Gizeh.* London: Field & Tuer, 1883.

Pinch, Geraldine. *Egyptian Mythology: A Guide to Gods, Goddesses, and Traditions of Ancient Egypt.* New York: Oxford University Press, 2002.

Rapoport, V., N. Mityakov, V. Zinichev, et al. "Electro-Acoustic Sounding of the Atmosphere." *Radiophysics and Quantum Electronics* 48, no. 1 (January 2005).

Reader, Colin. "A Geomorphological Study of the Giza Necropolis, with Implications for the Development of the Site." *Archaeometry* 43, no. 1 (February 2001).

Redford, Donald B. *Egypt, Canaan, and Israel in Ancient Times.* Princeton, N.J.: Princeton University Press, 1993.

Reisner, George A. "The Harvard-Boston Egyptian Expedition." *Harvard Alumni Bulletin* 24, no. 7 (June 22, 1922).

Romer, John. *The Great Pyramid: Ancient Egypt Revisited.* New York: Cambridge University Press, 2007.

Schoch, Robert. "Redating the Great Sphinx of Giza." *KMT: A Modern Journal of Ancient Egypt* 3, no. 2 (1992).

Schwaller de Lubicz, R. A. *Sacred Science: The King of Pharaonic Theocracy.* Rochester, Vt.: Inner Traditions, 1982.

Shaw, Ian. *The Oxford History of Ancient Egypt.* New York: Oxford University Press, 2002.

Smith, W. Stevenson. *The Art and Architecture of Ancient Egypt.* New York: Penguin, 1965.

Tiffany, John. "Was Ice Age America Victimized by a Massive Supernova?" *The Barnes Review* (September/October 2006).

Tyldesley, Joyce. *Ramses: Egypt's Greatest Pharaoh.* New York: Penguin, 2000.

Verner, Miroslav. *The Pyramids: The Mystery, Culture, and Science of Egypt's Greatest Monuments*. New York: Grove Press, 2001.

Wallbank, Walter T., and Alastair M. Taylor. *Civilization: Past and Present*. Vol. 1. Chicago: Scott, Forsman, 1949.

Wang, Show-Ran, and Hsin-Hsiung Huang. "The Effects of 60 Hz Magnetic Fields on Plant Growth." *Nature and Science* 5, no. 1 (March 30, 2007).

Wenke, Robert J. "Egypt: Origins of Complex Societies." *Annual Review of Anthropology*, no. 18 (1989).

Wilson, David. *The New Archaeology*. New York: Knopf, 1975.

Wilson, John A. *The Burden of Egypt: An Interpretation of Ancient Egyptian Culture*. Chicago: University of Chicago Press, 1951.

Zook, H. A., J. B. Hartung, and D. Storzer. "Solar Flare Activity: Evidence for Large-Scale Changes in the Past." *Icarus* 32 (1977).

INDEX

Page numbers in *italics* refer to figures.

BOOKS OF RELATED INTEREST

Before the Pharaohs
Egypt's Mysterious Prehistory
by Edward F. Malkowski

The Spiritual Technology of Ancient Egypt
Sacred Science and the Mystery of Consciousness
by Edward F. Malkowski

Lost Technologies of Ancient Egypt
Advanced Engineering in the Temples of the Pharaohs
by Christopher Dunn

The Giza Power Plant
Technologies of Ancient Egypt
by Christopher Dunn

Forbidden History
Prehistoric Technologies, Extraterrestrial Intervention,
and the Suppressed Origins of Civilization
Edited by J. Douglas Kenyon

Forbidden Science
From Ancient Technologies to Free Energy
Edited by J. Douglas Kenyon

The Sphinx Mystery
The Forgotten Origins of the Sanctuary of Anubis
by Robert Temple with Olivia Temple

The Sirius Mystery
New Scientific Evidence of Alien Contact 5,000 Years Ago
by Robert Temple

INNER TRADITIONS • BEAR & COMPANY
P.O. Box 388
Rochester, VT 05767
1-800-246-8648
www.InnerTraditions.com

Or contact your local bookseller